D0855057

DETROIT
PUBLIC
LIBRARY

A PRETTY GOOD CLUB ★ ★ ★ ★

A PRETTY GOOD CLUB

THE FOUNDING FATHERS OF THE U.S. FOREIGN SERVICE

MARTIN WEIL

W · W · NORTON & COMPANY · INC · NEW YORK

Published simultaneously in Canada by George J. McLeod Limited,
Toronto. Printed in the United States of America.

First Edition

Library of Congress Cataloging in Publication Data

Weil, Martin.
A pretty good club.

Bibliography: p.
Includes index.
1. United States. Dept. of State. Foreign Service.
I. Title.
JX1706.Z5W4 1978 353.008'92 77-25104
ISBN 0-393-05658-9

1 2 3 4 5 6 7 8 9 0

To

My Mother and Father

CONTENTS

INTRODUCTION

THIS IS THE story of a small group of Christian gentlemen who founded the profession of diplomacy on a permanent basis in America. It is also the story of their experiences manning the desks in the State Department and in embassies abroad during the stormy period that saw Communism triumph in Russia, Hitler rise to power, and Franklin Roosevelt mobilize America to fight a global war.

The men they served—Woodrow Wilson, Franklin Roosevelt, Cordell Hull, Harry Truman, Dean Acheson—are much more widely known than any of the career diplomats themselves. Yet their span of service alone calls for a proper appreciation of their activities. It is rare that a secretary of state remains in office for even a decade; it is constitutionally forbidden today for a president to do so. By contrast, Joseph Grew's career in the foreign service spanned forty years—from 1904 to 1945—and William Phillips served equally long. Loy Henderson served thirty-five years, as did James Dunn. George Kennan was a Russian expert for thirty years, Charles Bohlen even longer. Jay Pierrepont Moffat and Sumner Welles had contributed well over twenty years of their lives to the State Department when tragedy cut them both down in their prime.

These men—the career diplomats—are the permanent stewards of the ship of state, ever ready to assist the helmsman from administration to administration. They and the influence they wielded, particularly in the great confrontations with Nazi Germany and Soviet Russia, are the subjects of this book. Throughout their careers they retained the stamp of their original New England education, and it is with that education their story begins.

This book germinated in the Bureaucracy and Policy Study Group at Harvard's Institute of Politics in the late 1960s. It was nourished by two men in particular—Richard Neustadt and Ernest May. Without their inspiration, enthusiasm, and support, this volume would have been inconceivable. The skillful editorial pencil of Ed Barber, my editor, has contributed immeasurably to the style and grace of the narrative. Like all who have made their way through the written record of twentieth-century American diplomacy, I am indebted to the gracious and efficient librarians and archivists who tend these records. I owe, finally, a special debt of gratitude to those who shared their personal recollections of these events with me.

To do a book on the State Department, you would need Drew Pearson for gossip, Karl Marx for social forces, Henry James for social nuances and Max Weber for institutional patterns.

—I. F. STONE

To most people the State Department means Jimmy Byrnes and then a lot of Anglophiles in striped pants, who have good manners and have married rich wives. Actually the fact is that American foreign policy is frequently made by a series of decisions at the lower levels, taken by men most Americans have never heard of and often after raging conflicts within the Department.

—JOSEPH ALSOP

I

THE AMERICAN DIPLOMATIC PROFESSION

* * * * * * * * *

I call that a complete and generous education, which fits a Person to perform justly, skillfully, and magnanimously, all the offices both of public and private life, of Peace and of War.

—MILTON

1 | IN SERVICE TO THE NATION

DURING THE NINETEENTH century, American diplomacy was an upper-class avocation, the province of wealthy, eastern seaboard Brahmins with a taste for European society and the leisure to indulge it. Diplomacy itself did not attract people looking to make a career out of it. Most overseas posts of any importance were filled by politicians between jobs or merchants, bankers, or lawyers on leave from their regular professions. The rapid development of industrial and financial empires during the Gilded Age absorbed the energies of the most ambitious and adventurous men of affairs. Diplomacy was the thin layer of chocolate on the Boston cream pie—a sweet crust on top of a substantial career dedicated to accumulating personal wealth.

Like all prosperous parents, the Yankee businessmen of New England sought to give their youngsters advantages they had lacked. Private schools and tutors soon appeared in emulation of European society and as protection against the immigrants streaming into the public schools. Nowhere did these desires find finer expression than in the stern Christian headmasters of Groton, St. Paul's, Andover, and Exeter. In these schools the future leaders of the foreign service took their education. Groton headmaster Endicott Peabody saw his responsibility as the molding of the character of the next generation of American leaders, and he sought to inculcate a public morality that would serve the entire nation. Trained for the clergy at Cheltenham and Cambridge, Peabody was eager for Groton to do for American public life what Eton and Harrow had done for Britain. Six British prime ministers of the nineteenth century had graduated from Eton and cabinet meetings at times resembled a Harrow class reunion. Peabody's ambitions were no less grand. Among his early charges were teenagers Franklin Roosevelt, Averell Harriman, Dean Acheson, and Sumner Welles. "If some Groton boys do not enter political life and do something for our land," he declared, "it won't be because they have not been urged."[1]

A Groton education was for men only. As Peabody explained: "The private schools . . . have the advantage of commanding the services of men teachers alone. There are indeed many women who are altogether efficient instructors—some certainly superior to the men, but it is the belief of many parents that their sons during the period of adolescence . . . should be under the direction and influence of the male mind and personality and they act accordingly." The emphasis on exclusive male instruction in a school of boys did not spring from any derogation of the abilities of women but rather from a way of life that valued family and home as the cornerstone of the community. As it was man's role to protect and support his family, it was woman's role to nurture home and hearth. Boys needed male role-models during their upbringing, and women required teachers of their own sex. Harvard and Radcliffe maintained this distinction until well into the twentieth century.

The moral core of the home was faith in Christianity. "The American home," wrote Alfred E. Stearns, headmaster of Phillips Academy Andover, "is distinctly a product of our western Christian civilization."[2] Home and Christianity were seen as the foundation of an upright civilization. Without the strength of both, the nation must inevitably disintegrate. And out of this moral culture sprang the doctrine of service that infused the young men who were to found the American profession of diplomacy. Stearns underscored the tradition of practical service to the community that arose from Christian teachings. "The highest test of Christian discipleship," he wrote, "is love manifested in unselfish service and sacrifice. The truth established by the Master Himself is that . . . only he who loses his life for the welfare of others truly finds it—and finds it here and now, not in some dim and uncertain hereafter." Alfred S. Drury, headmaster of St. Paul's, expressed this spirit most vigorously. He regarded "the life and teaching of Jesus Christ as the greatest subject in the school, always and everywhere. . . . The school might make one condition for its diploma: the ability to recite the Sermon on the Mount."[3]

No individual was a more practical embodiment of these public ideals than President Theodore Roosevelt. Speaking to the Pacific Theological Seminary in the spring of 1911, he enunciated the precepts that guided his own life. In an age enamored of the creation of great fortunes, he gave credit to the individual who founded a great business enterprise, but also warned that "it is a debasing thing for a nation to choose as its heroes the men of mere wealth." These sentiments gave heart to a number of youngsters from wealthy backgrounds who sought to do more with their lives than add to their families' fortunes. Roosevelt, like Peabody and Stearns, stressed the practical necessity to the country of a sound home life and religious training. In a lecture entitled "The Home and the Child," he stated: "It is so elementary that it seems hardly necessary to say that everything in our civilization rests upon the home. . . . No community can afford to think for one moment that great public service . . . will atone for the lack of a sound family life. . . . Multiplication of divorces means that there is something rotten in the community." Speaking of women's suffrage, he echoed Peabody:

> I do not believe that the question of woman's voting is a thousandth or a millionth part as important as the question of keeping, and where necessary reviving, among the women of this country, the realization that their great work must be done in the home, that the ideal woman of the future, just like the ideal woman of the past, must be the good wife, the good mother, the mother who is able to bear, and to rear, a number of healthy children.[4]

Out of the home, quite literally, came the future of the country, and, to Roosevelt this meant the hardihood of the Yankee stock from which he descended. If the home faltered, the nation would inevitably decline. "Two-thirds of our increase," he explained, "now comes from the immigrants and not from the babies born here, not from young Americans who are to perpetuate the blood and traditions of the old stock. . . . Nothing else takes the place or can take the place of family life. . . . If you do not believe in your own stock enough to wish to see the stock kept up then you are not good Americans, you are not patriots. . . ."[5]

Roosevelt's ideal of Christian service was as strong as that of Peabody and the other New England headmasters. "I plead for the training of children in the Bible," he declared. "Our success in striving to help our fellow-men . . . depends largely upon [leading] our lives in accordance with the great ethical principles laid down in the life of Christ, and in the New Testament writings which seek to expound and apply his teachings."[6] Roosevelt, in fact, personified what E. Digby Baltzell called "a national inter-city metropolitan upper class" that was emerging at the end of the nineteenth century and sought to protect its way of life through privately funded boarding schools and colleges.[7]

The recipients of this education, responding to Roosevelt's inspiration and the moral fervor of their schooling, looked beyond the commercial horizons of their parents' universe. Educated in European history and languages, accustomed to foreign travel, bored with the prospect of tending the fortunes others had created, and impregnated with the doctrine of Christian service, many of them looked to government for challenge and excitement. Some, attracted by Roosevelt's reformism, joined the Progressive Movement, as their offspring in turn would flock to the New Deal a generation later. A smaller group, however, enchanted by the exotic appeal of foreign lands, and fluent in French and German, sought a career serving their country abroad.

Joseph Grew—Back Bay, Groton, and Harvard—was one such. He began in 1904 a career in diplomacy that spanned half a century. His biographer explains why he rejected the domestic alternative: "It meant coming to terms with the State Street of his father or the South End of the Irish immigrant. He rebelled against the former and had no inclination to rub shoulders with the latter." Rejecting both the mundaneness of business and the crudities of the working class, these young Harvard graduates sought an overseas calling. Grander in aspiration than their parents but equally as ambitious, they entered diplomacy in high excitement.

Grew and his generation of diplomats began their service as private secretaries to ambassadors or ministers. The private secretary at the time was as casual a job as that of chief of mission. More recreational than anything else, it provided a post for "young men of independent means seeking a few years in world affairs and European society before settling down to serious occupations."[8] Grew, however, was no timeserver. At times his zeal for the job was so strong that it interfered with the leisurely pace of the amateur. In his first job, at the age of twenty-four, Grew devoted three months of night work to indexing ten years of correspondence in the Cairo consular office. His superior, unimpressed by this unusual effort, ignored the index. At a subsequent assignment, Grew suggested the use of carbon paper to save labor; still later he urged the American diplomatic corps to wear a uniform in imitation of European diplomats. Both these suggestions were received coldly. Grew was undeterred; bent on a career in diplomacy, he was naturally alert to improvements that would have a long-term effect. A song learned from a British colleague became a favorite of his:

> The building of ambition
> Is fraught with strife and pain,
> But if your castle tumbles down,
> Just build it up again.[9]

Grew's castle rose bit by bit as his dedication won him a reputation for efficiency and competence. The Vienna embassy under his energetic management as first secretary won accolades from the Department of State for the quality and completeness of its reports. When the ambassador went on vacation for the summer, Grew became acting chief of mission at the early age of thirty-one. He was already drafting diplomatic notes for the ambassador as a routine matter. He next went to Berlin as first secretary in 1914 and repeated his Vienna performance. Grew thought of the embassy as an "organization" and drew all the threads of activity into his own hands. A small hierarchy with himself at the pinnacle managed the embassy's business, supported by all the office machinery contemporary technology could supply.[10] In this, he was assisted by a carefully chosen staff, heavy with Groton-Harvard alumni. The small fraternity in Berlin included Hugh Wilson and Alexander Kirk, two future stalwarts of the foreign service.

In Washington, the third assistant secretary of state, William Phillips, made sure that Grew got the people he wanted, and, equally important, did not have to suffer those he disliked. Phillips, a close friend of Grew, traced his lineage through Wendell Phillips and John Jay. He had traveled the Back Bay-Groton-Harvard track two years ahead of Grew and had abandoned State Street with the same sense of adventure, drawing equally reproving glances from his business-minded relatives. Casting about for something more stimulating than "the pallid career of family trustee," Phillips met Joseph Choate, American ambassador to Great Britain, during a weekend at Biltmore, the great North Carolina estate of George W. Vanderbilt, "said to be the finest private residence in the country." In early 1903, Choate, favorably impressed, wrote Phillips and offered him the position of "private secretary (unpaid)." Phillips accepted and happily embarked for England. While Grew did his apprenticeship in Cairo, Mexico City, St. Petersburg, Vienna, and Berlin, Phillips saw service in London and Peking, joining the department itself in 1907. Phillips showed in Washington the same innovative impulses Grew had first exhibited in Vienna. Gradually and with much difficulty he made his office "a funnel through which all papers on Far Eastern matters had to pass." His efforts were crowned by the creation of a Division of Far Eastern Affairs in late 1907, the first geographical office in the department.[11]

Grew's coterie of assistants in Berlin, Phillips and William Castle, Jr. (Harvard '02) in Washington and Hugh Gibson at the legation in Belgium all felt themselves members of an exclusive club—founding fathers of the American diplomatic profession. Grew's wife, fittingly, was a direct descendant of Benjamin Franklin, the first American to shine in European diplomacy. An intense *esprit de corps* enveloped these young aristocrats. William Phillips acknowledged the inspiration of Theodore Roosevelt. "One of T.R.'s greatest contributions to the nation," he recalled in his memoirs, "was the responsibilities which citizenship carries with it. . . . Government service, which before 1900 had not been a popular career, now began to attract young men from all over the country. The idea of a permanent foreign service . . . was born at that time."[12]

Relief in escaping the boredom of State Street reinforced the excitement of opening up a new professional niche. Grew and his colleagues keenly felt the historical significance of their careers. Grew and Phillips, in particular, kept diaries from the first. "Contemplating the lengthening row of leatherbound volumes containing his papers," Heinrichs writes, Grew at the age of forty "saw unfolding a career which already contained historic value." The sense of sharing an unique and historic experience bound together the original group of career diplomats, creating loyalties and friendships that were to last a lifetime. "The Service would have been far from a congenial career all those years," Grew later recalled, "if it hadn't been for the little group of men who have known each other intimately, and when serving at different posts, have kept up their friendship." Waldo Heinrichs describes this feeling of comradeship:

> Service spirit bound the secretaries closely together. The career only deepened and circumscribed existing ties. They possessed a common background, common experience, and a common liking for old wines, proper English, and Savile Row clothing. . . . Indeed the Diplomatic Service most nearly resembled a club.[13]

The regal splendor and pomp of prewar European court society represented the golden age of civilization. Grew's letters home from Berlin contained "a minute account of parties and court functions." Phillips's memoirs present in loving detail numerous recitations of social occasions. The actual business of diplomacy often seemed merely an agreeable accompaniment to the pleasures of membership in an international society of elegance and sophistication. This "freemasonry of European professionals," as Heinrichs termed the transnational fraternity of career diplomats, developed" a corporate identity apart from their national identity."[14] The genteel and leisurely life of an international elite, laced with the agreeable obligations of negotiation, representation, and reporting, made a very pleasant life. Dickering with friends from the local foreign office, chatting genially at fancy social events, and dreaming up elegant-sounding clichés in the warm confines of a paneled study made for a varied and integrated existence. Indeed, the well-modulated life of an embassy often held more appeal than the combative and intellectually demanding routine of the department in Washington. Hugh Gibson viewed his job as assistant secretary of state as a disagreeable interlude before returning to the pleasures of Warsaw society. Although Castle preferred the department, and Phillips enjoyed the excitement of official Washington, others felt more comfortable abroad. Many retired there.

The disdain for business never left those who had consciously rejected it for a public calling. "If you ever hear of me starting in on State Street," Grew wrote to Hugh Gibson, "please send flowers as the end will not be far off." Gibson at one time even argued against salary increases for ambassadors and ministers. "I am not in favor of raising salaries," he told a reporter. "As a matter of fact, if salaries were raised the jobs would be sought by a bunch of incompetents with political pull." True to his standards, Gibson had to turn down Herbert Hoover's offer of the Paris embassy in 1929 for financial reasons and accept Brussels instead. Grew, for his part, as minister to Denmark in 1921 confined his acquaintances to those in the Copenhagen bluebook. Feeling that he should broaden his horizons, he met some prominent Danish businessmen and visited their factories. But his interest waned. "He attended one dinner of Danish merchants," Heinrichs relates, "but found the protocol of *skaaling* severe, the food heavy, and the conversation dull." Phillips had better success in breaking out of the courtly minuet, but he also felt more at home in the company of tiaras and top hats. The occasional necessity for mingling with the proletariat aroused sheer revulsion.

> Trips to the fair and the beach with the children were occasionally cut short because of "the dirty, smelly crowd of all the rabble of Copenhagen." [Grew] noted that a group of Danish-American singers whom he had entertained were listed as carpenters, plumbers, housepainters, and gardeners, and bluntly commented in his diary, "They look it."[15]

If businessmen were disagreeable and labor unions distasteful, communism was anathema. As Christian gentlemen, the diplomats were horrified at the assault upon family, religion, and simple decorum that gained popularity with the Bolshevist revolution in 1917 and the American jazz age of the twenties. "Small wonder," wrote Andover headmaster Stearns, "that Russia, weltering in the tragedy of communism, should rage with unconcealed venom against the Christian home."[16] When American businessmen looked toward communist Russia as a new lucrative mass market, the diplomats deplored what seemed to them a morally blind opportunism. And the stirrings of labor unrest in America equally alarmed them. The Boston police strike shook Grew. "Bolshevism and anarchy are pretty near our gates," he wrote from his study in Copenhagen, "when that sort of thing can happen."[17] He praised members of the nobility and others, "clearly gentlemen," who broke a dock strike in Copenhagen by loading the ships themselves. It was "the one and only answer to the Unions."[18]

The vituperative politics of the New Diplomacy seemed of a piece with the Teapot Dome politics of the twenties—a violation of the civilized codes of personal honor and fair dealing. Heinrichs writes:

> The peace of Brest-Litovsk, remarked Hugh Wilson, who viewed things the way his friend Grew did, marked the end of the era of "scrupulous courtesy" and "good manners" in international dealings and the beginning of the era of "diplomacy by vituperation." This manifestation of the threatening new Russia struck home most forcibly to a diplomat of the old school like Grew. Bolshevists were not gentlemen.[19]

Grew found the Soviet entrance into European diplomacy at Genoa and Rapallo in 1922 "profoundly disgusting." Aware that the standards of decorum they treasured ultimately rested on no more than an agreement as to their legitimacy, the diplomats were very sensitive to attack on the forms of behavior. The learned codes of conduct were all that separated civilization from barbarism—especially for an elite who felt that the bonds of society were fragile even in the best of times.

The unsettling changes occurring in the world about them did not disturb the diplomats' enjoyment of their own company or of the profession they had chosen for themselves. There the center did hold. Bonds of friendship and loyalty formed that carried through the years. Looking back on his career at midcentury, Phillips lamented the disappearance of a "family feeling" in the foreign service. Jay Pierrepont Moffat, who entered the diplomatic service in 1919 fresh out of Harvard, recalled the atmosphere: "In those days the Department was still like a club: the outsider was regarded with a faint air of suspicion, but a member, even a junior, was treated with absolute trust."[20]

2 | THE WARSAW MISSION, 1919–21

THE APPOINTMENT OF Hugh Gibson, son of a California banker, as the first American minister to Poland in 1919 offered the young diplomats a firsthand look at a fledgling government living in the shadow of the new Soviet Russia. "He had a scintillating mind," wrote Jay Pierrepont Moffat, who served under Gibson at Warsaw, "and a razor-like wit, fortunately tempered by a keen sense of fun. He knew Europe as did few Americans; he was on terms of intimacy with the key men in a dozen foreign offices."[1] During his service at the legation in Belgium during World War I, Gibson assisted Herbert Hoover in his relief activities. They became close friends. Hoover, with the support of Colonel House, persuaded President Wilson to appoint Gibson minister to Poland. He was only thirty-six, the youngest minister in the diplomatic service, when he arrived in Warsaw in the spring of 1919. Gibson's second secretary, responsible for organizing the operations of the mission as Grew had been in Berlin, was young Arthur Bliss Lane, twenty-five years old. Son of a wealthy and aristocratic New York City merchant family, Lane had moved from private school to Yale and then to Rome as private secretary to Ambassador Thomas Nelson Page. His family and close friends called him Muggins. Like Phillips and Grew, Lane rejected the unexciting job of maintaining a fortune that others had created. He sought adventure abroad.

Gibson and Lane by choice and by temperament became honorary members of the Polish aristocracy. Lane, in particular, judged Warsaw as he judged New York—by the elegance and lavishness of the entertainments enjoyed by the idle rich. Before assignment to Warsaw Lane had expected that he and Gibson would be sent to Prague. In anticipation he wrote to Gibson inquiring about the golf scene in the Czech capital. "I don't believe," Gibson answered, "there is anything in the way of a golf course at Prague but it might be well to bring along your clubs. Perhaps some of that rolling country can be put to good use."[2] Although Warsaw also lacked a golf course, it proved rich in other entertainments. The centerpiece was the Club des Chasseurs, an aristocratic redoubt where the young American diplomats took most of their meals. They were graciously welcomed into the fold. "They have very courteously made us all temporary members," Lane wrote to his parents, "including all the many privileges thereof." The club compared favorably to those in New York. "The Club des Chasseurs is a very exclusive aristocratic club where one meets the members of the famous old Polish families who pride themselves on their lineage. It is beautifully equipped and is every bit as comfortable as the best clubs in America."[3]

Lane enjoyed the company of his Polish friends and sent home a steady stream of letters detailing the sumptuous life of the nobility. "We lunched at the Countess Potocka's," began one typical account. "She and her sister have a beautiful palace . . . with a huge courtyard in front. Old Count Gulokowski . . . one of the largest landowners in Galicia was there and I found him very pleasant. We sympathized with ourselves when we came out of the palace after lunch and we knew well how sorry our friends at home must feel for us in 'starving Poland.' We only had eggs cooked with shrimps, beefsteak, mushrooms, potatoes, string beans, and vanilla ice cream and cake; not to mention beer and burgundy."[4] If for any reason the food should decline in quality under the stress of war, all was not lost. "It is a great relief," Lane wrote, "to know that one has always got the finest opera to fall back upon in the evening."[5] Occasional disappointments, however, could not be avoided. Lane, who had great affection for his racing horse Bull Run, could not overlook the "poor quality" of the horse jumping at the Cours Hippique. To compound the matter, the tennis courts, fissured by the winter frost, were "most disappointing." A final blow was lowered in the evening of the same day at the opera itself. "The cello flatted terribly in the last act," Lane sadly recorded.[6]

With no sense of incongruity Lane time and again equated events in Warsaw with the activities of the nobility. "All of Warsaw was there," he wrote of one reception, "and it was quite gay to see all of the noblesse in their bright uniforms."[7] The events at the Cours Hippique marked "the first time this season that all the Warsavians had a chance to turn out in their gala attire." When he planned a dinner to repay those who had invited him to their homes, the list of "Warsavians" narrowed even further. "All Warsaw seems to consist of the Radziwill family," he noted, "and this dinner will be practically all Radziwills." And he added in explanation: "I thought I might as well get in right with some of the people who own horses!"[8] Gibson, ten years older than Lane, had a little more perspective.

When Lane moved to London at the end of 1919 he was replaced by Jay Pierrepont Moffat, a descendant of John Jay and a brilliant student at Groton and Harvard. Moffat, intent on a diplomatic career from adolescence, became private secretary at the Hague in 1917 at the age of twenty-one. Returning to Washington two years later, he passed the oral examination ahead of all his competitors and was assigned to Warsaw as third secretary of legation.[9]

Gibson rented the famed Blue Palace to house the legation. Moffat and the other secretaries of the legation moved in and shared the expenses. Its sixty rooms, large garden, library of rare manuscripts, and collection of valuable paintings endeared Gibson to the nobility. "He quickly became a prime favorite in Polish society," Moffat wrote, "and no gathering was complete without 'our dear Gibson.' " Amidst preparations for battle and the lingering misery of World War I, Moffat affectionately remembers:

> Never had Warsaw known such a "season" as the winter of 1919–1920. The great families, Potockis, Radziwills, Lubomirskis, Sapiehas, after having lived in the country for decades, made a point of returning to Warsaw and opening their palaces. With their eighteenth century standards, they felt that they were testifying to their faith in Poland's stability by making its capital for one brief winter the most brilliant in Europe.

Moffat was most struck, however, by the country estates of the Polish aristocracy. Never before had he seen such opulence. America had nothing to equal the manors and chateaux of Polish feudalism. He marveled at Lancut, "the fairy-tale chateau of Alfred Potocki."

> No description could do justice to the house or to the princely state with which it was maintained. . . . We never dined twice in the same dining room. Once we ate from plates carried by Napoleon on his invasion of Russia and abandoned during his retreat. We had coffee in a drawing room where the furniture and pictures came from Versailles, bought by an ancestor during the French Revolution. There were galleries, halls of sculpture, an orangerie, even a theatre.[10]

Moffat's wonderment extended to the feudal system that supported the landlords. He had never before realized its virtues. "Life was still feudal," he began, "but it was devoid of sham." There was no false pretension on the part of the peasants, no counterfeit humility by the nobility. Each order knew its place and gloried in it. "Landlord and peasant had made common cause during the partition. . . . This had welded a strong bond between them. . . . The more lavish the castle and its invariable hunt, the greater the pride of the peasants." The nobility, of course, must show interest in the lives of the peasants to keep this "strong bond" intact. "There were some ten thousand peasants on the estate, happy enough, loyal enough, but not to be tempted beyond a point." Sympathetic interest in the minor problems of peasant life, an occasional scolding, a few coins, a pill, a small present for the newborn —these simple gestures won the loyalty and affection of the peasants. "The system worked," Moffat concluded, "and it would work so long as the landlords were willing to give so much of themselves."[11]

Just how much they were willing to give is evident in Lane's account of a dinner conversation with Princess Radziwill, "literally perhaps the most interesting evening I have spent in all my life." Lane relates:

> She said that her husband was revered and loved by all his servants on his vast estates and that after he died the serfs would attend service almost daily at the little chapel where he was buried in respect to their former master. However, he was known as the man with the strong fists and would knock his servants down with great agility. The Princess said that she could not keep a cane or riding whip in the house, they were all broken on the servants' backs. She said they seemed to like it.[12]

The view from the chateau was a pleasant one—happy peasants, benevolent lord, harmonious community. It seemed sad that the "misery and torture and carnage" of Bolshevism might soon destroy this rural idyll. "And yet we instinctively knew," Moffat lamented, "that the Polish way of life, twentieth century feudalism however benevolent, was doomed to die."[13] The peasants, content in their station, would never rise against the landlords on their own. These simple people were vulnerable, however, to the siren call of Soviet propagandists. "The landlords were no longer safe," he later explained, "as in many regions the peasantry was in a ferment stirred up by infiltrating Soviet agents."[14]

Moffat admired the determination of his friends to fight unflinchingly against threats to "the Polish way of life." Princess Radziwill, for one, had no doubt but that the Bolshevik rabble could be subdued only by the harsh means that her own servants so liked. "The only salvation of Russia [is] the knout and the scaffold," she told Lane.[15] Like the Trojan soldiers who fought on even when all hope was gone, these aristocrats would concede nothing.

> To them Bolshevism was sheer evil. It was anti-Christ. The memory of relatives massacred, of houses burned over their heads, of property torn from them was too near, too vivid. It confirmed in them a super-conservatism, a resistance to reform. . . . They were living in a bygone world, mistaking the gesture for reality, but they were governed by a code, and that code included intense loyalty to friends and unflinching defiance of foe.[16]

The new Polish government was a pathetic affair. After a century and a half of partition Austrian Galicia, German Posen, and Russian Poland did not smoothly fuse together into a unified state. "The difficulties of forming an administration," Moffat later wrote, "of unifying three financial systems, three judicial systems, and three sets of military traditions at times seemed almost insuperable."[17] The most serious threat to national survival in the eyes of Moffat and Gibson was from the East. By early 1920, the Bolsheviks had defeated all their internal enemies and were free to concentrate their armies, if they wished, against Poland. Should the Russians take Warsaw, Poland would fall into their hands; the spark would leap to a restive and sullen Germany. Europe would blaze with social revolution. "The impending campaign between Poland and the Soviets," Moffat learned from the club members at the embassy in Berlin,[18] "might well determine the future social order of Europe."

A Polish-Soviet war, however, was neither as inevitable nor as imminent as Moffat imagined. Through the mediation of the Polish Communist Julian Marchlewski, a secret Polish-Russian armistice had been arranged in the summer of 1919. The Bolsheviks desired calm in the West while they dispatched the White generals Denikin and Kolchak in the South. The Polish chief of state, Marshal Joseph Pilsudski, chose to hold his fire until Lenin had defeated the British-backed armies. Then he could launch his offensive as the last hope of the West against the Bolshevik menace. The allies would aid him in restoring the 1772 boundaries of Poland, he felt, only if their own interventionist plans had first failed. As the Whites collapsed in early 1920, Pilsudski prepared to act. The Bolsheviks, however, did not want war with Poland and began to shower Warsaw and allied capitals with one peace proposal after another. The Communists had not abandoned the dream of world revolution. They concluded, however, that a generous peace with Poland and the Baltic states would help the revolution more than territorial conquest. Peace, wrote *Pravda,* was "the most advantageous condition for introducing Communist ideas in the minds of workers of all the world and for the victory of world revolution." The Bolsheviks offered to settle on the line dividing the Polish and Russian armies, considerably more generous than the ethnographic frontier known as the Curzon line agreed upon at the Versailles conference.[19]

Pilsudski's ambition, however, was to create a great Polish empire controlling the borderlands. The Polish sphere of influence would stretch from the Baltic to the Black Sea, anchored in alliances with the new Baltic republics in the north and Rumania in the south. The Ukraine and White Russia would become confederal provinces of Poland, nominally independent but in reality protectorates of Warsaw. Pilsudski's desire to create a Polish empire in Middle Europe may have been unrealistic, but it was not fanciful. He hoped to transcend the harsh dilemmas of Polish geography by permanently reducing the power of Russia in the borderlands. Versailles Poland was ethnically correct but strategically unsound. As a professional soldier, Pilsudski intended to rectify this error.[20]

Russian Foreign Minister Chicherin's peace offer was, therefore, unsatisfactory on two counts. First, it did not extend to the Dnieper, Poland's prepartition border, and thus left Kiev, largest city in the Ukraine, outside Polish control. Second, it did not permit the defeat of the Red Army by Pilsudski's legions. A careful historian of this period concludes: "The chief of state felt that a lasting settlement embodying his eastern program could only be achieved after a victory over the Red Army; any other kind of peace would bring no permanent solution." Pilsudski's response to Chicherin's overture reflected these calculations. He refused a general truce on the grounds that the Bolsheviks were untrustworthy and insisted that the site of negotiations lie behind Polish lines. The Polish reply demanded the ancient boundaries of 1772, and employed a peremptory tone calculated to be offensive. Count Wladyslaw Skrzynski, undersecretary in the Polish Foreign Office, later wrote: "The [Soviet] proposals for peace were not given any serious consideration. When, however, parliamentary and democratic policy did not permit them to be left without an answer, the question of the place where negotiations might be held was raised in such an offensive spirit that the whole question stopped at that point."[21]

The Russians, realizing that Pilsudski wanted war, belatedly prepared to receive the attack. His armies struck on April 26, 1920. Pilsudski correctly anticipated the advantage of an early offensive. His forces met little resistance and occupied Kiev, ancient capital of the Ukraine, in less than two weeks.

While Pilsudski prepared his attack, he also sought allied assistance. After speaking with the marshal, Gibson—unfamiliar with the conspiratorial politics of Eastern Europe—telegraphed Washington predicting an imminent Bolshevik offensive that might spell the end of Western civilization. Only immediate shipments of arms and matériel could bolster the valiant Polish army in its brave opposition to the Communist aggressors. He reported on January 17, 1920, four weeks after the first Russian peace offer, that "failing to conclude an early peace, the only alternative left to the Bolshevists and one that doubtless accords with their designs, is to attempt the military conquest of Poland." As evidence Gibson offered "the clear motives" of the Bolsheviks for wanting to attack, and reports of individuals returning from Russia that "the next great objective was to be the conquest of Poland." The final argument was contributed by the chief of state. "General Pilsudski told me this afternoon that he knew definitely that the Bolsheviks were pushing their preparations for an attack on the Polish front." Gibson pleaded for clothing, shoes, rolling stock, munitions, and food to aid the Polish army in its "defensive campaign." Without Western aid morale might collapse with a dreadful domino effect in Europe. Polish capitulation "would be quickly followed by a similar collapse in Czechoslovakia." Austria would fall next. "That brings us to Italy," Gibson continued and added ominously: "What the results would be there and in other . . . western countries, the Department is in a position to know." Indeed, Gibson reported, "Success in a campaign against Poland . . .

would give a fresh impetus to the Bolshevik movement throughout the world."

Gibson's dispatches treated the prospect of a peace settlement as a danger nearly equal to a successful Bolshevik invasion. By threatening to sign a peace treaty with Russia out of despair, Pilsudski stimulated a Gibson telegram to Washington urging immediate aid for the Polish army. Gibson's reports posed a choice—aid Poland or force her into signing a peace of subjection.[22] "Without material support on a large scale," Gibson wrote to Lane, "it will be impossible for the Polish army to resist the Bolsheviks much longer. They will either have to make the best terms they can by way of a treaty of peace or be conquered and treated as a conquered territory . . . matters are fast approaching a crisis."[23] If aid were not sent, Gibson wrote to the secretary of state, and the Allies encouraged Poland to conclude peace, "she will undoubtedly do so on the best terms she can secure. In that event what measures does our Government consider desirable to prevent the spread of Bolshevist doctrines to more western countries?"[24]

Moffat also viewed with foreboding the prospect of a settlement on the eastern frontier. He noted the Soviet willingness to draw the boundary "more or less along the line the Poles now hold," and feared that the populace might support it. "It is too early yet to estimate the popular reaction to this appeal. Things are not going too well. The radicals, of course, ask for nothing better than peace with Lenin and Trotsky, and there has been a very carefully organized and apparently successful propaganda among the peasants."[25] Moffat faithfully reported Pilsudski's view that peace was dangerous, a radical plot to undermine the Polish government. Cooler heads prevailed in London and Washington. Lloyd George urged the Polish government to make peace with the Bolsheviks and refused to send any aid. The secretary of state cabled in answer to Gibson's urgent plea for help: "I feel that it would be most unfortunate if the Polish government should conclude from the silence of this Government in the matter that there is implied such military and economic assistance as might determine the Polish government in refusing to enter into armistice negotiations with Bolshevist Russia."[26]

Moffat, like his Polish friends, wanted a victor's peace, restoring the historical greatness of Poland. As Pilsudski's columns approached Kiev, he wrote: "The news from the front . . . was most conducive to real enthusiasm, and people are beginning to hope again of some sort of a peace with the Bolsheviks."[27] Two weeks later, during the brief period the Polish flag flew over Kiev, he wrote: "With just a little common sense, Poland will succeed and become a great nation. Though at times I doubt it, I still think that the necessary grain of common sense will be found."[28]

Moffat and Gibson alike sometimes wondered if the Poles were a Christian people or a lesser order of humanity. Moffat described with condescending affection the naive enthusiasm of the Poles on achieving nationhood.

> The Pole is by nature sanguine. He lives in the present. He has the happy faculty of closing his eyes to gathering storm clouds and concentrating on transient sunshine. Although he subconsciously sensed the dangers threatening the country from without and within, the average Pole preferred not to think about them. . . . He gave free rein to enthusiasm, to buoyancy, to optimism.[29]

It would not be easy to implant the Anglo-Saxon virtues of responsibility and hard work into such a childlike race. "The Slav is incurably easy-going by temperament," Moffat wrote. "They do not seem to realize that with a country to make it might behoove them to play a little less. . . ."[30]

Joseph Grew was equally puzzled by his first diplomatic encounter with a culture outside of Western Europe. As chief American negotiator at the Lausanne Conference in 1923, Grew had his first encounter with Turkish diplomats. Heinrichs records Grew's assumption "that the Turk was an Oriental and thereby essentially different from and inferior to the Westerner."[31] Grew alternated between treating these lesser creatures as rug merchants—wily bargainers who were master bluffers and highly untrustworthy—and regarding them as insecure children who would respond to trust and affection.

Despite their reservations, neither Gibson nor Moffat wished to see the magnificent estates in the border regions leveled by the communists. At the height of the Polish offensive, Moffat made a trip into the Polish-occupied Ukraine in the private railway car of the British military attaché. The touring party reached the front sooner than they imagined, for Budienny's Cossacks had launched a successful raid behind Polish lines. Moffat could soon hear rifle fire in the fields alongside the tracks. They pulled into the Szepetowka railway station and darkened the car for the night. Moffat's thoughts and those of his companions turned to brighter times: "In happier days Szepetowka had been the station for Count Joseph Potocki's fabulous estate of Antoniny, and we tried to picture it as it must have looked with coaches and four drawn up for the laughing and carefree guests arriving from St. Petersburg, and the fourgons to transport the servants and the mountains of baggage."[32] As the Bolshevik counterattack swept toward Warsaw, Moffat reported the anxieties of his friends. "The Poles are beginning to arrive" at the embassy, he wrote, "and with tears in their eyes ask you to send out their jewels in the pouch, so that they will have some capital abroad if they must again become refugees."[33] The British ambassador, Horace Rumbold, confided to Moffat that he had much to lose if Warsaw fell. "Rumbold said that it would be most disagreeable for him personally as he had all his china, paintings and silver here and did not feel that he was in a position to suffer the loss calmly."[34]

The Bolshevik counterattack reached the outskirts of Warsaw before the Poles rallied and saved the city from occupation. Moffat reported the happy aftermath to Castle, who replied: "Your account of Adam Tarnowski's rescue of his valuables from the Bug was very interesting. I wonder whether he also fished up some of the thirty-two Bolshevists whom he had the honor of shooting."[35] Such solicitations for the welfare of the nobility won the Warsaw mission high praise from the Polish elite. Polish Foreign Minister Prince Eustachy Sapieha, in an instruction to Polish diplomats abroad, referred to Gibson as Poland's "great friend." When Gibson returned to the United States in April 1920 for consultation, the Poles were distressed to learn that he might not return. Adam Tarnowski exclaimed, "It cannot be, it cannot be. He is too good a friend of ours."[36]

Gibson, however, was not idle in Washington. He bent every effort to serving the interests of his Polish friends and eradicating the nightmare of Bolshevism. He fought hard but in vain to get an American line of credit to Poland for purchase of war materials; the indifference of the War Department and the hostility of the Treasury blocked the effort. "Lubomirski and Smulski [of the Polish legation] are camping in the Department," Gibson wrote to Moffat. "I feel desperately sorry for them. . . ."[37] As he saw it, the American attitude to Russia would determine the policy on Poland. "I don't feel that it is any use to try to deal with Poland or Finland or Roumania separately. We have first to find out what we want to do about Russia, and how we can go about it." Gibson's choice was clear. "If . . . we really do want to see the Bolsheviks cleaned up or even held back from swarming over Europe, the Poles seem to be the only people who can do it and we ought to at least foot the bill."[38]

American policy, however, was softening after the abortive stab at intervention in Siberia. The British were negotiating a trade agreement with the Soviets. Gibson was aggrieved. "We yesterday announced the removal of trade restrictions with Russia," he wrote to Moffat on July 8, 1920, "a step that was taken over my dead body."[39] Gibson funneled his energies into the only remaining avenue of support—a presidential statement of principle. "I have been pushing like hell for all I am worth to get the President to make a statement in regard to Poland and Bolshevism in general," he told Moffat.[40] In the form of a communication from the secretary of state to the Italian ambassador, Gibson finally won this small victory.[41] The end of the war saw Poland holding a considerable amount of territory east of the Curzon line—a rough ethnic frontier. Gibson wanted the American government to endorse the new boundary. Allen Dulles sympathized. "I realize the importance of what you say about the Poles need of territory in the East for expansion and for her surplus population," he wrote to Gibson.[42]

As Soviet armies closed on Warsaw, the diplomatic corps packed to leave. Moffat went to the station to see the diplomatic train off. He described the scene to Gibson, expressing his sympathy for the harried diplomats who in the midst of crisis maintained their gentlemanly poise. Then an unexpected sight caught his eye.

> On the next track stood a refugee train, and into this poured a swelter of humanity. They sounded like so many cackling geese. They stormed the compartments, climbed over the roof, struck each other, and generally behaved in a manner that made us pray like the pharisee, "Lord I thank Thee that I am not as other men." With this republican sentiment, I am, etc.[43]

Moffat had never witnessed scenes such as this. Even stranger to him was the necessity of dealing with Jewish refugee problems. He wrote to Gibson: "I have been having a delightful time holding the hands (figuratively, of course) of our numerous Hebraic friends who are in trouble." One of these was a Judge Fisher, representative of a Jewish relief mission, who sought permission to cross into Bolshevik territory in pursuit of his relief work. "He told both Redecker and myself that he anticipated only the most cordial cooperation in Russia, that he

Hugh Gibson at his desk in Warsaw, 1919. YALE UNIVERSITY LIBRARY, ARTHUR BLISS LANE PAPERS

Joseph Grew as undersecretary of state, 1925. HENRY MILLER NEWS PICTURE SERVICE, INC.

The American minister, Hugh Gibson (seated), and staff—Warsaw, 1919. Left to right: Lt. Col. Elbert E. Farman, military attaché; F. R. Dolbeare, secretary; Capt. C. A. Abele, naval attaché; Arthur Bliss Lane, second secretary. YALE UNIVERSITY LIBRARY, ARTHUR BLISS LANE PAPERS

The Executive Office Building, home of the State Department until 1947. U.S. DEPARTMENT OF STATE

The Warsaw Ghetto, 1919. YALE UNIVERSITY LIBRARY, ARTHUR BLISS LANE PAPERS

George F. Kennan, 1947. WIDE WORLD PHOTOS

expected 'to be recognized' and to be able to make himself understood by means of Yiddish, in which he is proficient. This latter remark is rather a give-away on the general religion of the Bolsheviks." The May Day parade in Warsaw underlined the fact of Jewish predominance in the communist movement.

> May Day passed off on the whole rather quietly. There were great processions all morning with red banners, about 75% of which were covered with Yiddish inscriptions. You would have thought from seeing the streets that it was a Jewish holiday. The main focus of infection was in the square just in front of the legation.[44]

Moffat considered it a happy coincidence that the Polish national holiday came only two days later. "It was rather an advantage to have May Third so soon after as it rendered a comparison possible. On May Third not a Jew was to be seen anywhere and it was a true Polish holiday."[45] Moffat viewed peace sentiment as Jewish-tinged and therefore suspect. "The situation is at present rather depressing," Moffat wrote to Gibson, disappointed that Pilsudski's offensive had not aroused more support in Warsaw. "The dissenters and pacifists are doing their best to embarrass the Government, a general strike is threatened . . . and a certain class of Polish citizens are scarcely covering their smiles with their whiskers."[46]

Gibson offered his own opinion of the character of the Bolshevik régime when he returned to Warsaw after the end of the Polish-Soviet war to discover a Soviet legation in the capital. He began with a description of the head of the legation, Leo M. Karakhan. Karakhan had been assistant commissar of foreign affairs before his assignment to Warsaw. He later became famous for his successful negotiations with China and Japan. Gibson drew this sketch: "Karakhan, a slinking little rat, is said to be an Armenian Jew of a sect that feeds chiefly on the Old Testament; I can't remember their botanical name off-hand."

Moffat and Grew also had encounters with Soviet diplomats. Moffat's diary records his first impression of the Soviet delegate to the League of Nations: "Then Litvinoff, with the malevolent look of an untidy Jew, rose to speak."[47] Grew, whose daughter later married Moffat, had his first face-to-face negotiation with a Soviet diplomat at the Lausanne Conference in 1922–23. He described Russian Foreign Minister Chicherin as "a Bolshevik bird of prey, with malignant eyes and a beak nose."

Gibson's friends and aides knew how much he liked Jewish stories, especially practical jokes, and kept him well-supplied. A Warsaw embassy subordinate, Benjamin Thaw, Jr., wrote to him in loving detail of an encounter on a train with a Jewish-American tourist. Thaw knew German but Mr. Eppstein did not. When they found themselves together in the dining car, Thaw took the German bill of fare, looked it over for both of them, and falsely announced that there was nothing to eat except ham and eggs, which he ordered for two. Thaw reported the hilarious denouement. The waiter set down the order and Eppstein said: "Help yourself; I don't care for ham."[48] One of the best tricks of all was pulled by Ensign J. L. Olmsted, editor of the 1922 *Lucky Bag*, the Annapolis yearbook. Olmsted had the photograph and biography of graduating senior Leonard Kaplan perforated so that they might be removed from the yearbook by the students. Kaplan's caption read: "This is Porky, of whom it is said that he was born in the township of Zion, county Cork, in a state of ignorance on March 17, 1900." A friend mounted a news clipping of this episode on a card and sent it to Gibson with the delighted comment: "Can you beat it?"[49] Grew added to Gibson's collection a mounted clipping of Harding's appointment of a rabbi as minister to Persia, the first time in history a rabbi had represented the United States in a foreign country.[50]

Gibson returned these two favors by putting little Jewish squibs in his letters. He wrote to Lane, for instance: "On Christmas night . . . Mike found an orchestra of yids who were about the most disreputable specimens you ever saw."[51] Assistant Secretary of State William Castle, Jr., a club member who decided after the war to become a permanent policy officer in the department, ran a personal news service on Jewish activities at home. First of all, he observed, they were trying to shylock Poland in postwar banking arrangements. There were "a great number of Jew Bankers who are naturally irritated with the agreement because it prevents them from making 50% on their transactions. . . ." As Castle told it, they tried to win him over by sending a non-Jewish lobbyist to make the case, but he was too smart for them: he unmasked their "noble representative, Mr. Mason, whose American name, I imagine, covers his Semitic origin." Castle asked Gibson for help in combating sharp-dealing Jewish financiers: "it would be particularly useful if you know of any instances in Poland where American citizens (your co-religionists) in Poland have been cheated out of the proper number of marks exchanged for dollars."

Day by day their tentacles spread. "They are more and more entering the political field along with the Irish," Castle wrote, "and their grip in finance is appalling." He passed along a story told him by Major Reagan of the War Department. He had recently met a man who had changed his name "from yours or something of the sort" to a Jewish name "because there was no show in business in New York for a Christian." Castle liked to keep things in perspective. His verdict on the story: "significant if unimportant." Castle felt duty-bound to stand up to the Jews, even at considerable personal risk. He drafted a letter for the secretary's signature castigating Louis Marshall, head of a Jewish relief organization. "I should not mind [being the scapegoat]," he wrote Gibson, "if the Jews could be a little bit muzzled, or at least forced to become American citizens, in fact as well as in name."[52]

After Gibson left Warsaw to lobby for Poland in Washington, Moffat took up the cause. He inveighed against "the activities of Massel, of the Hebrew Sheltering and Aid Society. He has already perfected his organization to send a quarter-million Jews to the U.S. . . . which would be wonderful if performed in a more worthy cause." Moffat shared his concern with Gibson. "I don't know quite what you can do to remedy this situation, as it has grown a great deal worse since you left. I think a very severe enforcement of delousing, including shaving of beards and heads, would help a little."[53]

Moffat may have picked up the idea of shaving heads and beards from a letter he had received two weeks earlier. A Polish-American Jew, Aron Offen, had written to the embassy to tell of an encounter with soldiers of Haller's army, a volunteer brigade of Catholic Polish-Americans. "Stop Jew!" they had commanded. One of them "got hold of my beard and began to cut it or rather saw it with a saw." The soldier yanked Offen's hair and struck him over the head, damaging his hearing. "After he got through with the barber job, he asked me to pay for 'trimming' my beard but he let me [go] without pay. Now I look terrible . . . totally defaced."[54] Moffat offered a solution and a warning:

> I think an uncompromising representative of the Commission on Immigration would succeed in weeding out a great many as mentally, physically or morally unfit. And as for the rest, unless the Department gives absolute discretionary powers and a man who is not afraid to use them, we shall have to swallow even if they do cause a revolution. It is such an obvious method to increase Jewish numbers and political influence in the United States that if we were not a blind country with a muzzled press, they wouldn't play their hands so rawly.[55]

Moffat's complaint about the American press referred to the coverage given to the report of a special commission sent by President Wilson to examine the Jewish situation in the new Polish nation. The three-member commission, chaired by Henry Morgenthau, could not agree on a joint report. Morgenthau issued a report in his own name and the other two members, Brigadier General Edgar Jadwin and Mr. Homer Johnson, wrote a "minority" report. Jadwin and Johnson were considerably more critical of the Polish Jews than was Morgenthau, who felt that summary executions and the beating and robbing of helpless citizens were inexcusable, whatever the provocation. Jadwin and Johnson suggested that anyone concerned about persecution of the Jewish minority in Poland should be equally alarmed at the oppression of the vast majority of the Russian people by a tiny cadre of Bolsheviks. "Is not the effect of domestic disorder in Russia upon Poland and upon the Peace of the World quite as important a subject for regulation by the Nations as is the limitation upon the majority's treatment of minorities?" they asked. Remove the Bolshevik threat to Poland, they added, and the nation will then be able to "create a governmental system insuring equality, protection, and prosperity to all elements of its population."[56] "It is a curious sidelight," Moffat noted, "that although [the 'minority' report] was issued the same day as the Morgenthau report, it was never published in the American papers."[57]

The various excesses against the Jews documented by both reports were overlooked or minimized in Gibson's dispatches to Washington throughout 1919. The American minister responded slowly to State Department pleas for information on the Jewish situation in Poland. He wrote to his mother: "I am blessed if I think it is worth the time as our Jewish friends come dashing in and tell us every time they hear of anybody who made a face at a Jew. . . . "[58] Gibson's reports consistently emphasized the provocative actions of the Jews and summarily dismissed the notion that killings that did occur had any anti-Semitic causes.[59] First of all, he explained, many Bolshevik agents were Jews. A good number of Polish officers "have seen the Jew as a Bolshevik or his agent in nefarious practices." Secondly, Jewish traders hoarded food during the current time of famine in order to drive up prices. "There is no doubt," Gibson stated, "that this class carries on business by methods that would not be tolerated in the United States." Third, the Jews were "very active" in smuggling food through military lines into Germany. It is what the Jews do, not who they are, that arouses the Polish "sense of justice." "If a Jew is injured," Gibson wrote, "it is called a pogrom. If a Christian is mobbed, it is called a food riot."[60]

Lane, who was in Warsaw during this period, also found the concern of his government over the condition of the Jews somewhat wearying. When Frederick Dolbeare phoned in that the beating to death of five Jews in one town was really "a perfectly natural outcome of poor food conditions," Lane was relieved. "That settles that," he wrote. "Now we can breathe freely until the next report comes that the Jews are being mistreated."[61] It came quickly. Charles Evans Hughes, who had been the Republican candidate for president in 1916, delivered a speech in Madison Square Garden protesting "well authenticated" atrocities against Jews in Eastern Europe. "If America stands for anything in her service to humanity, then now let America speak," he declared.[62] Lane was not interested. "People ought to keep their mouths shut if they don't know what they are talking about," he wrote. Besides, Hughes was just forcing them to do a lot of bothersome work, "making investigations, preparing reports, and then sending them off by telegram." "I should like to get out of here soon," Lane wrote to his parents, "but due to Mr. Hughes and the telegrams we have to send in this regard to prove that he is a nice old mutt I suppose that I shall have to stay on for some time more."[63] When Gibson departed for Vilna and Pinsk for a firsthand investigation of the atrocities, Lane confidently predicted, "I am sure that he will find that they are greatly exaggerated."[64]

The foreign service officers had at first been hopeful that the Morgenthau report would match their own views. Phillips asked Frederick Dolbeare to read it for him because he thought "early publication would help the Polish government." Dolbeare reported otherwise. "I think Uncle Henry did his best," he wrote to Gibson, "and was conscientious in his effort but—" Gibson agreed. "I think it will be just as well," he answered Dolbeare, "if the report is never published. I look forward confidently to more Jewish troubles in the spring." Gibson, hoping to answer Morgenthau's findings, had offered to go to Paris to help prepare a rebuttal. Grew advised against it. Gibson was already too identified publicly with a pro-Polish position. "It might be just as well for you to be able to prove an alibi in the future," Grew counseled.[65]

It was not long before Gibson became the target of Jewish criticism for the tenor of his reports to the State Department, which had become public under congressional pressure. Felix Frankfurter and Justice Brandeis confronted Gibson in a Paris hotel room and demanded that he cease being a propagandist for the Polish government. Frankfurter, whom Gibson called "the hot dog of war," charged that Gibson "had done more mischief to the Jewish race than anyone who had lived in the last century." Known in America as "fair-minded and humanitarian" because of his efforts to free Nurse Cavell during the World War, Gibson's name on a document carried weight. His reports had gone round the world and "destroyed the effect of months of Jewish work." Frankfurter and Brandeis insisted that Gibson "had no right" to make reports to the State Department on Jewish matters and should have "refused" on the grounds that he lacked sufficient information. According to Gibson's account of the meeting, Frankfurter issued "a scarcely veiled threat that the Jews would try to prevent my confirmation by the Senate."

Gibson boiled. Did he not say that stories of excesses against the Jews were exaggerated? "Yes, I said it and it is true." Had he branded the entire Jewish race as gunmen? No, only a certain criminal element. Gibson's anger spilled over into a long letter to Phillips. He accused "prominent Jews in Paris" of being "interested in agitation for its own sake rather than in learning of the situation. . . . They made it clear to me that they do not care to have any diagnosis made that is not based entirely on Jewish statements. . . . My statements . . . were received with incredible and manifest hostility. . . . Their efforts were concentrated on an attempt to bully me into accepting the mixture of information and misinformation which they have adopted as the basis of their propaganda." In Gibson's eyes there was no major Jewish problem in Poland. The rumpus was mostly a result of Jewish-American agitation. "These yarns are exclusively of foreign manufacture for anti-Polish purposes," he wrote to his mother. What was really behind it all? There were "two principal directing forces," he informed Phillips: "(1) To weaken Poland in the interest of Germany. (2) A conscienceless and cold blooded plan to make the condition of the Jews in Poland so bad that they must turn to Zionism for relief." He concluded with a somber warning. If Zionist agitation developed to the point that Poland were refused an American loan or forced to accept reduced borders on the argument that the Poles were not fit to rule minorities, the Polish people would undoubtedly and wrongly attribute the humiliation to the Jews living in Poland. Gibson predicted the awful consequence: "And if the people in their resentment do rise up and massacre Jews on a scale never before known, the blood guilt will be on the foreign Jews who with wicked disregard of the facts or the danger to human lives have played on this tremendously delicate situation."[66]

Gibson rode out the criticism and remained as minister to Poland.

After leaving Warsaw, Gibson was successively minister to Switzerland, ambassador to Belgium, ambassador to Brazil, and once again ambassador to Belgium. When a vacancy appeared in Berlin in 1937, Gibson turned down the offer to serve as ambassador to the Third Reich. He pleaded finances, but perhaps it crossed his mind that the New Deal was loaded with Frankfurter's recruits and that he might have a very uncomfortable time securing confirmation. He retired in 1938 after thirty years in the service.

Lane transferred to the London embassy when Moffat arrived to replace him. He then served as assistant to Undersecretary Grew in 1924 and 1925 before turning to Latin American affairs as counselor of embassy in Mexico City and minister to Nicaragua, then back to more familiar ground as head of the Soviet listening post in the Baltic states in 1936. After a tour in Yugoslavia he served as head of mission in Costa Rica and Colombia during World War II. At the war's end Lane became ambassador to the postwar Polish government, returning to Warsaw after a gap of twenty-five years.

Though two years younger than Lane, Moffat outstripped his contemporary and was soon regarded as the most outstanding young officer in the service. After an interlude in Japan he spent two years in Constantinople before returning to Washington as the first White House protocol officer in 1925. Moffat was bored with the triviality of that job, but before reassignment to Switzerland in 1927 he met and married Lilla Cabot Grew, daughter of the undersecretary. In early 1932 Moffat became chief of the Division of Western European Affairs, reporting directly to Undersecretary William Castle, Jr. Castle, a close friend of Herbert Hoover, left the State Department when Roosevelt took office, but Moffat stayed on. William Phillips, a contributor to Roosevelt's 1932 campaign and a close friend dating back to the Wilson administration, became the new undersecretary. Joseph Grew was appointed ambassador to Japan in 1931 and stayed in that post until Pearl Harbor.

3 | THE EDUCATION OF JUNIOR FSOs

THE UPPER-CRUST CLUB of which Phillips, Grew, and Gibson were founding members and Moffat a brilliant young associate dominated the foreign service during the twenties and thirties. Two-thirds of the secretaries serving in Europe between the Spanish-American War and the outbreak of World War I went to Harvard, Yale, Princeton, or a foreign university. Of those recruited between 1914 and 1922, three-quarters attended prep school, particularly at St. Paul's and Groton. "They were virtually without exception," writes Heinrichs, "well-to-do." Indeed, the State Department discouraged those without private incomes from applying. When Hugh Gibson said that he came from a simple home, he meant "no butlers or footmen." Hugh Wilson remarked that a diplomat understands "instinctively the social gradations of any cosmopolitan group."

The merging of the consular service with the diplomatic service in 1924 and the establishment of a formal examination system for entrance did not weaken the control of the old guard. Grew, as undersecretary of state in the mid-twenties, fought hard to protect the club from dilution. He even declined to testify regarding the merger before Congress on the grounds that those "who talk through their nose and spit on the floor will cut a lot more ice than those who talk like Englishmen." Willam Castle found consular "standards of civilization" lower, as shown in "a fondness for Y.M.C.A. standards and phraseology." "Gibson's picture of a person in a 'sweat'," Heinrichs writes, "was a consul at an embassy dinner." During a confrontation with Wilbur Carr, the chief of the consuls (or "The Little Father of the Consuls," as Grew identified him), Hugh Wilson spoke frankly. The diplomats, he told Carr, "have a higher thought which enures to the good of the Service. They have all felt that they belonged to a pretty good club. That feeling has fostered a healthy *esprit de corps.*" The adoption of a unified promotion list would end it.[1]

Although Carr prevailed (because of his greater support in Congress) in instituting a single promotion list, the diplomats in practice triumphed. A good part of the diplomats' triumph sprang from the fact that the new recruits, many of middle-class and midwestern origins, willingly accepted the values of the club. As the diplomats had modeled themselves on the courts of prewar Europe, so the eager youngsters from the public schools adopted the mannerisms and cast of mind of the club elders. I. F. Stone comments: "If you look through the foreign service register, you will see that a majority of the FSOs do not come from east coast prep schools. But the guys from the midwest schools soon come to conform to the east coast preppy patterns."[2]

The examination system reinforced this tendency. The written test, which required a superficial acquaintance with Western culture, was fairly objective but only marginally important. Alger Hiss, who prepared the written tests in the late thirties, was instructed to make them as difficult as possible so that candidates could be failed at will.[3] The oral interview before a panel of foreign service officers was really all that mattered. Style, grace, poise, and, above all, birth were the key to success. The standards were similar to those of a fashionable Washington club: "Is he our kind of person?" No one who clearly was not would pass. If a black slipped through the net, he was sent to Liberia until he resigned. Women were sent to the jungles of South America.

Jews could not be handled as crassly, but they were made to feel unwelcome and shut out of the better assignments.[4] Those who had the proper background, however, had a great time. Henry S. Villard, who entered the service in 1928 as a Near Eastern specialist, recalls: "Those who made the grade took immense pride in their abilities and enjoyed a unique sense of camaraderie, akin to that found in the congenial circles of a close-knit professional club."[5]

It was a pleasurable and heady sensation for a young foreign service officer to mingle informally with the mannered elite of Europe. And the manners rubbed off. Felix Frankfurter recorded in his diary the impression one journalist gained of Robert Murphy, Roosevelt's representative in North Africa from 1940 to 1942. "One trouble with Murphy," Frankfurter wrote, "is that although he is up from the ranks, he is like so many people, who have not had the advantages of the so-called well-born, but wish they had them, more 'Grotty' than the men who actually went to Groton in the State Department. . . ."[6]

Murphy was neither rich nor Protestant.[7] He was born to German Catholic and Irish Catholic parents in Milwaukee in 1894. The family eked out a living, and it was only Murphy's good work in grammar school that won him a scholarship to the preparatory academy of Marquette University. He picked up shorthand and typing at a local business college while recovering from an industrial accident. These clerical skills were his entrée to official Washington. Inspired by Senator Robert La Follette, he began to attend law school at night, and chose Washington as the site of his studies because he had been offered a civil service job as a stenographer-typist in the office of the third assistant postmaster general. He worked by day and studied at night.

Murphy's injured foot kept him out of the service in World War I, but he served abroad nonetheless as a stenographer-typist for the American legation in Berne, Switzerland. There he met Hugh Wilson and Allen Dulles, and proved valuable to the mission beyond his clerical skills because he spoke German readily. Murphy did not have to hire a private tutor or attend school in Europe to learn German; he had grown up in a faithful fragment of Bavarian culture in Milwaukee.

He returned to the typing–night school routine after the war, but the chance to join the counsular service and return to Europe, at least for a while, held great appeal. His first assignment was to Zurich, but he was shortly transferred to Munich where he stayed for four years, three of them as acting consul general. No city in Europe was a better replica of the German-Catholic neighborhoods of Milwaukee than Munich. Any talent Murphy might have had for a legal-political career in Milwaukee was readily transferrable to the diplomatic-commercial world of Munich. His quick intelligence and easy camaraderie won him many friends among the Bavarian elite. Bavaria had traditionally been a semiautonomous principality, ruled by a Catholic dynasty, "the popular and enlightened Wittelsbach family." Murphy developed an affection for the "popular monarchy" and shared local distrust of the Weimar Republic.

> Few Bavarians [he recalled] welcomed the Weimar Republic; most of them were thoroughly suspicious of it and especially of the Social Democrats who were the republic's principal proponents. In fact, as I soon learned, Bavarians did not expect the republic to endure long; they were impatiently anticipating the restoration of some form of monarchy which would bring back their own Wittelsbach royalty.[8]

The Catholic nobility attempted to recapture the gay atmosphere of prewar Munich when Bavaria enjoyed its own court and diplomatic corps. "They treated the consular corps," Murphy wrote, "as if it were their pre-war diplomatic corps." Murphy lacked none of the entertainments that had so enchanted Grew, Phillips, and Moffat during their early years in diplomacy. He, too, learned of the charms of the Golden Age of prewar, predemocratic court life.

Murphy learned about international politics at first hand from his colleagues in Munich, most of them veteran diplomats from the old school. His most influential teacher was the Papal Nuncio, Monsignor Eugenior Pacelli, later Pope Pius XII. Murphy respected "his intimate knowledge of international politics" and had "many enlightening conversations" with the Nuncio.[9] The anticommunism of the Church meshed well with the aspirations of the Bavarian upper classes for a Catholic monarchy. Murphy's training in Munich prepared him to advance in the foreign service when a unified promotion list emerged. By that time he had been fully socialized in the manners and values of the foreign service club.

James Clement Dunn followed a similar path. Six years older than Murphy, he had dropped out of high school in Newark and worked as a bricklayer for his father, a New Jersey construction boss. He laid bricks during the day and studied architecture with his brother at night; eventually he worked full-time for the new architectural firm of Dunn and Dunn.[10] The war introduced him to diplomacy, as it had Murphy. He won a spot in the naval attaché's office in Havana and then entered the State Department as a clerk. After four years in Spain and then Haiti, he became first secretary under William Phillips in Brussels in 1924. Dunn by this time had married a Chicago Armour and acquired the finances as well as the dress and manners of an old-school diplomat. Phillips was delighted with him. "He is just the right type," he wrote, "and I am looking forward much to my association with him."[11] Dunn's arrival in the inner circle of the club was confirmed when he succeeded Moffat as White House protocol officer.

THE RUSSIAN EXPERTS

One particular class of newcomers had a greater likelihood of establishing a distinctive outlook on international politics, namely, the area specialists. Unlike those absorbed from the consular service or sent immediately to a post after passing the oral exam, the area specialists received a rigorous training in the language, history, and culture of a particular country.

George Kennan was the first foreign service officer trained as a Russian specialist. Like Murphy and Dunn, he found an identity in diplomacy that was both enjoyable and comforting. He willingly conformed to the habits of the service, pleased that he had "a role to play."[12] Kennan sent reports of gargantuan length to the department. They were rarely read carefully or in full, but that was beside the point. The reports were graded, and the grades influenced promotion decisions. Rumor had it that longer reports got higher grades.

The only overseas experience the twenty-three-year-old vice-consul brought to his first permanent post at Hamburg in 1927 was an early acquaintance with Germany. In 1912, at the age of eight, he had spent six months in Germany, easily absorbing the language. His father spoke German, and one of his uncles was German-born. Kennan's training for Russia took place in Berlin and the Baltic capitals of Tallin and Riga. He got his best early experience with the Russian language during a Christmas stay at a monastery near the Soviet border, "a bit of old Russia, seventeenth-century Russia, in fact, unspoiled in a way that would have been hard to duplicate anywhere in Russia proper."[13]

In early 1929, Kennan moved to Riga, a city also redolent of old Russia. He was quickly caught up in "an intensive foreign colony social life," which included, in particular, "the remnants of the former British commercial colony of Tsarist times." Kennan liked this world, resplendent with "vodka, champagne, gypsies, sleighs or drozhki with hugely bundled coachmen waiting at the door. . . . " It was a cameo of prerevolutionary Russia. He reminisced:

> Riga was in many respects a minor edition of Petersburg. The old Petersburg was of course now dead, or largely dead—in any case inaccessible to people from the West. But Riga was still alive. It was one of those cases where the copy had survived the original. To live in Riga was thus in many respects to live in Tsarist Russia—it was, in fact, almost the only place where one could still live in Tsarist Russia.

Kennan clearly preferred the old Russia to the new. As Moffat and Lane had viewed Soviet Russia through the filter of Polish society ten years before, Kennan viewed the Communist régime through the nostalgic eyes of the social elite of Czarist times. The Riga legation, indeed, "was partially manned by people from the staff of the old embassy at Petersburg."[14]

Two years of study in Berlin served to reinforce the impact of these initial impressions. The purpose of the program was to provide "a background in Russian language and culture not dissimilar to that which would normally have been assumed on the part of a well-educated Russian of the old prerevolutionary school." His private tutors were Russian emigrés, victims of the revolution.[15] From Berlin Kennan returned to Riga as a member of the Russian section of the legation, the American listening post for Soviet Russia. The young diplomat's official responsibility was economic reporting, but his mind kept wandering back to the past. He read all of Chekhov's works in anticipation of preparing a biography. "There could . . . have been no finer grounding in the atmosphere of prerevolutionary Russia than this great body of Chekhoviana. . . . And the fact that it was read precisely in the atmosphere of the Baltic States, where more of the prerevolutionary Russia was still present than in Russia proper, gave it a special immediacy."[16]

Kennan's account of a weekend trip to the Baltic port of Liban includes a passage almost identical in flavor to Moffat's imaginings of Count Joseph Potocki's "laughing and carefree guests arriving from St. Petersburg" to vacation at his now deserted estate.

> In the summer days before the war, this beach teemed with the society of imperial Petersburg and Moscow. . . . The uniforms of officers and midshipmen, . . . ladies with long dresses and bustles, and with huge, many-colored beach parasols, children playing in the sand under the supervision of French and English governesses, flags, bunting, yachts, military bands—all these lent to this plain landscape, already tinged with the melancholy of the north, some of the glow and pomp of the capitals.

This gaiety would never return. Kennan intoned: "But this is 1932 and the month of November."[17]

The villains emerge in the next vignette, a walk through the depression-hit factory district. At intervals sit "pretentious houses, the residences of the owners . . . buildings which the mighty have abandoned." Will this "highly organized and pretentious civilization" flourish once more? "Or are these buildings already museum pieces . . . to be inhabited, like many a building in Russia, by people for whom their dignity and pretension are only a nuisance, and their original function a matter of indifference?"[18]

At the age of twenty-eight, Kennan in spirit was already an old man sadly recalling a world that had disappeared. His mind awhirl with the captivating remembrances of his colleagues and teachers, he fell in love with an imagined civilization and idealized its rulers. The youth from Milwaukee needed to concede nothing to Grew or Phillips in his affection for the prewar revelries of European society. Nor did he lag far behind in his aversion to the uncultured masses who would eventually populate the beaches formerly reserved for the titled elite.

The Soviet régime offended Kennan's sensibilities. He felt a mixture of snobbish disdain and moral repugnance in witnessing a government that had repudiated a way of life he esteemed. On the eve of his departure for Moscow after Roosevelt granted recognition in 1933, Kennan's mind was set in an unforgiving mold. "Never—neither then nor at any later date—did I consider the Soviet Union a fit ally or associate, actual or potential, for this country."[19] Kennan viewed the régime through the dark prism of emigré life in the Baltic states. The experience of growing to "a mature interest in Russian affairs" in the anti-Soviet capitals of the Baltic states in the 1920s had left its mark before Kennan ever set foot in Russia. "The brief and bloody periods of rule which the Russian and local Communists had enjoyed in Riga and Tallinn in 1919 left no pleasant traces," he dryly recalled.[20]

Loy Henderson, who served as chargé d'affaires in Moscow from 1934 to 1938, had witnessed this episode of Communist rule at first hand as a member of the Red Cross relief mission to the Baltic states and western Russia in 1919 and 1920. He had joined the foreign service two years later and in 1925 was assigned to the Eastern European division (EE). His job was to trace the connection between the Communist International and the American Communist party. He split the work with Ray Murphy, an expert on domestic communism: Henderson monitored Communists abroad, synthesizing reports from American missions; Murphy kept tabs on those at home. Murphy was aided by close liaison with the red-sensitive FBI. When Arthur Bliss Lane transferred to the field from his job as special assistant (U-2) to Under secretary Grew in 1925, he noted: "The volume of U-2's correspondence with Hoover of Justice is perhaps not realized. During the month of May I received 27 letters from him and sent him 65 personal letters, excluding those letters transmitting Scotland Yard reports on revolutionary activities in the United Kingdom."[21] Most of these FBI communications ended up in Murphy's files, a constantly attended catalogue of suspected Party loyalists. Murphy was not a member of the foreign service, and, indeed, looked and acted more like a gumshoe than a diplomat.

The chief of the Russian division was Robert Kelley, Harvard Phi Beta Kappa and a student of the history of Russian foreign relations. Kelley was distinctly anti-Soviet and had brought Ray Murphy into the department to be trained as an expert in Soviet subversion around the world. Kelley's principal function before 1933 was to find reasons for not recognizing the Soviet Union. Murphy was his permanent lieutenant in the department while the foreign service experts shunted back and forth between Eastern Europe and the department. Kelley also initiated the practice of taking a scholarly approach to the Soviet Union and monitored Kennan's training in Berlin.[22]

After two years under Kelley's aegis, Henderson continued his education in Soviet affairs in the Russian section of the Riga legation and then returned to the department for two more years of Comintern watching before joining the American mission in Moscow in 1934. His distrust of the régime was as deep-seated as Kennan's.

Elbridge Dúrbrow, who served on the Moscow-EE shuttle in the thirties and forties, joined the foreign service in 1930 and served in the *cordon sanitaire* capitals of Warsaw and Bucharest before assignment to Moscow in 1934 for three years. He also formed some preconceptions. "I had some misgivings when we went to Moscow with Bullitt in 1934," he recalls, "I got a little prejudice against the Russians from the Pilsudski régime when I had been in Poland."[23]

Charles Bohlen entered the foreign service in 1929 and spent the next three years in Paris studying Russian affairs in the company of emigré intellectuals before joining Kennan and Henderson in Moscow. While Kennan absorbed Czarist culture in Latvia, Bohlen practiced the Russian language at the Serebrakovy sisters' pension in neighboring Estonia.

> The Serebrakovy sisters came from Leningrad, which they always referred to by its pre-war name of St. Petersburg. Both were strongly anti-Bolshevik and lived in the hope that someday the nightmare would pass away and they would return to old Russia, complete with Czar and aristocracy. One of the sisters was well educated and had been a teacher in the Smolny Institute, a school for the daughters of the Russian nobility.[24]

Bohlen was treated like a son of the Russian aristocracy. Study in the morning, late lunch around four o'clock, a nap, a walk in the woods, late supper, and conversation around the samovar into the night. "Life in the Serebrakovy sisters' pension," Bohlen concluded, "undoubtedly followed the centuries-old style of the leisure class of Czarist Russia." Bohlen, like Kennan, also spent time in Tallin, staying with an émigré timber merchant "full of the curiosity which characterized the pre-Revolution Russian intelligentsia."[25]

Kennan, Bohlen, Durbrow, and Henderson were the leading Russian experts in the foreign service. Together they suffered the petty slings and arrows of daily intercourse with the Soviet bureaucracy. The cumulative effect of these annoyances is easy to underestimate. Michael Forrestal, son of the first secretary of defense and later White House aide to President Kennedy, saw the results a decade later during a visit to Moscow. He wrote his father:

> Since we have so little real knowledge about this country . . . our attitudes change day by day depending on the more or less pleasant experiences we have had. . . . So many of our State Department personnel acquire such a cynical attitude after the first six months here . . . because they deal with the massive and immovable organization known as the Soviet Government. . . . In dealings with the Government one feels as if one is punching a mass of featherbeds. They react to no stimulus, they have invented the most amazingly consistent system of excuses and dilatory tactics and are impossible to shock or prod into any kind of action. They make extravagant demands on the Embassy, so that it becomes a constant war of nerves.[26]

The xenophobia of low-level Russian bureaucrats, fearful of consorting with foreigners, made life a continual nightmare for the foreign service officers who had to manage the routine business of their government with their counterparts. When one had to struggle for weeks merely to get adequate shelter and transportation, it became easy to interpret inertia and timidity as deliberate malice. Liberal journalist I. F. Stone appreciated the problem. "If you have ever paid a visit to Moscow," he commented, "you will feel the oppressive Victorian inertial weight of the Soviet bureaucracy and the striking contrast with the friendly nature of the Russian people. This had to affect anyone who spent time there."[27]

The foreign service officers were not, however, simply visiting Moscow. They were interpreting the régime to their own government. And unavoidably their personal experiences in gaining cooperation from the Russian government in handling their day-to-day business affected their estimate of the value of Russia as a potential ally for the United States. Soviet scholar Samuel N. Harper during research trips to Russia in the 1930s noted his distaste for "the complaining sessions into which social evenings in the foreign colony usually degenerated."[28] "We regarded ourselves," Kennan recalls, "as a lonely and exposed bastion of American governmental life, surrounded by a veritable ocean of official Soviet ill will. . . . "[29] "I feel personally," Michael Forrestal observed, "that the attitude of the Embassy people is a little too bitter in light of the fact that what they report home is accepted as the fact."[30]

Although they hated the government, the Russian experts professed great affection for the Russian people, those lovable stupid peasants. Echoing Moffat's Polish stereotype, Bohlen reports that "the average Russian is an easygoing person with a certain distaste for sustained labor." He found the Russian people docile, simple, and unaffected, "primitive in the best sense of the word." Lest one romanticize the peasantry, however, it was well to remember that "the average Russian is unquestionably on a lower level of cultural development than the average American." Furthermore, unlike his enlightened American counterpart, "the average Russian . . . is still the victim of many superstitions, gullibility, and other characteristics of his peasant ancestors, who lived for centuries in darkness." Bohlen illustrates the charming idiocy of this race with a well-chosen anecdote. A Russian workman, rewarded for moving some furniture into the embassy with a Polish zloty, was puzzled at the markings on this strange coin. In the United States, of course, we test a coin by biting it. Not so the Russians. They placed it on a rock and mangled it with a sledgehammer. Bohlen draws the moral. "In proving it was real, they destroyed the coin, thus fulfilling the curious Russian logic of destroying that which they desire."[31]

Returning from one trip to Moscow, Bohlen ran into a friend who asked him if he had noticed any changes. "The place still smells the same," Bohlen replied, dragging out every word. George Orwell, commenting on high bourgeois revulsion for the lower classes, distills the essence of class distinction in Britain into "four frightful words which people nowadays are chary of uttering but which were bandied about quite freely in my childhood. The words were: *The lower classes smell.* . . . Very early in life you acquired the idea that there was something subtly repulsive about a working-class body; you would not get nearer to it than you could help." Bohlen concludes a chapter of his memoirs entitled "The Smell of Malshora" with the sentence: "the dank smell of the station . . . the odor of wet sheepskin coats, of sawdust spread on the floors to absorb moisture, of disinfectant, of pink soap, of human sweat, and of the cheap Russian tobacco known as Malshora—still remains for me the smell of the Soviet Union."[32]

From 1934 to 1937 the Great Purges occurred in the Soviet Union. These nightmarish events left a deep impression on Kennan. "To be forced to follow their course, day by day," he recalled, "and to write analytical dispatches about the entire process, was unavoidably a sort of liberal education in the horrors of Stalinism. . . . The effect was never to leave me."[33] Henderson as chargé d'affaires shared the task of writing reports on the purge-trials. He was equally horrified, and, like Kennan, recognized the utter degradation of the Stalinist régime.[34]

The rising menace of Nazi Germany might have been expected to temper the views of the Russian experts. Stalin's program of "socialism in one country" might have appeared less threatening to peace in Europe than Hitler's demand for *Lebensraum*. The inauguration of the United Front policy in 1935 also betokened a desire to forgo revolutionary tactics in favor of a defensive alliance against fascism. The experts did not, however, waver a bit in their relentless opposition to the Soviet Union or in their utter cynicism about all its claims. Any signs of friendliness were viewed merely as a smoke screen to lull the West. The assumption that American and Russian national interests could never be compatible remained unshaken.

Indeed, the moral imperative to reject all proposals initiated by the Soviet Union extended to assuming that if *Pravda* said something, it must be untrue. The Russians claimed that Germany had aggressive designs on Soviet territory. Therefore, it was probably not true. The wily Stalin was merely creating a war scare to provide a cover for the slaughter of his political opponents. Kennan seemed more inclined to believe Hitler than Stalin. He accepted Hitler's assertion that he sought only "territories now or previously controlled or inhabited by Germans." Therefore, Russian fears were probably groundless and certainly exaggerated. The United Front policy was no more than an ideological cover for encouraging an internecine war among the capitalist states from which the Soviet Union might stand aloof, and then move in for the kill after the contestants were weakened. Russia, in any case, would unceremoniously repudiate any "undertaking regarding military assistance, unless this happened to coincide with her interests at the given moment."[35] Soviet efforts to strengthen defenses in the West were "militarism." A diplomatic campaign to discourage an Anglo-French accommodation with Hitler aimed at Russia was "a cynical policy of driving the wedge between one's neighbors." Defending his analysis in retrospect, Kennan notes that Russia shares responsibility for provoking the Nazi invasion by maintaining an army on the western frontier. "Hitler dared not leave so imposing a force intact on his flank," Kennan explains, "at a time when his inability to invade the British Isles was compelling him to widen his strategy into an attack against Britain's Mediterranean lifeline."[36]

Kennan's tolerance for Hitler's geopolitical dilemma reflected more than a backlash against Stalin. His fondness for Germany traced back to childhood and was reinforced by association with his colleagues in the German embassy in Moscow. Gustav Hilger, counselor of the German embassy during the 1930s, recalled that the diplomatic corps in Moscow was "one great family, whose members led a very active social life among themselves and engaged in intensive exchange of opinions." Friendships were formed "which rested on such strong personal sympathy and so much mutual trust that they lasted even beyond the war and its aftermath."[37] The American diplomats, it appears, had a closer relationship with the German embassy than with their British colleagues. As German ties with Russia quickened after Munich, the American representatives were kept abreast of the conversations by their German counterparts. Although the hawkish Ribbentrop reigned in Berlin, the German mission to Moscow was headed by Count Werner Friedrich von der Schulenburg, a nobleman of ancient lineage. He opposed Hitler's adventurous policies and even went so far as to encourage his British colleagues in Moscow to urge their government to give a categorical guarantee to Czechoslovakia. No other action could deter Hitler from launching Germany into a catastrophic conflict. Schulenburg failed in this *sub rosa* approach, but his courageous opposition to the Nazis did not diminish. He was later executed for participation in the 1944 conspiracy against Hitler.[38] It is not surprising, therefore, that Kennan and the other American diplomats in Moscow, on friendly terms with their anti-Hitler German counterparts, should initially misread Hitler's intentions. Like the European experts (sometimes known as Europeanists) in the State Department, who saw Germany through the mediation of the Wilhelmstrasse, the Russian experts could not at first grow exceedingly alarmed about a régime that sent them such cultured and moderate colleagues. Kennan's respect and admiration for the proud aristocrats who scorned Hitler increased during the war, when he maintained contact with Count Helmuth von Moltke, great-grandnephew of the famous general, and Gottfried Bismarck, grandson of the legendary chancellor. "The older Prussian aristocracy," he writes, "was divided; but from its ranks came some of the most enlightened and courageous of all the internal opposition Hitler ever faced."[39]

The Europeanists' closeness to the German embassy in Washington tended to make them unsympathetic to those who urged protests against Hitler's actions. The Hanfstaengl imbroglio was a case in point. Ernst Hanfstaengl, a member of the class of 1909 at Harvard and a close aide to Hitler, received an invitation from Senior Class Marshal Eliot Cutler to serve as one of his aides during the 1934 commencement. Hanfstaengl accepted at once and gave the news to the press, whereupon, in Moffat's words, "all the Jews in Christiandom arose in protest."[40] Cutler decided to withdraw the invitation and asked William Phillips, a Harvard overseer, if he would be the intermediary. Phillips asked Moffat for advice. Moffat was glad to help out. He liked Phillips but considered himself brighter. "Bill Phillips . . . is not a deep student," he recorded in his diary, "nor does he really get into any problem at all deeply. But his general approach to matters is a common sense one." Moffat advised standing firm, for if the invitation were withdrawn, "the repercussions would be pretty serious." In particular, Hitler would consider that "freedom of opinion in American universities" was a farce. Furthermore, if Harvard acted "in response to Jewish pressure," she would herself show less than total faith to the "principle of intellectual tolerance."[41]

The opposition to Hanfstaengl, in fact, extended beyond the Jewish community; indeed, it included President Conant of Harvard. Although Conant felt that any alumnus had a right to attend a graduation ceremony, he did not view the opposition to Hanfstaengl as "Jewish pressure." He felt it was motivated by insight into the nature of the Nazi régime. "Those who understood the implications of what had been going on in Germany since March, 1933," he recorded in his memoirs, "were disturbed by the prospect that a personal friend of Hitler's would be a commencement aide." When Hanfstaengl in the capacity of an alumnus offered to found a traveling fellowship, Conant turned him down cold. Refusing to allow "Hitler's henchmen . . . to use Harvard as an American base to spread approval of the Nazi regime," Conant argued that Nazi attacks on the German universities had been so flagrant that Harvard could not accept a gift from anyone associated with that régime. In short, he determined that the principles of free inquiry that Harvard symbolized required issuing a rebuff to Hanfstaengl—the exact opposite of the argument Moffat had advanced.[42]

The growing evidence of fascist aggression created a painful dilemma. How to oppose the Nazi threat to the cherished cultures of England, France, and Italy without supporting Soviet foreign policy? After a tour in Australia, Moffat returned to the department in July 1937 as chief of the Division of European Affairs. As Roosevelt's policy stiffened, Moffat fretted. When the president's quarantine speech, aimed at isolating the Axis nations, came over the radio, Moffat discovered that it was more dramatic than he had expected. "The sentence regarding the quarantine of nations was a surprise," he noted. Moffat feared that it might "ultimately drive us much farther than we would wish to go." A few days later, he clarified his reluctance. Speaking for his fellow diplomats, he said: "Those of us who have lived abroad were a unit in pointing out that we could not go on to take sanctions, no matter what their form, without risking retaliation; . . . that if effective and Japan were completely downed China would merely fall a prey to Russian anarchy and we would have the whole job to do over again and a worse one. . . ." Moffat's judgment was clear. Better a Japanese protectorate in China than the possibility of communism. Anthony Eden's efforts to win American support for a firm stand against Japan aroused Moffat's ire. "I am still convinced," Moffat wrote, "that he would like to see us embroiled side by side in the Far East. . . . This is a tall order, however, and I suspect that in his heart of hearts Eden does not think he will fall into the trap."[43]

Moffat could see no point in forging an antifascist alliance. "My personal preoccupation is to prevent at any costs the involvement of the United States in hostilities anywhere, and to that end to discourage any formation of a common front of the democratic powers." The editor of Moffat's diary takes pains to point out that these sentiments did not arise out of simple isolationism. She explains:

> A fairer interpretation of his views, as expressed in his diary and supported by the testimony of his friends, is that he agreed in many points with his father-in-law, Joseph C. Grew. Both men saw the danger that war against the fascist dictatorships might destroy their menace but augment the power of the communist dictatorship. Thus one adversary would be replaced by an even more powerful one.[44]

As war approached, Moffat grew more and more apprehensive. When the British government decided on conscription in April 1939, he was disturbed. "Personally, I fear that more than any one measure it may be the straw that breaks the camel's back and goads Hitler into desperation. . . ." When Hitler attacked Poland, Moffat despaired. "The issues are so terrible, the outlook so cloudy, the probability of ultimate Bolshevism so great, and the chances for a better peace next time are so remote that if one stopped to think one would give way to gloom."[45]

Hugh R. Wilson, a charter club member and American ambassador to Germany in 1938, did what he could to calm the growing anti-German feelings in the United States. "Certain elements" will work "frantically" to bring the United States into war, he wrote, "and with motives which do not appeal to the vast majority of the American people as real cause for war." Wilson applauded the rectification of the Versailles Treaty at Munich. There were "two sides" to the Sudeten problem, he wrote Secretary of State Cordell Hull, "and not only the Czech side." None of this was really America's business, but he would "deplore" the fact if continued animosity toward Germany in the United States "spoiled" the possibility of creating "a better Europe." "For if our press keeps up its hymn of hate while efforts are made over here to build a better future, this attitude will . . . retard if it does not destroy, the realization of the achievement of real peace in Europe. . . ."

Hugh Wilson could abide a Nazi peace. He had a deep affection for Germany and warm admiration for Hitler's pacification of the German working class. Wilson thrilled to the Nazi *Kraft durch Freude* (Strength through Joy) program, which organized recreational activities for the German worker in lieu of wage increases. It made the life of the workingman "richer and fuller" in contrast to "mere increases in salary" which go into "idiotic things as a rule." He compared one director of the program to "a Hull House worker under Jane Addams," and equated the labor camps "to the efforts we were making in the CCC." This program so captivated Wilson that he took the liberty of expressing Roosevelt's interest "in the effort of the Germany government to enrich the lives of workmen" and sent an embassy officer to attend one of the camps. When Hitler praised *Kraft durch Freude* at a diplomatic reception as a measure to eliminate class warfare, Wilson noted his "obvious intensity and sincerity." He asked the Fuehrer a question much on his mind—if such programs lessened the appeal of communism? Hitler replied that he "no longer feared Bolshevism for his country because of these movements."

The Nazi régime had solved the social problem Wilson wrote, in a way "which is going to be beneficial to the world at large." It would be tragic, he felt, if England and France chose to defy Hitler rather than learn from him. Three months before Munich, Wilson was urging a four-power conference to settle the internecine differences in the European community. "Could the way be paved so that such a meeting would be automatic?" he asked his counterpart in France, William Bullitt. Even if Hitler's territorial appetite continued ravenous, the conference need not fail. Merely turn Hitler to the East, solving two problems at once. Wilson's worst anxieties were realized when Chamberlain gave Poland an "unrealistic" guarantee and the Wehrmacht marched for Warsaw. Still he hoped against hope. "If a spirit should develop in Europe," he wrote Alexander Kirk, "which would permit a cessation of hostilities in the West to allow Germany to take care of the Russian encroachment, I for one should enthusiastically applaud and believe sincerely that the ends of civilization would be furthered thereby."[46]

Although Wilson's views were extreme, they represented the general tenor of the Europeanists' feelings about how to handle Hitler. Both the Europeanists and the Russian experts, though from different angles, viewed Nazi Germany through the filter of communism. There is considerable difference in tone, however, between Moffat's tart sarcasm and Kennan's odd mixture of moral outrage and cynical fatalism. To Moffat, Communist leaders were mortal enemies but also faintly ludicrous Semitic buffoons. Kennan, who did not share Moffat's prejudices, could not appreciate the humor. Knowing the enemy at first hand, he could not be satisfied with comic stereotypes. His hostility was coldly intellectual, thoroughly articulated, and buttressed with copious research. The Europeanists were simple partisans, the Russian experts trained ideologues.

On one point, however, all the diplomats, highborn and low, were united—that foreign policy should be run from the foreign office, not from the White House or Congress. A career diplomat who fancied himself a specialist in foreign affairs had little respect for the politician who viewed *his* mandate as a license to meddle in diplomatic business. Gripes about politicans in diplomacy extend far beyond annoyance at campaign contributors' being rewarded with the better embassies. The main contention is that diplomacy should in no way depend upon public opinion—a throwback, not surprisingly, to the glories of the Old Diplomacy. The diplomats consider themselves keepers of the sacred fire of "national interest." This flame, in their eyes, burns with a platonic regularity; it is endangered by the fickle breezes of public sentiment. Only the diplomatic priesthood, standing aloof from the vagaries of politics, can discern and protect the true and invariant interests of the nation. The phrase "national interest" in the mouth of a diplomat at times has the same quality as the phrase "military necessity" when uttered by a soldier. It is an ideological shibboleth employed to justify basing foreign policy decisions on the preferences of career officials rather than those of the public or its elected representatives.[47]

A demand for permanence or continuity in foreign policy is cut from the same cloth. Politicians come and go, but the diplomatic service is part of the permanent government. Continuity in policy is tantamount to granting the diplomats stewardship over foreign policy. Hugh Gibson makes the case:

> Only too often the opposition party, having denounced the policy of the party in power, feels it essential to scrap everything the old party stood for. . . . That is a body blow to our hopes of having a foreign policy. You can't have a four-year policy followed by another four-year policy. That is nothing but improvisation cut off in four-year stove lengths.[48]

Foreign policy, it appears, should owe nothing to the democratic process. Gibson recommends the British practice. "Let us assume a change in the British Government. A new Foreign Secretary comes in. . . . He finds a group of permanent officials who support him loyally and guide him as to the fundamentals of policy." If the new minister should choose to follow a "brand-new policy" instead of the "precipitate of centuries," he would be repudiated by the people and turned out of office. World War II, of course, was the fault of arrogant politicans who would not take the counsel of trained diplomats. "In general," Gibson writes, "war is brought about by deficient statesmanship on the part of political leaders whom the diplomat serves." It was the "usurpation of diplomatic functions by politicians and inept amateurs" that helped create "a worldwide mess of unprecedented proportions." And the chief sin of the politician is his readiness "to settle everything by the methods of domestic politics."[49]

Kennan's disgust at the intrusion of public opinion into the delicate realm of foreign policy is particularly strong. "Our government," he writes, "is technically incapable of conceiving and promulgating a long-term consistent policy toward areas remote from its own territory. Our actions in the field of foreign affairs are the convulsive reactions of politicans to an internal political life dominated by vocal minorities."[50] This state of affairs is pathological, "a neurotic self-consciousness and introversion" that has stamped American foreign policy with "a certain histrionic futility, causing it to be ineffective in the pursuit of real objectives in the national interest, allowing it to degenerate into a mere striking of attitudes before the mirror of domestic political opinion."[51] Kennan simply refuses to grant the chosen representatives of the American electorate a legitimate voice in the shaping of American foreign policy. In the foreign service lexicon, the "national interest" is what the diplomats say it is.

II

THE NEW DEAL AND THE FOREIGN SERVICE: THE 1930S

* * * * * * * * *

History will achieve no complete understanding of Franklin Roosevelt's Administration without knowledge of the intramural feuds which so frequently beset it.

—ROBERT SHERWOOD

4 | FDR AND THE FOREIGN SERVICE

ONE POLITICIAN WHO had full confidence in his own ideas about foreign policy was Franklin Roosevelt. His upbringing paralleled that of the leading Europeanists. A Hudson Valley aristocrat and cousin of Theodore Roosevelt, he graduated from Groton in 1900 and Harvard in 1904. Like Grew and Phillips, he paled at the prospect of devoting all his time to the administration of family affairs. He shared also their distaste for the Tammany brand of politics, but his ebullient personality and winning charm inclined him to seek at home the adventure they sought abroad. The possession of the Roosevelt surname doubtless helped to confirm the decision to enter politics.

While Grew and Phillips steeped themselves in the cosmopolitan culture of the European courts, Roosevelt plunged into the reformist politics of the Progressive Era. The intricate network of political relationships necessary for success in the polyglot Democratic party tempered Roosevelt's biases, in particular, his initial disdain for Catholic politicians. The large Jewish vote in New York and Roosevelt's reliance on Jewish intellectuals and reformers for some of his programmatic innovations made it quite impossible for him to indulge the anti-Semitic predilections of the diplomats. The Jews with whom Roosevelt was most familiar were a cultured intelligentsia, the offspring of the commercially successful German Jews who arrived in the United States prior to the floodtide of peasant immigrants from the Russian Pale at the turn of the century. Gibson and Moffat, by contrast, did not encounter American-educated, partially assimilated Jews in Eastern Europe. The Polish Jewish community was a beleagured and culturally distinct population, whose religious traditions the diplomats found eerie and ridiculous. Gibson and Moffat could scoff at Jewish claims of persecution in Poland, fully supported by Polish friends and diplomatic colleagues. Roosevelt could not afford to scorn their American compatriots crammed into tenements on the Lower East Side. Tolerance and respect for differences—personal, class, ethnic, regional—characterized Roosevelt, the Democratic politician, and caused him to take a less terrified view of the Russian revolution than his fellow patricians in the diplomatic service. He did not associate labor demands with conspiring Jewish communists. Sympathetic with the needs of his working-class constituents, he attributed industrial conflict to employer recalcitrance as well as union organization. Eleanor Roosevelt, who also enjoyed the variegated life of politics, commented to a disbelieving Caroline Phillips: "Yes, the Unions may be bad but the employers are *so* much worse that there is no comparison."[1]

Although of necessity less of an outspoken crusader than his wife, Roosevelt's own sympathies as well as his political experience made him understand the legitimate grievances that underlay radical appeals. On the one hand, he had no sympathy for the abuse of civil liberties or the denial of religion in Russia; on the other hand, he did not consider the régime a fountainhead of international subversion. The ideology of social reform struck a sympathetic chord in him. Beyond that, he respected the strength of the régime and was prepared to judge it by its acts, rather than its rhetoric. Unlike Kelley and Henderson, he did not preoccupy himself with conscientious tracing of the tentacles of the international communist conspiracy. Roosevelt was too responsive to the pulse of domestic politics to think much about Russia. The impotence of the American Communist party made it hardly relevant in his political calculus. The notion that it was a serious threat was laughable.

Roosevelt's stance toward Russia was more, however, than the residue of his experience in domestic politics. For six years during World I, he had been assistant secretary of the navy. He loved the sea and saw international politics through the eyes of a naval strategist. The only nations that could threaten American security were those who could challenge the American navy—the maritime powers of Britain and Japan. Historical ties to Britain converted the British navy into a close ally dominating the Mediterranean and the North Sea and thus protecting the United States from European powers who might assault the Atlantic seaboard. Japan was the real danger. Growth of Japanese sea power posed an eventual threat to the safety of the Philippines and the fueling stations stretching across the Pacific to Manila. The world of the Europeanists radiated out from a quadrilateral anchored on the choice embassies of London, Paris, Rome, and Berlin. The globe in the eyes of a Navy planner centered on Honolulu, stretched east to the Philippines, north to the Aleutians, and south to the Panama Canal. The diplomats considered the revolutionary doctrines of the Soviet régime the foremost threat to world peace. In naval eyes, however, the Soviet Union, a land power with no naval ambitions, appeared as a potential counterweight to Japanese designs.

Recognition, 1933

Before he took office in March 1933, Roosevelt had decided on recognition of the Soviet Union as a dramatic gesture he could take on his own initiative that might restrain the Japanese. Kelley accepted the inevitable but set to work churning out one memorandum after another listing the multitudinous conditions he believed the Russians should accept in return for recognition. He also emphasized the likelihood that the Russians would blithely violate any agreements they found inconvenient. He did everything in his scholarly power to thwart the successful completion of the Roosevelt-Litvinov conversations. Undersecretary William Phillips supported Kelley's campaign. Although he could not deflect Roosevelt from his course, he tried to throw obstacles in his path. The United States he argued, should not take the initiative. "I felt badly that the President took the initiative in the recognition of Russia," he later recalled. "Russia was eager to be recognized by the United States . . . and would have taken the initiative herself."[2]

When Roosevelt initiated negotiations through Henry Morgenthau, Jr., and William Bullitt, neither a professional diplomat, Phillips was irritated. His wife recorded that Bullitt "is plausible and clever and seems to have a great influence over Franklin; anyone with a Radical idea seems to gain influence over the President."[3] Bullitt had gone on a famous though futile mission to reconcile the new Bolshevik government with the Allied powers during the Versailles Conference and later married the widow of John Reed. He was eager to bring the two nations closer as a matter of personal vindication. Morgenthau, as head of the

Farm Credit Administration, sought a new market for American grain and farm implements. He also wished to prove his usefulness in the Washington arena to his old friend and Dutchess County neighbor, Franklin Roosevelt, whom he had served as conservation commissioner in New York. Roosevelt sidestepped the diplomats in initiating negotiations because they were clearly out of sympathy with his purposes.

Phillips used his influence, once Litvinov arrived, to make the terms of recognition as stiff as possible. If recognition were unavoidable, perhaps the terms could be arranged to void the result. His wife noted: "William says that he persuaded the President to insert into the terms the agreement that at the first sign of Soviet propaganda in this country through any Russian representative, our relations with Russia will automatically be broken off." Caroline Phillips herself considered recognition not only unwise but morally offensive. "We are only following the majority of the other 'Christian' countries," she wrote, "but in doing so I feel we have lost in moral standing. . . . It is sad and demoralizing when we lose our honor for expediency."[4] Joseph Grew in Tokyo echoed Mrs. Phillips's reservations. Recognition constituted a "serious sacrifice of principle and letting down of standards." The United States, he insisted, should never "palliate by recognition the things Soviet Russia has done and the things it stands for."[5] Officially, he expressed his alarm by raising fears that recognition might encourage the more militant elements in the Japanese government to reckless action. Closer ties with Russia, he argued, would not deter the Japanese but incite them. His son-in-law made the same point when urging a moderate stand against Germany.

The Europeanists, in hope of arousing public opinion against the recognition initiative, resorted to the classic weapon of bureaucrats on the defensive—the press leak. On October 20, 1933, Assistant Secretary of State Jefferson Caffery tipped off the United Press (UP) State Department correspondent that the department had uncovered an exchange of messages between Cuban revolutionists and Moscow communists. The Russians were seeking recognition, he implied, at the same time they were fomenting revolution 90 miles from the American coast. Caffery told the UP reporter he could use the item but not attribute it to the department. The New York news manager, however, decided to kill the story. Raymond Clapper, head of the UP Washington bureau, noted in his diary: "Coming just ahead of a development in the Russian thing, it looked suspiciously as if a plot being hatched to spike Russians, because one strong point of Bullitt and others is that communists must lay off propaganda in the United States."[6] Indeed, the timing was apt. On October 23, three days after Caffery's leak, Roosevelt invited Soviet President Kalinin to send a representative to Washington to discuss normalizing relations.

These various attempts to subvert Roosevelt's policy did not succeed. The president achieved his purpose and simply ignored the diligent citations of Soviet infractions that the Russian experts provided in subsequent years. Kennan felt that Roosevelt avoided a legalistic stance on the Litvinov agreements because he had a larger purpose in mind. "He obviously considered the resumption of relations with Russia to be desirable for the sobering influence it might exercise on the German Nazis and on the Japanese militarists."[7] When Moffat complained to State Department Counselor R. Walton Moore of the "unwillingness of Litvinoff to honor any of the promises he had made," Moore repeated Roosevelt's logic to him. "Our best and, in fact, only trump card," he explained, "was the fear of Russia, and if the Russians and ourselves should fall out, it would encourage the Japanese to acts of aggression."[8]

In the face of this settled conviction the diplomats could do little but complain in private at Roosevelt's highhandedness. "[To] such a degree our foreign affairs centralize with the President that no one here really knows what is going on," Moffat grumbled. "With regard to disarmament," he later added, "Bill Phillips and I are as much upset over the lack of clear guidance as can be. The President has now taken entire charge. . . ."[9]

Diplomatic Appointments: William Phillips versus Raymond Moley

Roosevelt's presumption that he could run foreign policy on his own extended to the secretary of state, Cordell Hull. "He has a hard time with the President," Mrs. Phillips recorded, "who is becoming more and more of a dictator and goes ahead without consulting Mr. Hull and often against his wishes." Roosevelt also had the characteristic weakness of politicians, a tendency to give the better embassies to party supporters. "Franklin R. is rather ruthless," wrote Mrs. Phillips, "and thinks only of handing out diplomatic plums to some of the many hungry Democrats just to be relieved from their ceaseless clamoring."[10]

The chief offender in this regard was Assistant Secretary of State Raymond Moley. A Columbia University professor and founder of Roosevelt's "brain trust," Moley knew nothing of diplomacy. "I've been digging through the Congressional Directory," Roosevelt explained to him, "and I find that the office of Assistant Secretary of State is the only one of importance that seems completely free of statutory duties." Moley would not be tied down with an administrative job but would still have an impressive title to win the respect of those he would see on behalf of the president.[11] Moley did have one informal assignment—to weed the Hooverites out of the department. Moffat noted Moley's remark "that he would certainly work to clean out the Department of all Republicans." Hugh Gibson and Hugh Wilson, in particular, seemed in danger.[12]

William Phillips, as undersecretary, took the responsibility for resisting Moley's encroachments. He knew, however, that Moley was Roosevelt's agent and that, therefore, he "had to be careful." Roosevelt had told Phillips directly how he felt. Mrs. Phillips noted her husband's words: "F.R. was very down on poor Bob Bliss and wants to drop him and also Hugh Gibson for a couple of years, anyway. He said H.G. had sold himself body and soul to Hoover."[13] Allen Dulles mournfully reported the news to Gibson. "Unless one has been in Washington since March 4th, it is hard to realize the extent of the movement to break with the policies, and the individuals who have been responsible for the policies, of the last twelve years. . . . I would guess that FDR felt that you were so closely identified with carrying out Hoover's policies in European disarmament and other matters that he preferred to have you in South America." Moffat seconded Dulles's analysis. "Change of policy," he wrote to Gibson, "is easier with change of representatives. This is a rather tenuous thought but I believe it is the nearest reason one can fathom for the change."[14]

Moley, however, was limited in what he could do. Phillips, he later recalled, was "bitterly resentful of my status in the government."[15] They clashed initially over appointments. Hull had taken the job of secretary of state on the condition that he would have an undersecretary who would manage the administrative machinery of the department and do most of the entertaining of the diplomatic corps. He hated entertaining and blanched at the jibe of Kentucky friend Arthur Krock that he would have to "get a big house with butlers and footmen" if he became secretary of state.[16] Roosevelt preferred Hull for the secretaryship because Hull had supported his nomination and represented the southern wing of the party, which had only reluctantly accepted Roosevelt. Even more in his favor was Hull's unfamiliarity with foreign affairs: he cared only about trade treaties and would not steal the show from the master dramatist, who intended to be his own secretary of state. Roosevelt, therefore, accepted Hull's recipe for a career diplomat as undersecretary and chose Phillips, an old friend and an experienced diplomat. Hull could, as he wished, devote himself exclusively to policy.[17]

Hull's self-denying instincts extended to diplomatic appointments as well. Phillips was, therefore, free to arrange appointments as he wished. Moley noted that he "soon showed a preference for Social Registerites and career boys." Party chairman James Farley became so enraged at Phillips's choices that he commissioned Moley to protect the party faithful. They fought long and hard. Phillips really dug in his heels at appointing noncareer men to the lesser European posts, the most desirable career spots since the major embassies usually went to heavy contributors. Only the combined pressure of Moley, Farley, and Roosevelt badgered him into assigning historian and Democratic party publicist Claude Bowers to Madrid. Bowers's "charming lack of tonishness gave Phillips an attack of horrid misgivings," Moley recalled.[18] Likewise, the idea of sending another liberal historian, William Dodd, to the sensitive Berlin post upset the diplomats. Moley, wishing "to help infuse new life into the career service," boosted William Bullitt for an appointment in the department. Armed with a memo initialed by Roosevelt, Moley won Bullitt the position of special assistant to the secretary of state "despite the heated opposition of William Phillips."[19]

Although Phillips had to make a few concessions to Moley, he managed to protect the members of the inner club. Wilson and Grew remained in Berne and Tokyo. After strenuous argument by Phillips and the intercession of Norman Davis with the president, Roosevelt agreed to keep Gibson but in a lesser post—Brazil.[20] Gibson felt that Rio was a fate worse than retirement at fifty, but decided to accept the new post gracefully for the good of the service.

Although stoic in public, Gibson was bitter at his treatment by Roosevelt. He let off steam to Hugh Wilson when his replacement at Brussels was announced before he had heard a single word from Washington about his own fate. Gibson felt he was shabbily treated simply because the rabble in the Democratic party had no respect for their betters. "I am convinced," he sarcastically commented, "that our firm convictions against class distinction would prevent our supplanting a nigger messenger of 25 years service without any intimation as to whether he was to be thrown into the street or assigned to other work."[22] Gibson reserved his purest scorn for William Phillips. Phillips had habitually taken a leave of absence from the service whenever distasteful assignments loomed. Yet, because he had conveniently become a Democrat when Hoover began to fade, he plucked the coveted post of undersecretary. Phillips sent Gibson a note of congratulations on his new job, adding that he was confident it would be a "most enjoyable assignment." "I haven't replied to him," Gibson wrote to Wilson, "but when I see him I think I'll say that when he has done five years in Central America instead of getting out every time someone suggested an unpleasant job, I'll be glad to receive his congratulations on going back to the swamps. Hu-hu!"[23]

Although Phillips had to abide the unhappiness of those who thought he should have done even better for them, his overall success in defending the service was undeniable. Moffat and Kelley retained their key posts in Washington. And, most important, within six months Moley was forced to resign from the department after a monumental feud with Cordell Hull.

5 | CORDELL HULL AND THE EUROPEANISTS

CORDELL HULL WAS a crusty Tennessee mountaineer, equally suspicious of slick-talking northern intellectuals and well-polished society types. Neither Moley nor Phillips was his style. Yet Phillips won his trust and Moley aroused his wrath. One point in favor of the diplomats from the outset was Hull's innate conservatism and his feeling that he needed them to do his job. He had no desire to reform anything—except tariffs—and had no use for the zealous New Deal intellectuals that flocked around Roosevelt. He did need the diplomats to manage the routine business of diplomacy and to handle the housekeeping chores of assignment, rotation, cable drafting, and memo writing. The secretary did not want to be bothered with running the department and turned naturally to the permanent bureaucrats to run it for him. When Moley got in their hair, they complained to him that this radical busybody was undermining Hull's policies and being disloyal.

Hull's "policies" on day-to-day business were usually no more than to assent to drafts of cables and memos prepared by the country desk officers. After hasty perusal, he would add his initials. The documents went out under his name, but they rarely reflected his own independent opinions, which were few. On most matters Hull gladly accepted the suggestions and careful prose of his subordinates. When Roosevelt called him to the White House to discuss disarmament negotiations, Hull brought Moffat with him. Roosevelt asked for a briefing, and Hull turned to Moffat: "You know more about this so I leave the answer to you."[1] Elbridge Durbrow, who served as assistant chief of the Eastern European division during World War II, described a typical conversation between Hull and Soviet ambassador Gromyko.

> He usually had me in beforehand to discuss what might come up and how to handle it. I would sit a little behind Gromyko so that I could give Hull facial signals if he was getting into trouble or missing a left hook. Afterwards he would ask me, "Well, how did I do? Did I give away anything or not?"[2]

Hull was a willing pupil. He respected and needed the expertise of his subordinates. China expert John Carter Vincent recalled one instance when Hull signed a cable without reading it. Vincent had interrupted Hull's afternoon croquet game to get his signature. Hull merely asked, "Is it all right to sign this, John Carter?" Vincent assured him it was and he signed. Vincent later explained: "That was not normal. He normally read them through."[3]

Hull also lacked talent for intellectual debate. He grew bored and uncomfortable during a complicated discussion of issues and alternatives. He was incapable of making a logical and integrated presentation of a subject and felt inferior to those who could. Inept and palpably uncomfortable at press conferences, he relied heavily on the stock response: "We are looking into all phases of the situation."[4] Even when his subordinates wished to follow Hull's wishes, they usually found them impossible to discern. Arthur Krock, who knew him well, wrote that Hull sometimes talked "in cascades of words, rushing murkily over tangles of syntax."[5] Stimson found him "gentlemanly, rather slow, and a little 'senectified.' "[6] Herbert Feis, department adviser on economic affairs, recalled an early talk with Hull that "rambled somewhat with a downward beat." In a later discussion on conflicting trade policies, "the Secretary of State's comments faded out in obscure confusion." Secretary of Agriculture Henry Wallace, who witnessed Hull's confusion, remarked: "I think the Secretary is gradually reaching the state of Nirvana."[7] Hull's vagueness increased as his years in office lengthened. Inarticulate from the first, he gradually became incomprehensible.

Hull's insecurity as diplomat-in-chief made him an easy mark for the foreign service, even when he did have substantive ideas about a situation. As Axis belligerence increased, Hull's hillbilly displeasure at unneighborly behavior impelled him to a strong stance against aggression. "When you're in a pissin' contest with a skunk, make sure you got plenty of piss," he said to an associate, explaining his attitude toward the Axis. He had none of the society fears of the diplomats to restrain him, and his frequent visits to Henry Stimson's estate for croquet matches doubtless also shaped his outlook. Stimson's stern legalism appealed to Hull's idealistic streak. By the late thirties, in definite contrast to the Europeanists, he wished to edge away from isolationism. Arthur Krock recalls:

> Hull was always against isolationism. He continued to say, "I think we must educate the people not to believe in this anymore." Then he would have his difficulties with his own staff who were the ones who were so horrified at the "Quarantine Speech." They cut that out of the speech, and Roosevelt put it in again.[8]

The critical decision for Hull was not what he thought but whom he trusted. He did not choose his advisers because they reflected his ideas, but because he trusted them in good mountain tradition to be loyal to him. The Europeanists undercut Moley because they convinced Hull that whereas they sought to protect his reputation, Moley wished to undermine it. In this contest the diplomats' control of the cable- and memo-drafting process was a key advantage. Moley found himself time and again going to the White House to get changes made in a document drafted by the foreign service officers without consulting him and signed by Hull as it came through channels from desk officer to division chief to Phillips. Once Hull had signed off, the document went out under his name. The diplomats' control of the drafting process forced Moley to criticize a "Hull memo" or a "Hull cable" when he was really debating with a desk officer. Hull took the disagreements as personal attacks and feared Moley sought to build an internal cadre in the department to displace him.

Phillips encouraged his suspicions, and, unlike Moley, did not exploit his friendship with Roosevelt to cause Hull discomfort. "Being diffident," Feis writes, "Phillips never took advantage of his intimacy with the President to push his personal opinions or fortune."[9] He also took the advice of his assistants to urge Roosevelt to invite Hull over to the White House occasionally for a talk. When the end came for Moley, it was dramatic. He was propelled out of the State Department by the shock wave of Hull's open fury when the secretary discovered that Moley had cabled Roosevelt implying that Hull was intellectually incapable of leading the delegation to the London Economic Conference of 1933. Hull, who never tired of recounting the story of Moley's downfall, always included a capsule summary of a final talk with Roosevelt on the matter. Pulling his forefinger across his throat, Hull reminisced, "I cut the son of a bitch's throat from ear to ear."[10]

Historians, fascinated with the personal aspects of the Hull-Moley feud, have overlooked the larger rule it illustrates: that no individual could defeat the foreign service on its own ground. Moley's indiscretions did not cause his doom; they merely hastened it. Adolf Berle is another instructive case. Another Roosevelt New Deal lieutenant, he became assistant secretary of state in 1938. Like Moley, he had no line authority to draft cables on a regular basis. He accumulated a group of miscellaneous responsibilities that the political desks considered uninteresting or unimportant. As assistant secretary, he said his piece at Hull's frequent staff meetings, but no one cared. Elbridge Durbrow commented on Berle's status: "Of course, anyone could say anything at staff meetings, but he was not in the chain of command to get things cleared."[11] Non–foreign service appointees to the upper levels of the department were referred to scornfully as "drafting officers."

THE DUNN CONNECTION

The diplomats did not rely solely on control of the apparatus to defeat Moley. They also assiduously cultivated Hull's good will, and practice of this diplomatic art reached its highest refinement in bridging the transition between the Hoover and Roosevelt administrations.

Herbert Hoover had developed a great dislike for the Europeanists during his tenure as secretary of commerce. The diplomats had refused to cooperate with Hoover's foreign trade division because they felt he relied too heavily on Jewish economists for advice. Outraged at their snobbishness, Hoover determined to clean out the department if he became president. As Hoover's presidential campaign picked up steam, the diplomats began a letter-writing campaign to win his favor. Led by William Castle, Jr., they sent a steady stream of congratulatory letters to Hoover, praising him for his astute and brilliant statements on foreign affairs. Castle even emphasized the compatibility of Hoover's ideas with his own. They were, after all, both conservative Republicans and

Red-fearing Americans. When Hoover took office, he immediately turned to Castle for advice on diplomatic appointments. Castle soon became Hoover's most intimate foreign policy adviser.

Thus, the club prospered for four happy years. Although Secretary of State Henry Stimson was a vigorous executive and brought in his own staff, Castle's pipeline to Hoover prevented any sidetracking of the Europeanists. They advanced steadily in rank, and, through the vehicle of the foreign service personnel board, which they dominated, weeded out those who did not have the proper "representation" qualities. The appointment of Joseph Grew as ambassador to Japan in 1931 was emblematic of their success. He was the first careerist in the Tokyo embassy.[12] The Europeanists had smoothly allayed Hoover's fears and won his confidence. With Castle in the van they adroitly sidestepped a potentially hostile secretary of state.

Roosevelt's arrival upset this arrangement. His distaste for everything associated with Hoover led to Castle's swift departure. Gibson and Hugh Wilson were next on the list; Moley and Bullitt were leading candidates for undersecretary. Grew and Phillips, lifelong Republicans, hoped that the Groton-Harvard connection would preserve their careers but feared that it would not. There seemed little chance of seducing Roosevelt with kind words as they had Hoover. Hoover's dislike was purely personal and could be ameliorated with flattery. Roosevelt's objections were political; his policy bent closer to Henry Stimson's activism.

Since the president was hard to reach, the Europeanists went to work on the secretary of state. Although Hull's background was light years away from the polished gentility of the seaboard Brahmins, he did have certain points in common with them. As a southern conservative, he shared the northern Republican dislike for New Deal "radicalism" and the "leftists" around Roosevelt.[13] The courtly and gracious manners of the Old South blended well with the courteous and dignified bearing of the New England aristocrats. Indeed, the seaboard aristocracy included some of the fine old southern families. Caroline Phillips's ancestors came from the South, and she retained a fondness for the region. Mrs. Hull and Mrs. Phillips became close friends. Their husbands found enough in common to work smoothly together.

It is ironic, however, that Jimmy Dunn, son of a Newark laborer, should become the William Castle, Jr., of the Roosevelt years. Yet it was Dunn's intimate friendship with Hull, more than anything else, that guaranteed the Europeanists protection from periodic purges initiated in the White House. Dunn rose swiftly in the foreign service once he married Mary Armour, heir to the meat-packing millions. He bought an estate abutting the British embassy and was accepted as an intimate member of the foreign service club, although his overseas service was negligible. Dunn was a member of a small cadre of department officials who had resigned from the service to become permanent policy officers in Washington. Foreign service rules required that no officer could spend more than four consecutive years in the department between overseas assignments. Dunn resigned from the service in August 1930 and was transferred to the civil service payroll. His job as protocol officer and technical adviser on international conferences stayed the same, but in his new status he could hold it indefinitely and without interruption. The protocol job was devoid of policy. As one journalist described it, it consisted of "seating guests at White House dinners and receiving silk-hatted diplomats at union station."[14] Dunn himself, smart and ambitious, did not let it distract him from more substantive work. "On February 1, I hang out my shingle and start doing business as Chief of the Division of Protocol," he wrote to Gibson in January 1928. "It is going to be a scream. I have a wonderful time enjoying all the idiotic parties and this kind of work except when every now and then the old liver goes wrong from lack of exercise and then I feel like kicking the whole thing in the face and telling them all where to go."[15] Dunn had, in fact, asked Gibson to dissuade Coolidge from making him White House master of ceremonies, but Coolidge had insisted.

The conference job, by contrast, placed Dunn astride an important channel of diplomatic activity. The international conference was a popular mode of free-lance diplomacy during the Hoover and Roosevelt administrations. Secretaries of state and presidents seldom resisted the opportunity for free trips abroad complete with retinue, dramatic headlines, and a reception in the streets of the foreign capital. These provided a welcome contrast to the steady drumbeat of domestic criticism, now safely out of earshot. The Europeanists viewed these excursions with wry amusement, as publicity circuses that rarely had any practical effect. Hugh Wilson scoffed at the value of disarmament negotiations and referred to the League of Nations as the "League of Notions."[16] Nevertheless, these escapades disturbed the Europeanists because they often left the professionals on the sidelines. Government-to-government negotiations usually occurred through the local embassy, and communications were funneled through the relevant desk officer. Because of the heightened publicity attending conferences, the delegations tended to be overloaded with politicians and well-known civilian experts who tried to run their own show. With Dunn as permanent chief of the Division of International Conferences, the Europeanists had a sentry stationed at this vulnerable outpost, prepared to alert his colleagues to coming attacks on their monopoly control of American diplomacy. He could also use his position as "technician" to ensure a steady flow of briefing papers from the desk officers and to assign favored officers to staff positions. He thus found himself in a handy position to offer sympathy and instruction to Cordell Hull when the Tennessee senator arrived one morning to occupy the secretary's office. As protocol officer Dunn instructed him on the procedures of diplomacy, of which Hull knew nothing. As conference expediter he briefed Hull and accompanied him to the London Economic Conference in the anonymous position of secretary to the delegation. Dunn befriended his lonely and somewhat baffled chief and took his side against Moley.

Twenty years Hull's junior, Dunn became a surrogate son to his childless boss. Their wives became fast friends. The foursome frequently convened on Dunn's spacious lawn for croquet, a game the secretary took pride in playing. Since Hull lived in a hotel and shunned Washington social life, he found these outings particularly enjoyable. Hull returned Dunn's kindness with the loyalty of a clannish mountaineer who does not forget his friends. Dunn accompanied Hull to the Montevideo Conference of 1933 as secretary general. In early 1934 he became special assistant to Hull, and when Moffat's turn for an overseas rotation came up in 1935, Dunn, free of this requirement, replaced him as chief of the Division of Western European Affairs. In 1937, he became political adviser on European affairs. Moffat, back from Australia, managed the cable traffic for Dunn as chief of the Division of European Affairs. Dunn flew back and forth between his own office and Hull's "like an animated shuttlecock."[17] By the time Roosevelt and most of Washington officialdom began to devote serious attention to the European situation, Dunn had become Hull's closest friend and most trusted adviser. He was offered a post as minister two or three times in the 1930s. Each time he spoke to Hull, who said, "Do whatever you want," and added in the next breath, "but you don't want to go *there.*" Dunn stayed with Hull all twelve years.[18] Herbert Feis recognized the attachment in its formative days and tried to tip off Moley for his own good. Feis considered Dunn "a career officer who concealed beneath the conventional polished exterior of the old type of State Department official an astute mind and industrious habits." He made an appointment for Moley to meet Dunn. Moley couldn't be bothered.[19]

Dunn's friendship with Hull shielded the foreign service from harm much as Castle's friendship with Hoover had protected the diplomats. Hull insisted from the outset that overseas appointments be split fifty-fifty between career and noncareer people. At his urging, Republican Hugh Wilson was retained as minister to Switzerland. Most miraculous of all, Hoover's close friend, Hugh Gibson, survived the transition. "Hugh Gibson was another Republican whom I kept on as long as I could," Hull wrote, "because of his outstanding ability. But eventually the President wanted him out. . . ."[20]

Dunn's favored position was especially useful for getting early warning signals if any career officers were irritating the secretary. Dunn could see the smoke and douse the fire before Hull burst aflame with indignation. Moffat recorded a conversation with Dunn in early 1934. "He told me so many of the Service chiefs were behaving like spoiled children that the Secretary was beginning to get fed up." Gibson, unhappy at getting a South American post, had made "a perfect idiot of himself in Brazil," and even worse, his wife Ynez had been "patronizing" to Mrs. Hull. Frederick Dearing "didn't know his economic background at Lima." Francis White had shown "childish behavior"; Frederick Sterling balked at being assigned to Bulgaria.[21] "All together," Moffat wrote, recording Dunn's story, "the impression is gaining ground, in quarters where it ought not to, that our people are childish and all together above themselves."[22] Moffat passed the word along through the service network that things were getting out of hand, and Dunn reassured Hull that these incidents would cease.

If Dunn watched out for the interests of the Europeanists, Hull, in turn, defended his subordinates against attacks by Roosevelt. But it was heavy going. The president had no diplomats on the White House staff to moderate his distrust of the foreign service. Grew and Phillips were friends but hardly intimates. Beyond them, he only saw their colleagues as business required. The obstructionism of the service during the Litvinov negotiations sealed his suspicion that these Hooverite fops could be of no use to him.

Whenever the hectic business of the first term gave him an opportunity, Roosevelt sniped at the foreign service. A remark by the King of England that he wished to see America represented in London by Americans, not imitation Englishmen, raised the president's hackles. Those foreign service types were not only secret Republicans but ludicrous dandies as well. Roosevelt told Assistant Secretary of State R. Walton Moore to have the offending officer, Counsellor of Embassy Ray Atherton, transferred out of London. Atherton, a member of the inner club, was a good friend of Phillips, Dunn, and Moffat. Nonetheless, after extensive foot-dragging, he found himself minister to Bulgaria. Roosevelt won his removal, but the Europeanists made sure he got a promotion as solace.[23] This pattern was to be repeated in the future: a show of presidential ire would produce a transfer to a less important post, but the attendant promotion—often at Hull's insistence—put the exiled officer in line for a key position when the next round of rotations occurred. And by then Roosevelt might well have forgotten the original offense. In fact, when Moffat finished his second four years in the department in 1940, Atherton was appointed chief of the Division of European Affairs in his place. Roosevelt's episodic intervention could hardly compete with Dunn's constant watchfulness.

The Atherton episode inspired Roosevelt to issue an executive order barring the marriage of foreign service officers to aliens without permission. He would do what he could to keep America's representatives abroad as homespun as possible. Finally, he tried, though unsuccessfully, to break up the Europeanists' domination of the cable and memo process in the department. Regulations prohibited any foreign service officer from serving more than four years in the department between overseas tours. The key stateside policy officers—Dunn (Western Europe), Kelley (Eastern Europe and Russia), and Wallace Murray (Near East and Africa)—had all circumvented this rule by resigning from the foreign service and becoming officials of the department when their four years ran out. This powerful and permanent second-echelon cadre ran the department, easily outlasting the transients in the White House. Kelley and Murray had become desk officers under Coolidge and permanent officials in the late twenties. Intimately acquainted with the officers in the field and the foreign diplomats in Washington, their imprint was evident on most communications to the field or to the White House that went out under Hull's signature. Roosevelt could not frontally attack Hull's chief subordinates without risking an explosion by the secretary. Instead he sought to modify existing practice to prevent the situation from worsening. He instructed Moore to make it a "definite rule" that he would not reappoint to the foreign service any former officers who had resigned to become permanent officials. This rule would make any foreign service officer who hoped one day to be an ambassador think twice before becoming a permanent official. "Furthermore," he stated flatly, "I think we should discourage appointing any Foreign Service officers as officials of the Department."[24]

Roosevelt's strictures applied to the future but had little effect on the existing structure of the department. Dunn remained as the chief adviser on European affairs throughout Roosevelt's four terms and eventually became ambassador to Italy under Truman. Serving under Dunn was John D. Hickerson. Hickerson, who had been a foreign service officer in the twenties, returned to the department for a stateside tour in 1927. By 1930, he had been promoted to assistant chief of the Division of Western European Affairs, although he had never served in a European embassy. When his four years ran out in 1931, he transferred to the civil service and remained in basically the same job for the rest of the Roosevelt years.[25] Murray continued as chief of the Near Eastern Division until 1945 when he became ambassador to Iran. Kelley, upon leaving the Russian desk, was reappointed to the foreign service!

6 | THE NEW DEAL TURNS TO FOREIGN POLICY

ROOSEVELT OCCUPIED MOST of his first term combating the Depression. The nation's premier politician was well aware that the relentlessly isolationist Congress would fiercely resist presidential action in foreign affairs. The road to domestic change appeared smoother, and the potential for creating a permanent Democratic majority on the basis of innovative welfare programs made Roosevelt's political pulse race.

Roosevelt did not agree with Hull that the world could trade its way out of the Depression. The idea intrinsically had no appeal to him, for public opinion would not abide an activist foreign policy. Bored by ideas and programs that did not promise to increase his power, he instinctively turned to those advisers who blended intellectual arguments with political calculations. Arthur Krock offers this sketch.

> [Roosevelt] had no very strong convictions except that he wished well for his country. He wanted the American people to be strong and fine, and he wanted to go down in history as the benevolent—not dictator, because he never thought of it that way—but as the great American, strong President, who pulled his country out of a Depression, saved its system. . . . A man

> like that, without any kind of intellectual depth at all, when clever people came along . . . and he saw it was politically good, would follow them.[1]

Rexford Tugwell spoke Roosevelt's language. "Tugwell," Krock relates, "had the kind of advice Roosevelt liked. He said, 'You've got to make this labor-farmer combination, and the only way to make it as I say—through the A.A.A. and so forth,' and Roosevelt liked that."[2] Harry Hopkins had the same formula—snappy sociology that made political sense. Federal spending under a variety of labels—AAA, WPA, PWA, social security—would weld a working-class-farmer coalition to keep Roosevelt in office as long as he wanted. Krock continues:

> Also Hopkins knew that Roosevelt was not a convinced New Dealer by any political philosophy—that he didn't have much political philosophy. Hopkins, by impressing upon Roosevelt the political allure of that combination which the New Deal philosophy made, won Roosevelt's favor and confidence. It looked to him as if Hopkins had the golden key to perpetuity of power, which proved to be true.[3]

After his landslide reelection in 1936, Roosevelt's attention gradually began to shift to foreign policy. The Depression continued, but the survival of American democracy was no longer at issue. Huey Long was dead. Father Couglin's presidential candidate, William Lemke, had failed miserably. Nonetheless, the New Deal fared poorly during 1937 and 1938. The Supreme Court fight and the abortive effort to purge anti-Roosevelt Democrats in the 1938 primaries almost fractured the Democratic party. Southern Democrats formed a coalition with northern Republicans to stymie reform legislation. The New Deal had stalled. At the same time that Roosevelt was losing his grip over domestic affairs, certain sections of the electorate became more interested in events overseas. The Ethiopian War aroused strong feelings, especially among blacks and Italian-Americans. Jews had vocally opposed Hitler since 1933, and the arrival of many refugee Jewish intellectuals provided a source of leadership in the effort to force stronger protests out of the American government. The Spanish civil war brought the Catholic hierarchy into the fray and cemented a liberal antifascist coalition on the other side. The electorate, formerly divided primarily by economic circumstances, was being crosscut by ethnic and religious loyalties arising out of European politics.

Roosevelt, characteristically, redirected his gaze from the domestic stalemate to the opportunities abroad. The awakening of the electorate to foreign affairs suggested that as time passed he would gain more and more room for maneuver. The rising menace of fascism argued for an active presidential role. His naval experience told him it could not be ignored. One side benefit of an increasing emphasis on foreign policy would be the necessity to act more and more in the role of commander-in-chief. He would once again be running the navy—and the army and air corps as well.[4]

But until Hitler overran France and stimulated American rearmament, Roosevelt was preeminently secretary of state. He had endorsed Hull's "fine idealism" while others counseled against appointing him secretary of state. Hull would be content with speechmaking, a natural carry-over from his years in the Senate, and leave the fun of playing diplomatic chess to Roosevelt. "I think he just encouraged Hull to be almost an elder statesman mouthing principles," Krock recalls, "whereas, he, Roosevelt, was really running the show."[5] Roosevelt, like most other northeasterners, found Hull's ramblings virtually incoherent. His opinion of Hull's intellectual capacities was low, and in private he made fun of him. Hull had an Elmer Fudd speech impediment that Roosevelt liked to mock. "Hull was in a 'Cwist' mood today and the old boy was certainly good," he said to his secretary after a lively lunch in the Oval Office.[6] Hull's "twade tweaties" left the president unimpressed. He remarked in a cabinet meeting "how futile it was to think that we could be doing ourselves any good, or the world any good, by making it possible to sell a few barrels of apples here and a couple of automobiles there."[7] Roosevelt preferred to work with Undersecretary of State Sumner Welles, another Groton-Harvard graduate, who had been page boy at Roosevelt's wedding. (Unlike Phillips, Welles didn't resist.) Welles thought crisply and spoke concisely. The president fell into the habit of dealing directly with Welles, completely bypassing Hull except for an occasional ceremonial luncheon in the White House. "When it came to really doing the maneuvering on the great chessboard of diplomacy," Krock recalls, "he never let Hull have much to do with it at all. He would send for Sumner Welles to come over to the White House, and it was with Sumner that he would say, 'Now look, don't let old Hull know about this, but you and I will do so and so.' "[8]

Hull bridled at this treatment but never let it disturb his public facade of dignity and serenity. In classic feuding style, he never criticized the president to his face. Indignity succeeded indignity, but he never let his smile slip inside the White House. When a reporter asked Roosevelt who would have charge of the negotiations with Litvinov, Roosevelt replied, pointing to himself, "This man here." Many newspapers interpreted this action to mean that Hull, about to embark for the Montevideo Conference, was being deliberately shipped abroad so as not to interfere with the negotiations. Hull boiled over at this report and poured his outrage into Phillips's ear. Phillips pleaded with Roosevelt to set the papers straight, but the president refused. Hull saved face by postponing his trip and remaining in Washington during the negotiations.[9] He never confronted Roosevelt directly over this insult, but he burned inside.

Hull had decided to attend the now-aborted Montevideo Conference to repair his reputation abroad after the fracas in London. On the boat home from London, Dunn had urged Hull not to go to Montevideo, but the secretary responded, "I am going to that Conference because I've come out so badly on this one. I'm going down there to make up for the London fiasco."[10] By his "This man here" statement to the press, Roosevelt was inserting the knife again just as the original wound was about to heal.

As Roosevelt took control of foreign affairs, his New Deal lieutenants began to tread on Hull's toes. Their view of the world was quite different from that of the diplomats. The New Dealers—Harold Ickes, Henry Morgenthau, Henry Wallace, Harry Hopkins, Eleanor Roosevelt—developed an outlook on foreign affairs compatible with their domestic experience as quasi-socialist reformers. In their eyes the fascists were the prime enemy, Russia a necessary ally. The overriding fear of social revolution that animated the diplomats did not affect those who prided themselves on carrying out a peaceful revolution in the United States. The diplomats had little use, for instance, for the socialist Leon Blum, but Roosevelt admired the French premier. His reform legislation aroused strong opposition, but that indicated how desperately the reforms were needed. "Suppose Brother Hoover had remained President until April, 1936," Roosevelt said to a reporter, "carrying on his policies of the previous four years. . . . Had that been the case, we would have been a country this past April very similar to the country that Blum found when he came in. The French for 25 or 30 years had never done a thing in the way of social legislation." Roosevelt empathized with Blum's efforts to overcome the French equivalent of Hooverite reaction. "Of course I cannot say anything to even intimate that I am in favor of Blum—but if Blum can be kept there for a while he may be able to do certain things that almost every nation in the world has done."[11]

Though varied in background, the New Dealers were all committed to the use of governmental authority to correct social abuses. Henry Wallace and Henry Morgenthau came out of a farming tradition. Wallace, as a spokesman for the farm belt, worked to improve farm income. Morgenthau became chairman of the Agricultural Advisory Commission when Roosevelt was elected governor of New York in 1928. His recommendations to improve and expand rural roads, education, and agricultural research all became law. He solidified a rural political base for FDR in New York by redirecting state aid toward poorer counties. "Doing things for people at the bottom of the ladder," he commented, "this is revolution." After Roosevelt's reelection in 1930, Morgenthau became conservation commissioner. As the 1932 Democratic Convention approached, Roosevelt sent Morgenthau on a trip to the Middle West and South to survey rural opinion about the agricultural depression and about Roosevelt as a candidate. On this trip Morgenthau met Wallace and brought him to Roosevelt's attention.

Harry Hopkins, like Wallace, came from Iowa. After graduating from Grinnell College, he took a job as a welfare worker in New York City to see the "Big Town." The grinding poverty of the slums converted him into a zealous champion of the underprivileged. He continued in welfare work, rising to higher positions of responsibility. When Roosevelt was reelected governor, Hopkins became executive director and later chairman of the Temporary Emergency Relief Administration, the first of the alphabet agencies. He later did similar work as head of the Works Project Administration (WPA).

The political leader of the social reform movement in the 1920s, however, was not Roosevelt but Al Smith. In his governorship from 1922 to 1928, Smith fused together the forces that were soon to propel Roosevelt into the presidency and launch the New Deal. He united the growing voting power of the immigrant working classes with the missionary zeal of native Protestant reformers and Jewish labor leaders. The slum neighborhoods that the diplomats found abhorrent aroused a sense of social responsibility in people like Eleanor Roosevelt and Frances Perkins, Smith's choice to chair the state Industrial Commission. Through her involvement in the Women's Trade Union League, Eleanor Roosevelt met Rose Schneiderman and Maud Schwartz, two fiery labor radicals. Another close friend of Mrs. Roosevelt was Molly Dewson, who had served twelve years as superintendent of parole for girls in Massachusetts, worked for the Red Cross and the National Consumers League, and helped Felix Frankfurter prepare the economic briefs in the minimum-wage cases. Her advocacy of unemployment compensation, minimum-wage legislation, and old-age pensions reached FDR through his wife. By 1926 Eleanor was walking picket lines with Rose Schneiderman. When Roosevelt became governor, she suggested he appoint Frances Perkins as labor commissioner and sent Molly Dewson to see him with the same suggestion. Perkins got the appointment and became secretary of labor when Roosevelt reached the White House. On the fringes, but out of the same tradition, was Harold Ickes, a good-government Theodore Roosevelt Progressive from Chicago. Frances Perkins had also been an active Progressive. The New Dealers were united on the impulses for social reform that came out of the Progressive Era and were funneled through the social work profession into the Smith governorship and eventually the Roosevelt presidency.

These creators of the social welfare state were dispersed throughout the government. They were not permanent government officials like the foreign service officers. They constituted instead a loosely structured conglomerate sharing common values and a loyalty to FDR. As the American government moved in the direction of social responsibility, career opportunities opened up for people with a background in social work just as career opportunities had appeared in the early decades of the twentieth century for those interested in serving an expanding American presence abroad. The growth of the American governmental apparatus abroad and at home created career niches that the New Dealers and the diplomats filled. When the New Deal, tutored by East Side Mensheviks and checkered with sympathy for the Soviet experiment, turned to foreign policy, the foreign service—hostile to social reform—was solidly in control of the diplomatic apparatus. Throughout the Roosevelt years the social workers clashed with the Tory aristocrats over many issues of American foreign policy. In a highly diluted form, they performed in Washington a reenactment of the left-right conflicts that had riven European politics since the French Revolution and were boiling up once again with the rise of the Axis. In their more combative moments the New Dealers considered the diplomats "fascists" and the diplomats considered the New Dealers "communists."[12]

The occasional New Deal criticisms and insults aimed at the State Department during Roosevelt's first term became a systematic campaign of vilification during the second. In February 1937, Hubert Herring fired a salvo in *Harper's* magazine. A long and critical roasting of the department leadership culminated in the following conclusion:

> The stubborn conservatism of the older men sets the pace. The overregard for social privilege, the association with the diplomatic corps of other countries, the mingling with the expatriates of the "American Colony" . . . serve to create a foreign service with scant regard for democratic movements and little respect for members of those races customarily dismissed by Anglo-Saxons as inferiors.

Herring predicted that the mandate given the New Deal would soon extend to foreign affairs. The public will "turn to the President and ask when the cleansing of the New Deal so hopefully applied to the Departments of Labor, Agriculture and Interior will reach the sealed chambers of the Department of State."[13] Labor, Agriculture and Interior meant Perkins, Wallace, and Ickes, all quite radical in the eyes of the Europeanists. Hugh Gibson understood that this was just the beginning. "Did you see February Harper's on the State Department and the service?" he wrote to Lucy James.* "There is quite a drive going on and one of these days I will tell you some interesting details on where it all comes from."[14]

Part of the impulse for Herring's article may have come from the White House. Neither Eleanor Roosevelt nor Harry Hopkins had much use for the foreign service. Mrs. Roosevelt's biographer relates: "Harry Hopkins told her after his trip abroad in 1934 that American diplomats in Europe did not seem to know anything about the country they were in except what they were told by members of the upper crust, and they were not even interested in finding out from Hopkins what was going on in the United States."[16]

Only three months after Roosevelt's inauguration, as if in fulfillment

*Lucy James, a lifelong friend of Gibson and godmother to his son Michael, had her own ideas. During the 1936 campaign she had written to Gibson: "They are, *all* of them, Democrats and Republicans and Socialists alike, truckling to the Jews. Mind you, the Republican National Convention was opened by the prayer of Rabbi Snigglefritz of Philadelphia of the Congregation of some-kind-of-a-torah. The Herald-Tribune this morning carried a driveling editorial upon anti-semitism. The Jew is 6% of the population, and he is 60% of the present Administration and I should say he is 96% of Communism. . . . No one knows better than you!"[15]

of Herring's prediction, the White House abolished the Division of Eastern European Affairs and packed Robert Kelley off to Turkey to finish out his career.

The Russian division had been an annoyance to Roosevelt ever since his first tussle with Kelley over the recognition of Russia. He understood the difficulties Kennan, Bohlen, and Henderson faced in Moscow, but he had an overriding goal—allying Russia with the democracies as a deterrent to Germany and Japan. To harp on Russian discourtesies would merely serve Hitler's divide-and-conquer strategy. "The anti-Kelley group," Bohlen recalls, "was worried that the United States might lose an opportunity to work with the Soviet Union to counter the growing menace of Hitler."[17]

In early 1937, Roosevelt sent Joseph Davies to Moscow as ambassador to warm up the atmosphere between the two countries. Davies, a trust-busting lawyer for Woodrow Wilson and husband of the Post cereals heiress, was eager to serve Roosevelt in any capacity, and, as encouragement, contributed heavily to the 1936 campaign. He steadfastly overlooked the bloody purges and sent a steady stream of encouraging reports back to the United States. Official dispatches acquired a schizophrenic quality, paragraphs of Kennanesque gloom punctuated by a cheerful note of buoyant optimism added by Davies.

Kennan and Henderson were so distressed at Davies's attitude that they seriously considered resigning from the service in protest; however, decided to live with their frustrations and stay on. In their eyes Davies was stupid, dishonest, and publicity-mad. Bohlen attributes Davies's attitude to sheer ignorance. "He had gone to the Soviet Union sublimely ignorant of even the most elementary realities of the Soviet system. . . . He was determined . . . to maintain a Pollyanna attitude."[18] Kennan accused him of "a readiness to bend both the mission and its function to the purposes of personal publicity at home." Elbridge Durbrow: "I never worked with a more mentally dishonest man than Joe Davies." Why did Davies seek close ties with Russia? "Self-aggrandizement. He would succeed where others had failed." When Davies capped his tour of duty with a pro-Soviet panegyric entitled *Mission to Moscow*, the foreign service officers could not contain their scorn and referred to it freely as *Submission to Moscow*. Roosevelt had different ideas. He wrote on the flyleaf of his copy: "This book will last." Davies, indeed, was merely doing Roosevelt's work. As George E. Allen, court jester to Roosevelt, Truman, and Eisenhower, described it: "Steve Early, Roosevelt's press secretary, got Davies to write *Mission to Mos-*

cow for propaganda purposes. If they had said, 'Write about Yugoslavia,' he would have done it as quickly."[19]

On June 15, 1937, Undersecretary of State Sumner Welles summoned Kelley to his office and announced the abolition of the Division of Eastern European Affairs (EE). Kelley went to Turkey, and the division was merged with the Western European division into a single Division of European affairs (EUR) under Moffat. All that remained of Kelley's domain was a single room with two desks, one for Russia, the other for the Baltic states and Poland. The Russian experts saw the sinister hand of Eleanor Roosevelt in the reorganization, merely one more example of the "hands across the caviar" philosophy of the naive New Deal ideologues.[20]

The Europeanists did not oppose the reorganization—and did not inspire Hull to fight back—because they had their own quarrel with the Russian experts. Kelley's division, in stark contrast to the foppish dilettantism of the Western European division, engaged in extensive research. Before joining government service, Kelley had investigated the outbreak of the Crimean War in French archives. He carried these scholarly habits into the State Department with him. "EE did work no other division did," Henderson explained. "We did research work and gave sources for our statements. We had a wonderful library, *Pravda* and *Izvestia* from the first editions . . . the best Soviet library in the United States. The other desks opposed this. They said research was for professors, not diplomats."[21] The Europeanists and the White House shared a desire to abolish EE—the Europeanists to still the unflattering comparison between Kelley's scholarship and their own superficiality; Roosevelt to tighten relations with Russia. To satisfy the Europeanists, the research library was dispersed and EE became a subunit of EUR; to pacify the president, Kelley was transferred and Murphy ordered to destroy his dossiers on communists, foreign and domestic.[22]

As Hull became a spokesman for EUR, his reputation for principled idealism began to fade. Harold Ickes turned skeptical in March 1937, when Hull refused to issue passports for an American ambulance unit that wanted to go to Spain on the loyalist side. "I have been a great admirer of Secretary Hull's foreign policies," Ickes noted, "but this makes me ashamed."[23] Ickes' momentary distress congealed into fixed hostility as the State Department opposed his efforts to condemn the fascists. The Interior Department rarely had a claim to jurisdiction on specific foreign policy decisions, but Ickes could always find an opportunity to make a speech. In one instance, a hard-hitting speech on democracy versus fascism was cleared by the White House, but the State Department asked to look it over. Hull's associates sent it back to Ickes, "the worst mangled speech that I have ever seen." Ickes showed the butchered text to Roosevelt, who "cancelled practically every objection made by the Department of State." Ickes gave the speech in its original form; coming coincidentally on the heels of Eden's resignation as foreign secretary, it appeared as a rebuke to Chamberlain. The Europeanists were not pleased. And Hull was nettled at Ickes' excursion into foreign affairs and Roosevelt's encouragement of it. Ickes, taking a card from Roosevelt's hand, blamed it on the career boys, in league with the British aristocrats. "As the speech came back from the State Department, one might almost have guessed that some British fascist had been doing the censoring. Perhaps it was only some career man recently graduated from Harvard."[24]

Although Roosevelt often overrode Hull, he tried to soothe the secretary by having Ickes clear the final speech with him. Hull evaded the issue by saying that if Roosevelt had approved the speech the State Department had nothing more to say. As always he avoided a showdown that might imply resignation.[25]

Newspaper columnist Drew Pearson spearheaded the campaign for a New Deal foreign policy. Pearson's hostility toward the State Department dated back to the Hoover administration. In a widely read book of Washington gossip, published in 1931, Pearson excoriated everyone associated with the Republican administration. The socially conscious diplomats were an irresistible target for his lampooning pen. In a chapter entitled "Pink Peppermints and Protocol," he roasted the "career clique." Their creed, he wrote, is "snobbery, favoritism, self-protection, ultraconservatism, and assiduity in pleasing the Secretary of State." The diplomats hated him. Pearson's delight in revealing unflattering personal foibles was particularly infuriating. He accused William Phillips, for instance, of spending all his leisure time in the department manicuring his fingernails.[26]

Beginning in late 1937 Pearson began to give increasing emphasis to foreign policy in his daily column. The occasional and random sniping of the past evolved into a steady and focused attack on the foreign service, undergirded by ideological antifascism. One reason for the shift from titillating gossip to extensive and documented accusation was a marriage of convenience between the ardent New Dealers and Pearson consummated after the 1936 election. Wallace, Ickes, Hopkins, Morgenthau, Tommy Corcoran, Eleanor Roosevelt, and occasionally the president fed Pearson and his partner Robert S. Allen a steady diet of anti–foreign service gossip. Pearson satisfied his sources by printing their back-door remarks *in extenso,* vocally supporting their ideological line, and tipping them off to opposition attacks.[27]

The New Dealers argued that the State Department was in the pocket of the British Foreign Office, overawed by the skill and polish of British diplomats. Pearson hammered on this theme, sure to quicken the pulse of all red-blooded Americans. He wrote in April 1938:

> The American career diplomats hold the British Foreign Office in reverence almost as if it were the Deity. American policy in Europe, they contend, should do nothing to offend Britain. In fact, London is consulted on every move. This is the policy of Hugh Wilson, Hugh Gibson, Jimmy Dunn and others near the top, so all the younger career men strive to emulate them. Thus the adoration is self-perpetuating.[28]

When Roosevelt blessed the Anglo-Italian treaty, apparently approving the conquest of Ethiopia and the dispatch of Italian soldiers to Spain, Pearson blamed it on the "pro-fascist career clique" who had gulled the president into endorsing the treaty as a symbol of peaceful negotiation. The letter sent by British Foreign Secretary Halifax asking American support was almost identical to the letter sent to the Dominions asking endorsement of the Italian treaty. "State Department critics now are kidding the 'career boys' that finally the United States has attained dominion status," Pearson wrote. At the Naval War College, he added, the State Department was called "BAFO, short for British-American foreign office."[29]

Ickes agreed completely. "It is apparent," he noted unhappily, "that our State Department is firmly resolved to further the foreign policy of Chamberlain."[30] He commiserated with Morgenthau over the latter's efforts to block a State Department–sponsored loan to Franco Spain and to impose countervailing duties on certain Italian imports over Phillips's objections. On the latter point, Morgenthau later explained: "The President sided with the Treasury but, as so often happened, was unwilling to overrule Hull directly."[31] The department also prevented a loan to Finland because "some of the big European powers were opposed" and tried to discourage a Treasury luncheon with Czechoslovakian President Benes, Morgenthau complained. "If all of this does not spell a continued subservience of our State Department to Downing Street, then I do not know what it does spell," Ickes wrote in exasperation. He longed for the freedom to speak out against the department's "tender consideration of the dictatorships while pretending to serve the cause of democracy."[32]

Since Roosevelt would not allow the New Dealers to attack Hull in public, they turned to the liberal press for assistance. In May 1938, the *Nation* ran an article called "Hull of Downing Street." This criticism, aimed at weakening Hull's reputation and turning the president against the diplomats, was slightly off the mark. The Europeanists supported appeasement because they agreed with the policy, not because they automatically supported the British Foreign Office. In fact, their professional counterparts in the Foreign Office followed a historic *anti*-German policy traceable to the Crowe memorandum of 1906.[33] Chamberlain formulated foreign policy in isolation from and often in opposition to the Foreign Office. The American diplomats supported his stand because they feared Russia more than Germany. When strictly Anglo-American relations were at issue, they often took a stern anti-British stand.

During his two-year hiatus in Australia from 1935 to 1937, Moffat worked diligently to weaken British dominance in Australian trade. As minister to Canada in 1940–41, he did the same, seeking to edge the Canadians away from a Dominion mentality. As British policy in Europe stiffened after the absorption of Czechoslovakia, Moffat blamed British politicians for the accelerating drift toward war and its catastrophic social consequences. In his view, the First World War had spawned Bolshevism; and the second would extend its sway; and yet the British were making it inevitable. Moffat worked energetically as war approached to gain the extremities of the British Empire for American trade in return for the Lend-Lease goods to sustain the heart. Those who opposed the fascists grew more sympathetic to Britain as Chamberlain abandoned appeasement and Churchill came to the fore: Britain came to symbolize democratic resistance to fascist aggression. Moffat drifted the opposite way, growing more and more bitter at the British as appeasement waned. Perhaps Moffat felt, like Wilson, that the British had stupidly precipitated a war against Germany instead of making a settlement to turn Hitler to the East. Now, facing national extinction because of this idiocy, they wanted to spread the conflagration to save themselves instead of seeking an honorable truce. By July 1941, he was in deep despair. British propaganda was proving more and more effective. White House favorities Felix Frankfurter and Harry

Charles E. Bohlen, 1941. WIDE WORLD PHOTOS

Cordell Hull (left) and Robert Kelley leaving the White House in 1935. KEYSTONE VIEW CO.

Jay Pierrepont Moffat, chief of EUR, with Secretary of State Cordell Hull on the morning Germany invaded Belgium and Holland, May 10, 1940. WIDE WORLD PHOTOS

William Phillips, ambassador to Italy (left), FDR, and Hugh Wilson, ambassador to Germany, at Warm Springs, Georgia, November 1938. WIDE WORLD PHOTOS

William Bullitt, ambassador to France (left), with Undersecretary of State Sumner Welles at the White House, December 1938. WIDE WORLD PHOTOS

Hopkins seemed to him all but paid agents of Churchill. So, inevitably, the Americans would bail out the British—and all for *their* benefit. "For the first time," he wrote on July 14, 1941, "I came away with the conviction that it was . . . hopeless to avoid becoming involved in the war and that if and when we do become involved, we shall give all and get nothing, other than a good screwing to our trade by Great Britain."[34]

Moffat was proappeasement from background and experience. He backed British policies when they matched his own ideas and opposed them when they did not. It was easier to hide behind an isolationist, defer-to-Britain-who-has-the-responsibility argument than to reveal the anti-Soviet basis of his recommendations. Moffat was not, however, an isolationist by philosophy. He was prepared to intervene abroad when communism threatened, as the Warsaw episode made clear. And he was far from a lackey of the British. In 1938, however, the New Deal charge that the diplomats had sold out to Britain carried greater weight than the more accurate assertion that they were congenitally opposed to Russia. If the latter were the case, the only remedy could be to turn pro-Soviet, and the left-leaning press and the New Dealers had no desire to put *that* face on the issue—at any rate, not yet.

The New Dealers did sympathize, however, with Soviet efforts to contain Hitler. Ickes listened with a sense of inevitability to Soviet ambassador Oumansky's complaint that Joseph Green, State Department arms-export expert, was sabotaging a Soviet contract to have destroyers built in American shipyards. Roosevelt had given his approval. Hull agreed, yet Green so worded the permit that the ships could not be made to standard specifications. Oumansky's general view of the European situation, wrote Ickes, "corresponded exactly with my own." Chamberlain and the French were willing to give Germany a free hand in Eastern Europe "if only they can persuade Hitler to turn his attention to the East instead of the west of Europe." Even the purges and the Nazi-Soviet pact did not alter this analysis. Chamberlain had dug his own grave by trying to embroil Russia and Germany, and failing. "It is a terrible situation," Ickes wrote, "but I find it difficult to blame Russia. As I see it, Chamberlain alone is to blame." Ickes believed Oumansky's statement that Britain could have had an alliance with Russia had she wished. Now it was too late. The Nazi-Soviet pact was not a treaty between two devils. "I hate communism," Ickes stated, "but it is founded on belief in the control of Government, including the economic system, by the people themselves. It is the very antithesis of Nazism."[35]

Superficially the New Dealers and the Europeanists were united in condemnation of Chamberlain's blundering. But their reasons set them poles apart. The New Dealers criticized Chamberlain for excessive appeasement, the Europeanists for too little. The New Dealers resisted the equation of Stalin and Hitler as totalitarian dictators, believing that there were mitigating circumstances for the Russians. The Europeanists also rejected this equation, but on the grounds that Hitler's anticommunism was a point in his favor: one could still nurse the hope he would save Western civilization by turning East.

III

THE WAR YEARS

★ ★ ★ ★ ★ ★ ★ ★ ★

Not long after Pearl Harbor, President Roosevelt is said to have remarked jocularly to a friend that his State Department was neutral in this war and that he hoped it would at least remain that way.

—ROBERT BENDINER, Managing Editor of the *Nation*

7 | THE WHITE HOUSE FOREIGN OFFICE

IN A DRAFT of his 1940 postelection fireside chat, Roosevelt proposed to say that American citizens in high places were aiding and abetting the Nazis. The draft came back from the State Department with the words "in high places" circled in red. "Let's change the sentence," Roosevelt said, "to read—'There are also American citizens, many of them in high places, *especially in the State Department*. . . .' " [1] Roosevelt's distaste for the career diplomats was so great that he established an *ad hoc* foreign ministry to handle wartime diplomacy. This group was a heterogeneous mixture comprising New Dealers like Henry Wallace, Morgenthau, Hopkins, David Niles, Isador Lubin, and Jonathan Daniels; sympathetic millionaries such as Averell Harriman, Ed Stettinius, Myron Taylor, and Joe Davies, and sometimes simply men of compatible temperament whose company Roosevelt enjoyed, like William Donovan and Pat Hurley. He had to have special representatives, Roosevelt explained to Hurley, because he could not "get a damned thing done through the State Department." Always his own secretary of state, Roosevelt in time became his own State Department as well, especially in the delicate area of relations with Russia.

While Ickes agitated for the establishment of a propaganda agency—

eventually the Office of War Information (OWI)—to keep the New Deal image of foreign policy before the public, Roosevelt gave William Donovan authority to establish an intelligence operation separate from the State Department cable flow—eventually the Office of Strategic Services (OSS). The president, further limiting Hull's reach, lodged the responsibility for drafting and selling Lend-Lease legislation squarely in Morgenthau's lap. Morgenthau's attitude was clear: "stop the agressors in their tracks through every possible use of American economic and financial power." Hull was so resentful of the snub that he resisted testifying for the bill before Congress. The liberals blamed the foreign service officers for Hull's anger. Morgenthau records this conversation with Secretary of the Navy Frank Knox.

> "I don't think it's Cordell," Knox told me. 'I think it's some of those subordinates of his."
>
> "Yes, that's right," I said.
>
> "Yeah," said Knox, "let's organize a hanging bee over there someday and hang the ones that you and I pick out."
>
> "We won't leave many people over there," I said.[2]

The first one to go, most likely, would be Loy Henderson. After the German invasion of Russia, the White House moved quickly to add Russia to the Lend-Lease program. Henderson dragged his feet. The day before the invasion he had prepared a memo urging that the United States do no more than relax restrictions on exports to Russia if Germany attacked—exact a *quid pro quo* for all assistance, he proposed, and make it clear that Russia does not fight for the same ideals as the United States. Finally, should the Soviet régime fall, Henderson argued, we should refuse to recognize a Communist government-in-exile, leaving the path clear for establishment of a non-Communist government in Russia after the war.[3] Kennan echoed these feelings in a letter he wrote to Henderson two days after Hitler sent the Wehrmacht into Russia. "I feel strongly," he wrote, "that we should do nothing at home to make it appear that we are . . . extending moral support to the Russian cause in the present Russian-German conflict. . . . It has no claim on Western sympathies." The United States might send some material aid to contain the Nazis, but such assistance would "preclude anything which might identify us politically or ideologically with the Russian war effort."[4] The Russian experts feared that American aid and moral support might defeat Hitler at the price of extending Soviet authority over Eastern Europe.

Once the Lend-Lease bill passed, Roosevelt did not turn implementation over to the State Department. Harry Hopkins rode herd on Lend-Lease and enforced Roosevelt's insistence on no-strings aid to the Soviet Union, despite the gripes of bureaucrats who had to abide without protest the imperious demands of their Soviet counterparts. The concern of the military to hoard war material for American armies was likewise overriden. The Russian blood that would be mingled with American jeeps, airplanes, and ammunition on the eastern front was sufficient repayment. "The Russian armies are killing more Axis personnel and destroying more Axis material than all other twenty-five United Nations put together," Roosevelt wrote in May 1942.[5] Ever mindful of the political costs at home of high American casualty rates, Roosevelt was well aware that the more Germans that died in the East, the weaker would be the Wehrmacht that opposed American and British armies in the West. This political calculation merged into Roosevelt's vision of allied cooperation after the war's end and reinforced his insistence on presenting Lend-Lease as a show of American generosity to a valiant and trustworthy ally. A free hand with Lend-Lease might also assuage Russian unhappiness over the delay of the second front.

Hopkins, in turn, through the loyal Edward Stettinius, head of the Lend-Lease administration, and his general counsel, New Dealer Oscar Cox, ensured that the day-to-day operations of Lend-Lease conformed to Roosevelt's wishes. On the Moscow end, General Phillip Faymonville, head of the liaison mission in Moscow, reported directly to Hopkins, and shared the same philosophy of undiluted generosity. Faymonville was heartily detested by the army high command for his obeisance to Hopkins. He alone among army professionals had predicted that Russia, if aided, could hold out against the Nazis. Prevailing army opinion had been that Russia would collapse by August 15, 1941.

Similarly, in London Averell Harriman, destined to be an overseas Harry Hopkins during the war, managed Lend-Lease to Britain as Roosevelt's personal emissary to Churchill—"the London Office of the United States Government for the Conduct of the War."[6] When Henderson prepared a cable suggesting that American technicians supervise the construction of oil plants in Russia, Harriman at once protested that such an approach would merely make the Russians suspicious of American good will. He pointedly requested that all such proposals be cleared with Hopkins or Stettinius in the future.[7]

After Pearl Harbor, Hopkins became Roosevelt's personal emissary to Stalin on diplomatic matters, reporting directly to the president through the Map Room in the basement of the White House. This forerunner of the Situation Room allowed Roosevelt to conduct business with foreign capitals without using State Department cable facilities. Joseph Davies was resurrected to serve as liaison with the Soviet embassy in Washington, giving Russian ambassador Litvinov a direct channel to the White House around Loy Henderson. Roosevelt had short-circuited the Russian experts on both ends. "As you know," Hopkins told Davies upon offering him his new job, "the State Department is doing very little in making constructive suggestions to the President about the larger aspects of the Russian situation. Litvinov does not talk to the State Department. He talks directly to the President."[8]

Hull was not happy at this state of affairs. The diplomats may have been just as happy to have the "hands across the caviar" activities outside the State Department (keep the enemy at a safe distance), but Hull resented the insult implicit in the mushrooming of new agencies —propaganda, intelligence, economic—to handle overseas activities. Roosevelt's centralization of wartime diplomacy in the White House was making Hull a laughingstock. He had the title; Roosevelt had the job. Furthermore, when Hull did get some notice, it was usually a query as to whether he had any control over the "appeasers" at lower levels. "Does the good gray Secretary actually know what goes on in his department?" asked the *New Republic.*[9]

THE FRANKFURTER CIRCLE

Hull decided to cleanse the department's reputation by hiring the enemy. The wartime alliance with Russia elevated the New Dealers, discredited the Europeanists. To get a piece of the action, Hull began to search for a couple of "house" New Dealers, safe liberals who would dress up the department's image without being undercover agents for Harry Hopkins. Hull needed an Uncle Tom or two—men with the political coloration of the New Deal but a primary loyalty to him. Hull personally, of course, had no use for the New Dealers.[10]

After much backstage maneuvering, Hull landed his first catch—Dean Acheson, who became Assistant Secretary of State for Economic Affairs.[11] Acheson had everything—New Deal connections, conservative instincts, distrust of FDR, dazzling legal skills. An ardent interventionist and close friend of New Deal godfather Felix Frankfurter, Acheson was hailed by the liberal media as a refreshing contrast to Dunn and Co. He had argued a minimum-wage case before the Supreme Court and was known to share the New Deal distaste for the stuffy diplomats. His friends Archibald MacLeish and Ben Cohen were delighted at the appointment. Acheson's staff looked like a reunion of Frankfurter law students, including Eugene V. Rostow, Donald Hiss, Adrian Fisher, and Edward G. Miller. Hiss had clerked for Holmes, Fisher for Brandeis and Frankfurter.[12]

Acheson's enlistment in the anti-Axis ranks, however, did not stem from the ideological antifascism of the devoted New Dealers. He was not a social reformer but an American replica of an English aristocrat. Son of an Episcopal minister, scion of the house of Hiram Walker, groomed and refined at Yale and Harvard Law, he did not repudiate the high WASP culture that Roosevelt mocked. He was in appearance a perfectly sculpted Savile Row mannequin. As such, he epitomized the Anglophile eastern foreign policy establishment. One reporter, noting Acheson's "admiration for the English upper classes," drew this comparison: "Indeed, at bottom, Acheson is an Anglo-American in the same sense that LaGuardia is an Italian-American and Willkie was a German-American, not in the hyphenated sense but in the cultural sense in which every first generation American reflects his immediate national and family background."[13]

Paternal overlord of the Anglophile-New Deal alliance was Felix Frankfurter, a rare Jewish Anglophile and a link between the interventionist Yankee establishment and the New Deal reformers. By appointing Acheson, Hull was adopting one of Frankfurter's favorites as his own.

The support of Frankfurter and Acheson for the war had little to do with Russia and everything to do with England. Their reverence for British customs and institutions was so pronounced that they might better be termed Anglophiliacs. When Britain was cut, they bled. Isaiah Berlin termed Frankfurter an "Anglo-maniac," filled with a "childlike passion for England, English institutions, Englishmen. . . ." [14] Indeed, the England of Magna Carta and common law became for Frankfurter what the Russia of Tolstoi was for Kennan. Each rejected his own origins for a fairy-tale past adopted in academia—Frankfurter at Harvard Law School, Kennan in Berlin. And each played the role to excess, Frankfurter becoming a faint mockery of an English barrister, Kennan of a Russian aristocrat.

Frankfurter candidly admitted that on first encountering the urbanity and snobbery of his Harvard classmates, he was "scared stiff." Determined to be accepted by the Yankee establishment, he cultivated friendships with the Brahmin elite. Most of his close friends were Brahmins—Oliver Wendell Holmes, Jr., Henry Stimson, Franklin Roosevelt, Dean Acheson. His wife Marian was the daughter of a Christian clergyman with prerevolutionary ancestors. His desire to become a Brahmin by association is evident in his uncritical adoration of Justice Holmes. Holmes was an unabashed snob. His biographer Francis Biddle wrote: "He did not prefer, he said, a world with a hundred million bores in it to one with ten. The fewer the people who do not contribute to beauty or thought, the better." Apparently Frankfurter did not disagree. He referred to Holmes as the Master and quoted him unsparingly; he admitted himself that his admiration bordered on reverence. "Frankfurter's always giving you Holmes," said one of his students. "They don't make much of Holmes in Minnesota." When a friend casually mentioned that Holmes had a streak of vanity, Frankfurter erupted in defense at this blasphemy. The Brahmins, for their part, enjoyed being flattered by this brilliant Jew and let him into the club.[15]

Frankfurter became a vigorous patriot, celebrating the country that allowed him to be so successful. In particular, he made himself into a eulogizer of the governing class, singing the praises of the establishment that accepted him. His first mentor was Henry Stimson, United States attorney in New York City in the years before World War I. As a member of Stimson's staff, Frankfurter gave the utmost in effort and loyalty, winning Stimson's support in return. His filial devotion was unrestrained. One flowery letter to Stimson expressed gratitude for "the priceless privilege of your fostering friendship." He later gave Roosevelt the same treatment—and with equal success. Eleanor Roosevelt had little use for what she considered Frankfurter's effusive insincerity.

Devotion to Britain among those with prerevolutionary antecedents was tempered by memory of the redcoats. There were no such restraints on Frankfurter's passion. He dreamed of turning Harvard into a feeder university for the civil service in the tradition of Oxford and Cambridge. American laws would copy English statutes; American justice would mirror English criminal codes. When the British issued the Balfour Declaration in 1919 promising a Jewish homeland in Palestine, Frankfurter became an ardent Zionist. When the British opposed the creation of a Jewish state after World War II, Frankfurter opposed it also. His friend David Lilienthal recorded in his diary: "I admire the English but F.F.'s rhapsodies—a favorite subject—make me a little weary. There is something about it that troubles me; quite uncritical. . . ."[16]

Lilienthal was not the only one to notice. "Felix has very profound reverence with regard to British institutions," Henry Wallace dryly observed. "Felix is completely sycophant so far as the English are concerned," noted Frankfurter's Supreme Court colleague Frank Murphy. "Why do you always cite English cases?" Murphy once asked Frankfurter. "Frank, I'll make you a bargain," Frankfurter replied, "Whenever you give me a good Irish case on the subject, I'll cite the Irish case instead of the English."[17]

The highlight of Frankfurter's life was the George Eastman Visiting Professorship at Oxford during 1933–34. He accepted the offer with "a feeling of awe" and lavished such admiration on his Balliol hosts that they fell in love with him. Frankfurter, straining to be accepted, poured his heart into the creation of a profusion of glittering compliments. "English life became more vivid, part of my daily life," he later recalled, "and to that extent intensified my feeling for the institutions, political and constitutional, antecedents of our own political and constitutional life and more particularly our legal life." He summed it up himself. "Life that year was rich, abundant and stimulating. It was very happy for both of us at Oxford. I should sum it all up by saying that it was the fullest year my wife and I spent—the amplest and most civilized."[18]

After the fall of France, Frankfurter stepped up the propaganda. His archenemy, Assistant Secretary of State Adolf Berle, bristled.

> There are so many men around here—Felix Frankfurter is notable among them—who take the British whole without developing a strictly American point of view, that it becomes difficult. It is horrible to see one phase of the Nazi propaganda justifying itself a little. The Jewish group, wherever you find it, is not only pro-English, but will sacrifice American interests to English interests—often without knowing it. I think the process is unconscious, partly born of their bitter fear, and partly because the British actually have worked out more satisfactory relations with the Jews than any other country in the world. Then there is always the Anglophile group; and the British propaganda is working overtime.[19]

Other liberals also had doubts about Britain. Joseph Lash, Mrs. Roosevelt's protegé, noted the "suspicion of Britain as unregeneratively imperialist and dominated by the old ruling class." At a Hyde Park dinner during the summer of 1940, Frankfurter and Mrs. Roosevelt got into a mild argument over the reluctance of some American youths to oppose fascism by supporting a Tory Britain. Frankfurter gave his standard speech: Britain was the cradle and standard-bearer of Western values, and so on. Joseph Lash, who was there, was struck by Frankfurter's intolerance of anything less than adulation of Britain. "He could not see that young people might view Britain differently than he did and not respond with his sense of urgency to British needs. Mrs. Roosevelt shared Judge Frankfurter's admiration for England, but she was also sensitive to the charges that pre-war England had been a pluto-democracy."[20]

Dean Acheson was a perfect appointment for Cordell Hull because he represented the English side of the Jewish-British Frankfurter circle —conservative domestically, pro-British in foreign policy. Acheson would not use his berth as assistant secretary of state for economic affairs to promote the New Deal Keynesianism that baffled and infuriated Hull. He would confine himself to economic warfare against the Axis to preserve his beloved England.[21] Acheson, in short, was a friend of all the New Dealers but not a New Dealer himself. He had not dallied with communism in the thirties. What self-respecting Tory would? He loved New Deal society but stayed aloof from its politics. Only when the British Empire was threatened did he cement his ties with the liberals. Even more to Acheson's credit was his display of independence from FDR when he gracefully resigned as undersecretary of the treasury in 1933 rather than support Roosevelt's "radical" financial policies. Acheson was not enamored of Roosevelt. His feeling was of "admiration without affection." He thought Roosevelt a poor administrator and had no desire to be a court favorite. "Many reveled in apparent admission to an inner circle. I did not. . . . To me it was patronizing and humiliating. . . . It is not gratifying to receive the easy greeting which milord might give a promising stable boy and pull one's forelock in return."[22]

No attitude could have endeared Achesen more to Hull. Furthermore, when he had left the Treasury Department for private practice, he had opened the way for Henry Morgenthau to become secretary of the treasury. How much respect could Acheson have for the man who truckled to the president and got the job his own principles forbade him to take? Yet Acheson had worked hard on behalf of the Lend-Lease bill, and thereby had Morgenthau's respect. He could and would fight jurisdictional disputes with Morgenthau on Hull's behalf without being called a fascist. This was precisely what Hull needed. Two weeks after Acheson's appointment, Adolf Berle noted: "Acheson is a pet of Frankfurter's and I think the Frankfurter crowd can deal with the treasury crowd better than I can."[23]

And there was no doubt that Acheson would carry Hull's brief. He was the only assistant secretary not beholden to Roosevelt. When Hull called him in to offer the job, Acheson asked if the initiative for the appointment came from Hull. "I wouldn't consider it," he said, "unless I knew that it was really your own wish and you weren't doing it in response to somebody else's suggestion, particularly somebody higher up."[24] Hull was delighted. Whether Acheson cared for Dunn, Atherton, and Henderson, mattered little. A little liberalism was good for the department, especially in such a package! Hull later compared Acheson with the other assistant secretaries: "There's only one of him," he declared, "and he's *my* man."[25]

Rather than participating in the reinvigoration of the State Department, however, Acheson found himself in a backwater. The department, he recalled, "never did seem to find its place. . . . Few made any contribution to the conduct of the war or to the achievement of political purposes through war."[26]

Thus, Hull had acquired a conservative "liberal" from the Frankfurter circle, but foreign policy continued to issue from the White House.

8 | THE VICHY AFFAIR

AFTER THE AMERICAN landings in North Africa in November 1942, the wartime agencies staffed with New Dealers began a quiet tug-of-war with the foreign service for control of American activities in liberated territories. A key figure in this rivalry was New Dealer Paul Appleby, who was invited into the State Department by Secretary of State Hull a year after the successful probation of Dean Acheson as assistant secretary of state.

Pleased at Acheson's loyalty, his liberal reputation, and his struggle to defend the department's role in economic warfare, Hull was on the alert for other reliable liberals to strengthen his position. In the fall of 1942, Ed Stettinius asked Undersecretary of Agriculture Paul Appleby to be the Lend-Lease special assistant behind the line of military advance. Appleby, a charter New Dealer, saw a good opportunity for himself in organizing the liberated areas on New Deal lines. "There was an opportunity there for lend-lease to be perhaps the paramount civil organization behind the military, because of the need to bail out the people, get goods and services in, and help bring order."[1]

Hull got wind of this scheme and decided to try to lure Appleby into the department. Although Appleby was a full-blown New Dealer—not the lukewarm Acheson variety—he had never crossed Hull personally. This was not an easy accomplishment, since Appleby had sponsored commodity agreements that violated Hull's free-trade dogmas. Yet even in the one area where Hull presumably had strong substantive convictions, flattery could win the day. His ego had been bruised so many times that he would grant anything in exchange for a little obsequiousness. "There was no trouble of serious moment with Hull over [trade agreements]," Appleby relates. "Actually, our having got . . . the State Department to go along with these trade agreements was somewhat out of line with their general approach. . . . But because we were generally cooperative and because we made a recognizable effort to play up to State, we could get almost a blank check. . . ."

To prove the point, Appleby was in Hull's office one morning listening to the secretary "taking the hide off somebody on the other end" of the phone. When Hull put the steaming receiver back in its cradle, Appleby said, "Mr. Secretary, I come from a department you don't have to talk to like that." Hull would give the world to anyone who showed a little respect. "I know it," he said. "What do you want? You can have it."[2]

Appleby was also a good friend of Acheson, another point in his favor. As Appleby was getting ready to embark on his Lend-Lease mission, he got a call from Hull. "I've got a bigger job than that over here in State," Hull said. "Everything behind the line of advance of a nonmilitary sort will be under the leadership of the State Department." The State job seemed to offer a larger scope for action than the Lend-Lease position. All his top people, Hull added—Welles and the assistant secretaries—agreed that Appleby was "the man for the job." Appleby agreed to become head of the Office of Foreign Territories, little aware that the support of the cable-controlling political desks was more important than the endorsement of any number of assistant secretaries.

Appleby faced frustration from the outset because he did not have sole claim to the cables that dealt with his area of responsibility. "I think I counted at one time," he related, "something like eighteen people who signed Hull's name to messages abroad that had to do with what ostensibly was my responsibility. . . . The people were not under my jurisdiction, and no lines of reporting ran my way from them. So it was impossible in fact to do what I'd been called in to do." The source of Appleby's problem was simple. The European division was not about to give up its right to monitor and draft cables concerning liberated French territories.

No one deliberately withheld cables from Appleby. He saw all incoming messages that "had anything remotely to do" with ground over which allied troops had passed. Likewise, he was routinely sent all outgoing messages. Since cables addressed to him or necessary to his job also went to the European division, the Europeanists could draft answers to these cables and then clear them up the normal chain of command through Dunn, Welles, and Hull without consulting Appleby except in a perfunctory way. Who had ever cleared a cable on French politics with a thing called the Office of Foreign Territories? Unable to monopolize the cable traffic to and from North Africa and bypassed by the political desks, which habitually ignored oddball *ad hoc* offices not staffed by the foreign service, Appleby was impotent in his position. The foreign service demonstrated once again that power in the State Department meant control of the cable traffic.

The ability of the Europeanists to run rings around Appleby in the cable business was vividly demonstrated in the Marcel Peyrouton case. It all started with an incoming cable addressed in the typical organizational way: "To Hull, for Appleby, from Robert Murphy, signed Eisenhower." The message read: "Will State Department expedite transportation of Peyrouton from Buenos Aires to a place in North Africa?" The message landed in two places—Appleby's office and the French desk in EUR. As a convinced New Dealer, Appleby began to investigate the political coloration of Peyrouton. He was not going to be a party to installing a fascist sympathizer or an extreme conservative in territory liberated by American armies. "I didn't know who Peyrouton was—I'd never heard of him—and I began telephoning and verbal inquiries around to people there." First stop, quite innocently, was Ray Atherton, head of the European division, one notch under Political Adviser Dunn. Atherton was a prime example of the regenerative power of the foreign service in the face of Roosevelt's pruning. He had languished in Bulgaria ever since Roosevelt had forced his removal from the London embassy on grounds of excessive foppery.[3] When Moffat, after the maximum three years heading EUR, became minister to Canada in 1940 (he died of an embolism a year later), Atherton returned to occupy the most powerful career post in the department. Whether Roosevelt had forgotten, forgiven, acquiesced in weariness, or not been informed of the appointment, the man he had tried to get rid of now had the most powerful stateside job the foreign service had to offer.

Appleby, of course, was unaware of this history when he asked Atherton for advice. He tells this story.

> [Atherton] referred me to a man that he said was *the* greatest authority in the world on France and French politics. He was, as a matter of fact, on my small staff, a man who had been ready for me, assigned by the State Department when I came. I had not been very much pleased to find that they had picked a small staff for me, thinking they would hem me in. I hadn't been impressed by this fellow.
>
> I went to this man and asked who Peyrouton was. He thought a minute and said, "Well, he was a member of the French Cabinet." I said, "Oh, what Cabinet?"
>
> He thought a minute and he said, "The Vichy Cabinet." Then he named a post in the Cabinet which he'd had. Then he said, "He married—let's see, who was the woman he married? A daughter of a very wealthy businessman. What was her maiden name?" He thought for quite a while and thought out loud about what was Peyrouton's father-in-law's name. That was all he could tell me about Peyrouton—this greatest authority in the world on French politics.

Appleby decided that he had better widen his sources of information. He turned to a friend in Acheson's office, Eugene V. Rostow, and talked to the academicians at the Library of Congress and foreign correspondents at the Press Club. "By late afternoon I had quite a lot of information about Peyrouton and it didn't look good. . . . I found out that Peyrouton . . . was a reactionary who apparently had been quite happy in the Vichy régime to collaborate with the Germans. Of course, our purpose in establishing civil government was to build up the people who would not have done that. . . . It looked like he might be a fellow that we wouldn't want to elevate."

Late that Saturday afternoon, Appleby called a meeting for Monday morning to discuss Murphy's request. The next day—Sunday—he received a call from Atherton. A message was going out at once in reply to Murphy, Atherton said, and Hull had asked him to call Appleby and read it to him. The cable granted Murphy's request. It had been approved by the White House, Atherton added. Appleby was incensed. "The situation was quite plain to me, and I said on the phone that I understood the English language and I knew he was informing me—he wasn't asking me. Of course, in the circumstances there wasn't anything I could do except voice my objections and express my judgment that this was an unwise move and that it would be one that they would regret. I told him that I'd arranged to have a conference on this subject on Monday morning and that it was a matter that was certainly within my jurisidiction and hung up."

By Monday morning Appleby—no stranger to bureaucratic politics—had worked out a likely scenario to explain Atherton's maneuver. He cornered his adversary and before Atherton could open his mouth, left him embarrassed and speechless. "I'm going to guess how it happened," Appleby began, "and you tell me if I don't guess right."

> I guess that you picked this message up from a copy that came to you; that you went to Hull with it; that you told Hull we ought to comply with any request that came from Eisenhower; that the Secretary agreed that it was wise; but that he thought you ought to take it over to the White House and ask Admiral William D. Leahy about it; that you went over to the White House and told Admiral Leahy that Secretary Hull wanted to comply with this request and did Admiral Leahy have any objections to it instead of asking for Admiral Leahy's suggestions; that Admiral Leahy said, no, if the Secretary wanted to send a message he didn't have any objections; that said you came back and told Hull that it was cleared at the White House and he suggested you call me. Is that the way of it?

Atherton offered no rebuttal. "He hemmed and hawed and so on, but that was the way of it."

Appleby got the last word, but Atherton had first blood. And there was nothing Appleby could do. Too late he realized that Atherton "was undoubtedly afraid of me and afraid of the way I handled things." He talked to his friends Berle and Acheson, but as assistant secretaries they had no power over the political desks. He talked to Sumner Welles, but Welles knew that the Europeanists led by Dunn were much closer to Hull than himself. He could do nothing. Appleby decided to resign. "I saw it wasn't going to work. I was only there on loan at the Secretary's request. I wasn't going to fight for a function."

Appleby visited Hull for a final talk. The secretary startled him with a frank admission that he had no taste or talent for administration. He wouldn't interfere with foreign service control of the cable flow. "I'd be the first to sin," Hull said.

> I'd call a meeting in my office that would involve business I'd assigned to you, and I wouldn't call you. I'd call in the people that I've been in the habit of calling into these meetings. The way the Department has been organized and the way it has been functioning will take precedence over the fact that we've set up this new office. This new office wouldn't work unless I would make it my business to police the function of that office. I

> know myself too well to know that I wouldn't do that. It's not the kind of thing I do.

Appleby was dumbfounded. Like most New Deal intellectuals, he thought Hull was not only an inept tool of the career men but also fairly stupid—dumb and helpless. But here the paralytic revealed a perfect awareness of his own condition. "I didn't have any idea he understood this kind of thing in the way he did," Appleby said in amazement.

Appleby's position had actually been hopeless from the start. After the successful landings in North Africa on November 8–10, 1942, the scramble for control of civilian government in Algeria began. The diplomats wanted to use Robert Murphy's presence as a hook on which to hang a State Department mandate to coordinate liberated areas. They did not want to have their prewar monopoly of official information about events abroad diluted by the zealous New Dealers peopling the wartime agencies. If Lend-Lease, OWI, OSS, and so on began establishing overseas offices in liberated territory, there would be no end of headaches. Wallace Murray, head of the Division of Near Eastern and African affairs (NEA), had a claim to Algeria. So did Ray Atherton, responsible for Britain and France. In the interest of a "common defense against economic upstarts," Murray bowed to Atherton.[4] Atherton made the case for State Department primacy to Hull and to Hull's confidant, Assistant Secretary Breckinridge Long. Long shared Hull's distaste for the "radical boys."[5] Together they got Roosevelt to write a letter putting the department in charge of nonmilitary matters in occupied territories. Hull assigned this authority to the Division of European Affairs—namely, to Atherton. The Office of Foreign Territories, therefore, was formally under Atherton's command. Then Hull had his brainstorm and offered the job to Appleby, the New Deal candidate for the position—endorsed by both Henry Wallace and Dean Acheson. Conflict was inevitable. Atherton did not expect to have an ideological enemy dumped into his lap—in the very job he had created to ensure that EUR would dominate in North Africa. Hull did not bother to tell Appleby of Atherton's interest in the matter. Why discourage him? Hull needed a symbol, nothing more. Appleby seemed happy and Atherton could take care of himself.

Had he known something of the internal geography of the State Department, Appleby might never have walked into his office, Room 302A. The third floor of the Executive Office Building housed the geographic offices of the department—the heartland of the foreign service. The secretary, undersecretary, assistant secretaries, and other political types filled the second floor. The first floor and the basement were outer darkness. The second floor had prestige; the third floor, power. Dean Acheson had a spacious, southwest corner office on the second floor, Room 216, bounded by 17th Street and looking south to the Washington Monument. Cordell Hull was next door in 214. Yet Acheson, mindful of the pecking order in the department, recalled that the economic side was "below stairs" in Old State.[6] Along with Cordell Hull he was away from the center of action on the third floor.

The European division, prestige unit of the foreign service, as evidenced by Murray's deferral to Atherton, occupied the southeast corner. In the large corner office sat Jimmy Dunn, political adviser for Europe. Across the reception area was the office of Ray Atherton, chief of the division. Neither of their offices could be reached without passing through the anteroom. All the other EUR offices, housing the assistant chiefs and their assistants, were entered directly from the corridor. Reflecting the values of the Europeanists' world, the offices of Atherton and Dunn were flanked by the British and French desks. In 302A, next door to Dunn, sat Paul Culbertson and his secretary, Mary Maxwell. The previous January, Culbertson had celebrated his tenth anniversary as head of the French desk; he had been on the desk since 1923. Like Dunn and Hickerson, he was on the civil service payroll. His only service in Paris had been a four-month stint as a clerk in the American consulate in 1922.

Appleby's office was Culbertson's office. Atherton simply added another desk and told him that Culbertson was his "assistant," Maxwell "his" secretary. As long as he followed Culbertson's advice, he would be allowed to stay. But if he tried to operate independently, Atherton would know at once and he would be neutralized. The Peyrouton cable was Appleby's first significant problem. He at once crossed the hall to ask Atherton's advice. Atherton referred him to Culbertson, "the greatest authority in the world on France and French politics." Appleby went to talk to Culbertson, who impressed him as an empty-headed student of aristocratic lineage. He went elsewhere for help—and decided Murphy was wrong. Atherton loaded his gun and blasted Appleby to pieces. No outsider walks into EUR and defies the local boss.

Hull's effort to repair the department's "appeaser" image foundered on the solid refusal of EUR to abide any interference from outsiders on "political" questions. Acheson was tolerable because he dealt with economic arcana for which the Europeanists had little taste. Had Appleby confined himself to food and supply problems, his expertise, he might too have survived. Instead, he challenged the political judgment of the Europeanists and precipitated his own downfall. Assistant secretaries like Berle—feisty, quarrelsome intellects—might be irksome, but Berle never wrote a first draft and was outside the chain of command for clearing day-to-day cables. Appleby threatened to cut athwart the cable lines that led to reopened embassies in Europe—to cut the French desk out of the action and interpose himself. He was a sword aimed at the heart, a mortal threat.

Part of Hull's insistence on backing Murphy in the Peyrouton affair stemmed from Sumner Welles's opposition to the appointment. Hull and Welles had a longstanding feud because of Roosevelt's habit of conducting business with Welles without informing Hull. After Hull had signed off on the telegram Atherton devised to slay Appleby, Welles found out about it and had the order reversed. Hull flew into a rage and had the original order reinstated. He was not about to let Welles overturn a cable he had initialed. Eisenhower was somewhat puzzled at the yes-no-yes orders he received.[7] Indeed, had the Peyrouton decision not become enmeshed in the Appleby-Atherton, Welles-Hull conflicts, Peyrouton might never have arrived in Algiers. Hull and Atherton might well have accepted the damning evidence on Peyrouton (as French Minister of the Interior in 1940, he had enforced Nazi anti-Semitic laws) had it not been presented by their bureaucratic rivals. Policy became a weapon in the power struggle. Murphy was automatically right because Appleby and Welles—the internal enemy—disagreed with him.

Roosevelt had no way of knowing if Murphy was correct in wanting Peyrouton. He certainly would get no contrary opinion from the military. Eisenhower was too busy chasing the Germans to analyze desert politics. "We are going to get a new Governor for Algeria," Eisenhower told Churchill's representative, Harold Macmillan. "It's a guy called 'Pie-row-ton.' They tell me he's a fine guy."[8] His officers felt a comradeship with their French counterparts. "Most of our Army people," OWI's Jay Allen explained to Frankfurter, "are not only ignorant about all these things but on the whole, by inclination, rather more comfortable with the Vichysoisse [*sic*] crowd, the Nazified Frenchmen, than those who for their convictions of liberalism either had to leave France or were put in prison, etc."[9]

Patton struck up a lively friendship with General Nogues, the Governor General of Morocco. "It seemed to me a monstrous thing," Harold MacMillan wrote, "that General Patton should be so easily impressed by the gay hunting parties and the lavish entertainments which Nogues gave in his honour."[10] Nogues had jailed a number of allied sympathizers as rebels because they had aided the American landings. Patton deflected orders that Nogues correct this situation and even undertook to redraft a message from Roosevelt to the sultan of Morocco that Patton felt did not sufficiently emphasize the colonial status of the sultan.[11]

More important in strengthening Murphy's hand was Admiral William Leahy's position as chief of staff to the commander-in-chief—Roosevelt's liaison with the Joint Chiefs of Staff (JCS). Soon after Pearl Harbor General Marshall recognized the need for a staff officer in the White House to organize the flow of information and decisions back and forth from Roosevelt to the Pentagon. To bring the navy along—suspicious of a trap—Marshall suggested Admiral Leahy for the post. Leahy was former chief of naval operations and a Roosevelt favorite as well. He had served as high commissioner in Puerto Rico and recently as ambassador to Vichy. Roosevelt hoped that this old sea dog could keep the French navy out of German hands.

Leahy, a strong conservative, enjoyed the close relationship he established with Vichy ruler Marshall Pétain. These two old military men shared a similar view of the world—a preference for authoritarianism and a fear of communism. Harold MacMillan did not think much of Leahy's retrograde outlook. "Admiral Leahy was one of those men who, although unable to converse with any Frenchman in intelligible French, believed himself the supreme exponent of the French mentality. Even the keenest member of the Admiral's group had their doubts about his fitness for this post."[12]

Once the landing in North Africa was set, Leahy found himself in an enviable position—the voice of the JCS and a Vichy expert. His advice to Roosevelt carried double weight. When the president wavered under liberal criticism, Leahy brought him up short.

> Even the President raised some objection to any agreement with Darlan. I advocated that we should indefinitely continue to try to use everybody—good, bad, and indifferent—who promised to be of assistance in reducing the length of our casualty list. I did not believe the President's objections were based on the military point of view, but felt that he was being

> influenced by the public furor that was being stirred up because he was doing business with Darlan.

One of those stirring up the furor was Eleanor Roosevelt. Leahy sarcastically describes a White House dinner. "Mrs. Roosevelt, who appeared to be opposed to Darlan's efforts in our behalf, did most of the talking at dinner."[13]

Leahy kept pressing for closer American ties with Darlan. When Darlan tried to send orders to French officials through American channels, Roosevelt blocked the action because it implied American recognition of the legitimacy of the Vichy government—a far cry from Roosevelt's public stance of nonrecognition of any French government until the war ended. Leahy came up with the old saw. Darlan, a "very sensitive man," might be alienated, he said, and "if that happened it could cost the lives of many Americans." Leahy lost this one, but he succeeded in scuttling an invitation for talks in Washington between Roosevelt and De Gaulle in early 1943. The JCS had decided, Leahy told Roosevelt, that a conference with De Gaulle "might seriously affect our campaign." Roosevelt postponed the visit.

Leahy's antipathy to De Gaulle reflected his affection for the French right wing, and, in particular, his naval counterpart, Admiral Darlan. De Gaulle in their eyes was a traitor for repudiating Pétain and seeking a coalition of all anti-Axis forces in France—including the communists. Leahy spoke like a veteran Europeanist in analyzing the forces behind the near invitation to De Gaulle. "There were some reports," he wrote, "that this pressure was being instigated by a group of Jews and Communists in this country who feared Darlan's 'Fascist' attitude."[14]

The reports came from Atherton, who worked closely with Leahy. In the admiral the Europeanists had a White House spokesman on French policy who could gild their recommendations with the glittering words "military necessity." Atherton kept the admiral supplied with reports that De Gaulle was "tied in closely with the Communists."[15] Murphy echoed the same line. When Arthur Roseborough, head of the OSS French desk, pleaded with Murphy to intervene to free jailed Gaullists, Murphy wearily responded, "Art, old fellow, if you have nothing better to do in Africa than to worry about those Jews and Communists who helped us, why don't you just go home?"[16]

Murphy quickly became the Gibson of North Africa, drawing a hail of liberal criticism on his head for accepting the political analysis of his conservative friends. Welles dutifully issued a statement of support for him, as Phillips had for Gibson in 1919. And, ironically, one of the chief critics of the American envoy's approach was Felix Frankfurter—Gibson's nemesis a generation before. After a visit from Jay Allen, Frankfurter wrote that "the sum total impression left on my mind is that Murphy is a soft-spoken smoothie with easy charming manners, but lack of deep understanding of the forces at play. All that Allen said confirmed the impression that Murphy left on Harry Hopkins when the latter spoke of Murphy as a very shallow man."[17] Atherton had tried to foil Allen's appointment to Morocco by tipping off Leahy. The admiral called Robert Sherwood, OWI overseas director, for a talk. Sherwood, ardent New Dealer, friend of Hopkins, and a Roosevelt speechwriter, was not impressed by Leahy's claim that Allen "lacked discretion." The appointment stood.[18]

Frankfurter encouraged Acheson and OWI's Archibald MacLeish to fight against Murphy's line. "Archie and Dean [are] depressed to the point of violent utterance regarding the North African political policy," he noted in his diary. "Both talked as though we had thrown away everything which we had professed to be fighting for. . . . [I] told Dean . . . it was his job to fight as hard as he can for the views that seemed to him right."[19] In an attempt to quiet the liberals, Secretary of War Henry Stimson invited Morgenthau, MacLeish, and Frankfurter to tea a week after the landings to explain the military rationale behind the agreement with Darlan. He proved no more effective than Gibson had been with Frankfurter in the Paris hotel room. This time, however, Morgenthau led the charge. He made "a very passionate address" condemning Darlan and appeasement of the Fascists. If the State Department continued with this kind of behavior, he said, "in another ten years we will have another war on our hands."[20]

In another parallel to 1919, Roosevelt responded to the liberal outcry as Wilson had—he sent a Morgenthau mission, only this time it was Henry, Jr. Murphy tried to pacify the younger Morgenthau as Gibson had his father. But Morgenthau used his financial hook as printer of occupation currency to demand summarily the ouster of at least one "Vichyite." His finger fell on Maurice Couve de Murville. Murphy protested but to no avail.[21] Like the military commander who arbitrarily shoots a random civilian to intimidate a hostile populace, Morgenthau took de Murville's scalp as a warning to Murphy and the Europeanists.

In contrast to 1919, however, Murphy also had to contend with American officials in North Africa who disagreed with his analysis and tried to get their views before the president. Until the Morgenthau mission, no other government official could rival Gibson's firsthand reports from Poland. But in 1942, the situation was different. Appleby had been stymied from sending his agents to North Africa, but OWI and OSS could not as easily be excluded.

The struggle for the president's vocal chords is part of business as usual for most government departments. As war propagandist, OWI could draft foreign policy speeches for Roosevelt on the grounds of "domestic morale." This phrase became the propagandist's equivalent of the diplomat's "national interest" and the soldier's "military necessity." OWI drafted the "temporary expedient" statement that Roosevelt issued on November 17, 1942, to quiet liberal outrage. The Europeanists were not pleased at this apparent undercutting of Darlan. H. Freeman Matthews, who had served under Bullitt in Paris and later with Leahy and Murphy in Vichy, was wooing Vichyites elsewhere in Africa. FDR's statement, he wrote to Leahy, "certainly gave us some difficult moments and almost resulted in the Dakar people going home and deciding not to play."[22]

The Vichy imbroglio refueled the liberal attack on the foreign service. Hull paid dearly for his victory over Welles and his support of Atherton and Murphy against Appleby. Word of Appleby's ordeal reached the New Deal press and provoked increased sniping at the policy of collaboration with Vichy. I. F. Stone blamed the Peyrouton appointment on "Murphy, Dunn, Atherton and Berle," who were "among the principal architects of our pro-Vichy policy," and who secured Hull's assent "less than forty-eight hours before a departmental meeting at which Appleby was prepared to present the full facts on Peyrouton's malodorous past."[23] Stone also lashed out at the department's apparent disinterest regarding repealing the anti-Jewish Nürnberg laws that the Vichyites had enforced in Algeria. He wrote, "The European Division of the Department, which has always been pro-Franco and anti-Soviet, is also streaked with anti-semitism. . . ."[24]

Stone directed his fusillade at Samuel Reber, Groton and Harvard, second secretary to Phillips in Rome and currently an assistant chief of EUR, across the hall from Culbertson. In an earlier piece describing the department as "the last stronghold of appeasement," Stone had written: "Lower down in the bowels of the bureaucracy, is a figure like Reber. . . . Reber received his training in Rome under Breckinridge Long and William Phillips, socialite diplomats with strong leanings toward fascism."[25] Stone saw Reber as one of the neo-Papists in the department, glad to see the Third Republic go under, pleased with Vichy clericalism. Stone had gone to Reber to ask what the department was doing about carrying out Roosevelt's stated request that the Nürnberg laws be repealed. Reber said the department was "making a study of the question" and spoke "vaguely" of certain anti-Arab decrees which should also be repealed. "We're having it looked up in the library," Reber said. When Stone talked to French sources, Reber's story fell apart. The anti-Arab laws he mentioned turned out to be pro-Arab. The only "French Republican law" involved—another difficulty cited by Reber—was the Crémieux decree of 1870 conferring French citizenship on Jews, surely not a problem. When Stone took this information to the department, he received a denial that the department was even studying the question and referral to the War Department.

But earlier the State Department had claimed the army could not abrogate the anti-Jewish laws because "ours was not an occupying army and could not give orders to the civil population." Stone felt like a badminton shuttlecock, flipped back and forth from one excuse to another. "How can the State Department operate on the theory that ours is not an occupying army," he asked, "and at the same time declare that the carrying out of the President's request is the responsibility of General Eisenhower and the War Department?" Stone, exasperated at this runaround, charged in print that Reber was "extraordinarily vague and flighty on his facts and reflected the anxiety of some forces within the Department to find an excuse for abrogating the Cremieux decree."[26]

Stone's epitaph on Appleby's three weeks was apt:

> A strong powerful personality cannot survive in the State Department in opposition to the foreign service. He would be forced eventually to jump out the window. Everything is done by indirection. They always yield and fall back without conceding anything. Like all good bureaucrats they are masters of the negative, the gentle objection, the postponement, the misplaced paper, the need for further consideration.[27]

Journalist Edgar Ansel Mowrer resigned as deputy director of OWI in protest against the Vichy policy. Mowrer, author of the Pulitzer Prize–winning book, *Germany Turns the Clock Back* (1932), was the first American journalist expelled from Germany by the Nazis. He delivered a ringing indictment of the foreign service in a February 1943 speech to the French-American Club in New York. The higher officials of the

State Department, he disarmingly began, despite the charges of overheated radicals, "are not fascists."

> What occasionally—to uninformed outsiders—looks like sympathy for Fascism can better be described as conservative or "upper class" feeling.
>
> As it concerns American officials, this conservatism takes two forms. One of these is adherence to what the French call the *Internationale des Salonnards,* or the solidarity existing between members of what is called Society with a capital S all over the world. You can also call it the *Internationale of the People-you-meet-at-parties*—that is, you can if you happen to "belong." It happens that a large number of American diplomats and State Department officials do "belong." It is . . . natural for them to trust their own kind abroad. . . . In any controversy involving, let us say, on the one side, labor agitators and workmen, unwashed peasants, suspicious intellectuals . . . New Dealers . . . and, on the other side, diplomats, dukes, bankers, bishops, wealthy and pretty hostesses, etc. our salonnards just naturally gravitate to the latter.

Then Mowrer zeroed in on the central fear that suffused the diplomats' universe—Bolshevism. Since any association with Bolshevists spreads the deadly contamination, Blum's popular front was condemned from the start. "This is what made them . . . dub the oh, so bourgeois Third Republic, 'bolshevist.' This is why they desired the defeat of the Spanish Republicans, even though this defeat meant a vast strengthening of Hitler's Axis. . . . American conservatives believe Frenchmen who tell them that whereas in America democracy means Henry Ford and Rockefeller Center, Palm Beach parties and church-going, in France it means just the forty-hour week, atheism and revolution.[28] This is why Robert Murphy approved the French surrender and the destruction of Czechoslovakia; why, in my presence he often inveighed against the French Popular Front."[29]

The *Nation* devoted an article to Mowrer's speech, broadening the analysis to encompass the Vatican-led drive for a postwar clerical coalition against Russia—"the policy of creating as many centers of reactionary force as possible to withstand the certain postwar swing to the left." The North African landings, coming a month after Stalingrad, guaranteed Hitler's eventual defeat. Those who had appeased Hitler to stifle the Left were now anxiously moving to create a "Washington-Madrid-Rome" axis "before the people have a chance to get the smell of freedom in their nostrils." Archbishop Spellman's presence in Rome after a talk with Franco symbolized the Vatican's role as "the rallying point of the reactionaries of the Continent."

> A new Holy Alliance is in process of gestation. If it is finally born, it will be composed of conservative Catholic regimes in Poland, Hungary, Croatia, Slovakia, Italy, France, Spain and Portugal and will not only serve as an antidote to domestic radicalism in each country but provide a counterpoise to a victorious Russia at the peace conference.

Vichy and the parallel wooing of Franco were the first elements of the new alliance which "will retain the best features of fascism with none of its ugly by-products."[30] Henry Wallace absorbed the same analysis from a Latin American liberal, Enrique de Lozada.

> Enrique believes that the fundamental line in the State Department at the present time is cooperation with the Vatican. He thinks the State Department will cooperate with the Vatican to bring about a negotiated peace, that the Vatican is interested in the corporative forms of governmental organization, in other words, modified fascism. He thinks both the Vatican and the State Department want to see the war end in such a way that there will be semifascist governments in the United States and most of the other countries of the world. . . . The State Department line relative to South America, Franco and the Vatican seems to be definitely Catholic.

Wallace did not take the Peyrouton affair lightly. "I very much fear that this Peyrouton incident will ultimately have a more damaging effect on the President's reputation in world history than anything he has done."[31]

9 | FROM WELLES TO STETTINIUS

DRAWING ON THE momentum of the Vichy backlash, the White House readied a new reorganization of the State Department aimed at concluding the unfinished business of the 1937 EE purge. The reluctant agent of this new purge was Undersecretary of State Sumner Welles. The president had his way, but in the process left Welles vulnerable to attack. His removal in late 1943 and his replacement by Ed Stettinius allowed the Europeanists to recover considerably more than they had lost in the reorganization.

The Hull-Welles feud is amply documented, bred out of Roosevelt's habit of conducting business with Welles without informing Hull, and Welles's acquiescence in the practice. What has escaped attention in the fascination with this top-level rivalry is Welles's unique position as mediator between the Europeanists and the New Dealers—politically dependent upon FDR and the New Dealers because of Hull's hostility but also managing director of the foreign service at the top of the career pyramid. All the cable traffic ultimately passed through his hands coming and going. And he knew how to manage, a talent Hull lacked. The 1937 reorganization had been Welles's work. Roosevelt wanted to liberalize the department, but Welles skillfully balanced the old and the new. The Russian division was reduced—pleasing to the New Dealers

—and the remnant merged with the Western European division under Dunn and Moffat—gratifying to Hull and the Europeanists. Ray Atherton was bounced from London to Bulgaria, and Messersmith became assistant secretary of state, which made Roosevelt happy. But Hugh Gibson, Jefferson Caffery, J. Butler Wright, and Leland Harrison all came out with embassies. The service smiled. In fact, only in England, Russia, France, and Germany were there noncareer ambassadors. And the ministers and counselors were almost all career people. "The promotion of several 'career' men," read a *New York Times* editorial, "has strengthened the morale of the entire foreign service. . . ." The elevation of Far East expert Stanley Hornbeck to political adviser raised morale further. This irascible pro-Chinese academic was now safely adrift in the realm of "policy" with "no routine duties." Career Japanese hand Maxwell Hamilton ran the Division of Far Eastern Affairs CFE) and monitored the cables with Grew's outlook in mind. A week after the change Moffat noted: "Hamilton and Hornbeck are at odds on who is to control drafting of answers to incoming telegrams."[1]

In Latin America the White House gained a point. The chief of the Mexican division, Edward L. Reed—an irritant to Mexican ambassador and Roosevelt confidant Josephus Daniels—was shipped to Rome as counselor. Then, as with the Russian division, his fiefdom was merged with the Latin American division into a new Division of American Republics Affairs (ARA). To ice the cake, Welles chose his protegé, young Larry Duggan, to head the new division. Duggan was the youngest division head in department history. Welles had satisfied the White House and tightened his own control in an area he considered his private preserve.

To complete the performance, Welles sat for a long interview with the *New York Times.* "There is not much use in the government's spending money on a career service," he said, "unless the best men get a chance to serve in the best posts. The President favors this policy."[2] Welles posed as champion of the service while also delivering a few scalps for Roosevelt.

As Roosevelt's favorite diplomat, Welles was on friendly terms with many New Dealers, in particular, Eleanor Roosevelt. At the same time, he was the epitome of the polished and dignified diplomat, cool, correct, and distant. Beginning his career as a Latin American expert, he played a larger and larger role in European affairs as undersecretary, culminating in a 1940 tour of the European capitals in a last-ditch search for a European settlement short of war. Despite Hull's growing resentment, Welles played up to Roosevelt, hoping perhaps that in the event of a showdown he would end up secretary of state and Hull out on the street. In any case, he chose to please the White House and offend Hull when the choice had to be made. Hull who prized loyalty above all else, criticized Welles bitterly in private. Although Welles did not leak unfavorable State Department stories to Pearson, he was the only top official in the department friendly with the New Deal conduit.

Through Pearson, Welles kept in touch with New Deal thinking and got sympathetic notices as Pearson made his rounds of the Roosevelt loyalists. Hull undoubtedly blamed Welles for stories that actually leaked from the White House. Welles tried to play both sides and ultimately paid the price of divided loyalty. "Sumner Welles," Moffat noted a few days before Pearl Harbor, "is unofficially the peace maker between the Secretary and various New Deal elements. He found the role of peace maker a very ungrateful one."[3]

Welles had found himself in a very uncomfortable position when Eleanor Roosevelt began sending him regular memos on the difficulties Jewish refugees were having in getting permission from American consuls to enter the United States. Overzealous consuls tried in some cases to twist regulations to prevent any Jews at all from emigrating to the United States.[4] Welles had to reconcile White House protests with the values of the career service. Since Mrs. Roosevelt had a solid case, he went along with her and had some of the more obstinate consuls transferred to less sensitive posts. Those consuls who had cooperated with refugee organizations in filling the legal quotas replaced those transferred. Hull bridled at Mrs. Roosevelt's interference and Welles's coziness with her. Welles, in turn, estranged from Hull, needed Mrs. Roosevelt's support to maintain his own position. "I had great admiration for Welles," reminisced Loy Henderson, "but he had one vulnerable spot, Mrs. Roosevelt. Mrs. Roosevelt was the main backer of Sumner to FDR, the one man in the department she really liked. Welles was close to Pearson. This made people in the department uncomfortable."[5]

After the 1937 reorganization, the Eastern European division was reduced to a desk within EUR. It was still known as EE and still controlled the cable traffic to Moscow and Warsaw. At times Welles supported EE's efforts to restrict cooperation with Russia. At other times he sent the cables and memos back to be redrafted. When A. J. Drexel Biddle, ambassador to the Polish government-in-exile, suggested a stance of mediation between Russia and Poland, Henderson, Bohlen, and Durbrow sent Welles a memo through Atherton urging restraint.

Biddle's suggestions "are almost exclusively an outline of the immediate objectives which the Soviet Union desires to obtain in this controversy," they wrote. Welles initialed the draft response and it went out unchanged.[6] Similarly, when Roosevelt—perhaps trying to loosen his ties to the London Poles—asked that the department acknowledge a telegram from the Union of Polish Patriots in the USSR, Welles supported Henderson's refusal.[7]

On the touchy subject of freedom of religion in Russia, Welles tried to temper EE cynicism because he knew the importance of the subject to Roosevelt. When the Metropolitan of Kiev in October 1942 proposed an exchange of good-will missions between the Russian Orthodox church and the established church of Great Britain, the British ambassador in Washington, Halifax, asked Welles if the American government would approve. Welles, as he normally did on Soviet matters, sent Atherton a memo asking for a draft response to Halifax "setting forth the position you think we should take in this matter." Atherton sent the memo across the hall to EE and Bohlen drafted a reply. In fact, Bohlen wrote, the Metropolitan of Kiev had applied for a visa to visit the United States a year before. No action had been taken on his application and none was likely because "he has accepted and supported religious liberty restrictions in order to be permitted to exist." This proposed mission, Bohlen continued, was a cynical propaganda ploy. The Metropolitan "should be regarded more in the light of an agent of the Soviet government who is to be permitted to go abroad in order to demonstrate the Soviet contention that there is religious freedom in the Soviet Union."

Welles was not satisfied with this answer. He ordered the memo redrafted, "making clear that if the suggestion is accepted something might well come from it which would actually encourage the Soviet government to favor freedom of worship in the post-war years." Atherton and Bohlen gagged at this idea. They needed an ally and decided to wait until the American ambassador to Russia, Admiral Standley, returned home for consultation before responding. Standley, a conservative, was certain to back their position. At the same time he could claim to have what Bohlen called "the latest information" on Soviet religious policy. Meanwhile, the British decided to go ahead, thus giving EUR an escape hatch: the British *fait accompli* made an American opinion unnecessary. Furthermore, killing the issue would prevent Welles's taking it to Roosevelt for a decision. Who knows, Roosevelt might even invite the Metropolitan himself if he knew about it. Better to let the matter die quietly. "Since the British attitude is virtually decided," Bohlen wrote, "it would perhaps be unnecessary to present the matter to the President. . . ."[8]

Likewise, when Myron Taylor extracted a draft statement on freedom of religion from Archbishop Mooney to present to the Russians, Welles encouraged the initiative. Bohlen thought it a waste of time. "Any such approach to the Soviet Union," he wrote to Atherton, "would probably have little chance of success." Bohlen could see no point in encouraging the Russians to issue cosmetic and misleading statements about religious freedom in Russia. Welles understood Roosevelt's political problem and felt otherwise.[9]

The undersecretary was the prime contractor of the department. He routinely subcontracted the work that came to him to the specialists in the geographic divisions. Except when the White House squeeze was on, Welles did not overrule the desk officers. Personally, his views on Russia were closer to EE than to the White House. Larry Duggan's Latin American division was considerably more friendly to Russia than EE. Duggan, playing on his friendship with Welles, sent him a memo urging the State Department to let Spanish communists into Mexico to counter the fascists—and asked that Welles not show the memo to EE. Welles refused and sent it to Henderson, who killed the plan. Litvinov tried to use the Duggan route to bypass Henderson. He suggested in a memo to the department in 1942 a most-favored-nation consular convention. If an American citizen with Russian relatives died, a Soviet consular officer would have the right to obtain a share of the estate for the relatives in the Soviet Union. Instead of handing the memo to Henderson, Litvinov gave it to Duggan with instructions not to show it to EE. But Welles had enough trouble on his hands battling Hull without laying himself open to charges that he was conspiring with the Soviet embassy to bypass the Russian desk. He sent the memo to Henderson, who wrote a blistering comment. He predicted that the Soviet spy apparatus would keep a running list of all Americans with Russian names who had died. They would then discover some relatives in Russia and claim part of the estate. But, of course, no Russians with relatives in America would die—it would be a one-way street. The proposal died.

Although Henderson had to put up with annoying intercessions from the White House, he felt that, in general, Welles tried to support EE. He recalls a case in point: "Welles was strong on Russia until 1943. He was the only one in who said that we should break relations with the Soviet Union at the time of the Finnish attack. Oumansky came to me in late June, 1942, and said, 'Now that we are fighting Germany, can't you lift the State Department regulation on my going more than fifty miles beyond Washington without permission?' Since the Russians were doing the same thing to us in Moscow, I said, 'Well, can you lift it in Moscow?' He said 'No.' So, I talked to Welles and he said, 'No, it still stays.' But then days later he told me that it was lifted. Welles let me down because of the White House."[10]

In March 1943, Welles was forced by the White House to drop his posture of neutrality and participate in a purge of anti-Soviet officials from the department. The motivations are unclear. But one can speculate that the desire to get rid of Henderson and Atherton did not arise from fear that they could do real harm to the alliance with Russia. Welles was too good to traffic cop to allow that. And FDR did his important business outside the department anyway.

The primary motive appears to have been a desire to placate Soviet displeasure over postponement of the second front and discourage Stalin from signing a separate peace with Germany. Ever since Churchill had told Stalin in August 1942 that Roosevelt's promise of a second front in 1942 would not be fulfilled, the president had been nervous about Soviet intentions. Hopkins called in Davies for a talk about the problem on October 29. After criticizing the State Department's petty attitude, Hopkins stated his own philosophy. "I believe in the Soviets and in their good faith, but whether I did or not it is certainly a risk that we have to take whether we like it or not. We have got to trust them." The heart of the problem was to convince Stalin of this. A separate peace would destroy the Russianization policy of relying on the Russians to do the bulk of the fighting—supplied with American arms and machinery. Hopkins asked Davies to answer these two questions: (1) "If Stalin quit would he do it now or later?" (2) "What could we do now to most effectively give evidence to Stalin that despite his suspicions and resentment over the Second Front we were doing all we could and would do more and how?"

Next evening Davies talked with Litvinov. "He is almost despondent," Davies noted. "The faith of his government has been all but destroyed over the Second Front. . . . "[11] Soviet-American relations continued to deteriorate during the winter. In early March 1943, Litvinov visited Welles and left him a list of officials who were supposedly undermining American relations with Russia. He complained to Welles of "the apparent intention of many minor officials of the United States government to prejudice relations between the Soviet Union and the United States. . . ." Henderson was on the list.[12]

Indeed, had it been proper, Litvinov would undoubtedly have put a star by his name. When Litvinov came to Washington as Soviet ambassador after the invasion of Russia, Henderson was head of the Russian desk. They renewed the feud they had begun in Moscow in 1937 when Litvinov was foreign minister and Henderson first secretary of the American embassy. Henderson complained to Litvinov that he should take up his business with the department and not various White House agents. Litvinov ignored him and continued to deal with Davies and Hopkins directly, as Roosevelt wanted. When he did come to the department, he bypassed Atherton and went directly to Welles. In October 1942, Hull sent Henderson to Moscow to prepare a report on conditions in the embassy. He wanted to get him out of Washington for a few months to appease the Russians, but he had every intention of bringing him back when his assignment was completed. As a result, Henderson had to see Litvinov to get a visa. Litvinov was still steaming over Henderson's slaying of the proposed consular convention. "Well, Henderson," he said with venom, "I see you killed the suggestion for a semiconsular treaty."[13]

Litvinov complained to Standley about Henderson's attitude and suggested that American-Soviet relations would be improved if he were sidelined. Standley told Henderson and Henderson told Hull. "Litvinov doesn't decide these matters," Hull said heatedly. "It can't be tolerated." Henderson returned to his third-floor office on March 1, 1943. Three days later, Litvinov handed Welles his list of enemies. Henderson recalls: "Welles was a man of great strength. He seemed to falter in March, 1943. He had undergone a great change at that time . . . under great personal strain . . . maybe blackmailed. He had always been very friendly to me. All at once he froze up." Henderson felt Welles and Mrs. Roosevelt plotted to get rid of him—that Welles was dependent on Mrs. Roosevelt's leverage with FDR to protect himself from Hull's hostility, and, therefore, could not refuse her wish to get rid of Henderson. "We saw it as our job to explain things as we saw them," commented Durbrow. "Loy felt very strongly this way." He did not modify his views to suit Eleanor Roosevelt. Their first run-in had occurred in February 1940. Hull called Henderson one day to say that Mrs. Roosevelt was disturbed about the Finnish War, that some of her friends said that Finland was the aggressor, and that she wanted the department to look into the matter to see if its line was correct. "Tell Mrs. Roosevelt,"

Henderson said to Hull, "that I've been watching the situation from the beginning and I don't need to make a study. Russia is the aggressor." Mrs. Roosevelt followed up with a letter, and Henderson answered it the same way. She was "well intentioned," Henderson felt, "but was surrounded by left-wing New Dealers." In 1942, she tried to "plant a very strong left-winger as special assistant to the ambassador and sent a note to Welles on the subject." The candidate was an Ivy League divinity professor who frequently stayed at the White House and was a friend of Stalin. Welles sent the note to Henderson, who advised against the appointment. Welles then sent a note to Mrs. Roosevelt saying that Loy Henderson felt this man was not appropriate for the embassy. "This episode did not endear me to Eleanor Roosevelt," Henderson dryly commented.[14]

The first public attack on Henderson by an American (the Russians had been citing him in print as a "reactionary" since 1939) came on March 10, 1943. Two days before, Ambassador Standley had criticized the Russians for not publicizing American Lend-Lease shipments. Roosevelt moved quickly to dissociate himself from Standley's gaffe. Welles at once called up the heads of the foreign affairs committees and several other senators and asked them to attack Standley, which they did. One Ohio senator claimed that Loy Henderson was responsible for Standley's talk, that he was the hatchet man. Henderson explained the attack this way.

> One of his assistants was a close friend of Joseph Barnes, a left winger who was foreign editor of the *New York Times.* During the war Barnes became assistant director of OWI in charge of foreign work. He accompanied Willkie to Moscow. Barnes' dislike of me traced back to a time when he had been considered for a top appointive position. I was asked what I thought and I said that I thought he had bad judgment. He had the hatchet out for me.[15]

Henderson noted a continuing connection between Barnes and Welles. Barnes wrote the Russian section of Welles's 1944 book *Time for Decision.* Although Henderson saw Eleanor Roosevelt as his nemesis, enlisting the vulnerable Sumner Welles to carry out her designs, he also faced opposition from the Hopkins-Davies axis.

On March 12, Hopkins called Davies and asked him to come over to the White House for a talk about "this Standley business." He feared this latest outcropping of anti-Soviet feeling in the American government might encourage the Russians to seek a separate peace. Ribbentrop is "at this moment reported to be working for a separate Russo-German compromise peace, on highly favorable terms" to Russia. The Standley affair "was unfortunate, in view of the already serious deterioration and soreness over the Second Front, etc."

Next day Davies saw Roosevelt. The president was "seriously disturbed. The situation with Russia had deteriorated to a point where it was alarming." Standley would have to be recalled. "We had to keep the Russians fighting with us," Roosevelt said. Stalin considered Davies a friend of the Soviet Union. Would he go to Moscow as Standley's successor? Davies's health was too precarious to permit acceptance, but he agreed to go on a good-will mission to arrange a Roosevelt-Stalin summit.[16] The following morning Davies met with Henderson and Dunn at the State Department and then crossed the street for a talk with Hopkins.

Hopkins reiterated Roosevelt's feeling that there was only "one man to go" to Moscow, and that was Davies. Davies repeated that he could only go for a short trip and urged Hopkins himself to go over as ambassador. In any case, it was critical in light of the EE attitude that a Roosevelt loyalist be in the position. "I told him," Davies noted in his diary, "that the President's policy was being constantly thwarted by underlings in the departments, as he knew, and that it was particularly vital that the right man should be at the top [in Moscow] who was above all loyal to and sympathetic with the aims of the President."

Davies's health delayed his departure until May. En route he uncovered more evidence of State Department sabotage. He discovered to his surprise in Tehran that "Washington" had advised Minister Louis Dreyfus that Soviet activities had increased in Iran and that the Russians had resorted to "obnoxious pressure" to gain their ends. Dreyfus was instructed to have a "full and frank" discussion with the Soviet ambassador about the matter.

To Davies it was the same old story, "a recurrence of that disposition to always see something sinister in Soviet activities, sometimes seen among those 'low down' in the Department." He sent a full account of the situation to Harry Hopkins. No wonder Soviet-American relations have seriously deteriorated recently, he wrote. And then pointedly: "If officials are not in accord with their chief's policy, they should either play the game or get out."[17] Dreyfus explained to Davies that he disagreed with the State Department analysis. "Exactly the contrary was the fact," he said. "Someone pulled a fast one," Davies noted. The instruction to Dreyfus came from Wallace Murray's Near Eastern and African division. Murray's views paralleled Henderson's. (Dreyfus, a career diplomat, may have also been something of a chameleon. The record of his cables to the department indicates complete agreement with Murray.)

Davies returned to Washington in early June. Three weeks later, the word came down through Welles: Henderson and Atherton must go. British-American relations with Russia had sunk to a new low. Stalin had recalled his ambassadors from London and Moscow and had sent a lengthy cable to Churchill reviewing all the assurances that had been given in the last year that a second front was imminent. He concluded, Sherwood notes, "with words that could be interpreted only as charges of deliberate bad faith by the Western Allies."[18]

One can speculate, therefore, that Henderson was the sacrificial lamb, a guilt-offering to Stalin from Roosevelt.[19] Atherton's removal underscored the point, and, for good measure, Ray Murphy, foaming anticommunist and EE liaison with the red-hunting FBI, was banished from the European division along with his voluminous dossiers on Soviet espionage in the United States.

Atherton was sent to Canada as ambassador; Murphy, Henderson recalls, was "moved to a job on another floor. Some files he kept; some were taken away. He didn't talk to officers any more." Hull, angry at this latest attack on his subordinates, was determined to protect Henderson's career. Unless the White House would agree to make Henderson chief of mission somewhere, an unprecedented double promotion (Henderson was a Class Two officer), he would fight the transfer. Roosevelt agreed, and Hull told Henderson of the deal. "That would be unethical," Henderson said. "I don't want to push ahead of other men because I have the ear of the Secretary." Hull was adamant. "I don't want Roosevelt to feel he can do this to my officers. Where do you want to go?"

Henderson describes how he ended up in Iraq.

> There is an ethic in the foreign service that you don't oust a chief of mission to get his job. I looked around and found that in Baghdad we only had a resident, not a full minister. NEA said he wanted to retire. The post was going to be vacated. I went and told Hull. He said that it was a terrible post. Didn't I want a better one? I was made a full minister and it didn't upset anybody. FDR was very nice to me when he saw me before I left.[20]

The 1943 purge bore a similarity to the 1937 reorganization. Then FDR and the New Dealers working through Welles had ousted the head of the Russian division, downgraded Murphy, and exiled Atherton. Atherton had received a promotion to ease the pain—thus placing him in line for a key departmental position once the heat was off. Henderson was similarly treated in 1943. The differences, however, were significant. In 1937, the whole operation was conducted publicly under the guise of "strengthening" the service—promoting the deserving and dislodging the incompetent. That the identical job remained to be done again six years later is testimony to the regenerative power of the foreign service under Dunn's tutelage and Hull's protection. Henderson had more than amply filled Kelley's shoes. Murphy had quickly recouped. He assiduously monitored the increase in communist activity in the fertile soil of wartime America. "Communist-controlled" groups were blossoming everywhere to back the war effort. From Murphy's perspective, the alliance with Russia required heightened vigilance, not restraint. He ominously warned Henderson exactly a year before the boom fell: "Current communist tactics [are] to force from government service any public official who will not go along with what they conceive to be the best interests of the Soviet Union and the Communist Party of the United States."[21]

The 1943 purge carried no cover story that the changes were to benefit the service. It was quiet and surgical. The message was clear, but only to insiders. The *New York Times* did not devote part of its Sunday magazine to the shakeup. Welles granted no interviews. The *Times* allotted a few inches on an inside page to a bare announcement of the transfers—and completely disguised the facts. "Mr. Henderson," the story read, "while a specialist on Eastern European affairs, was selected for the Iraq post because of his competence and to promote a deserving officer."[22]

There is a mention of the Henderson affair in the Forrestal papers, a memo from one officer to another noting that Henderson "was completely removed from the sphere of Russian affairs during the war period, for advocating a strong line vis-a-vis the Soviets."[23] One can speculate that this information came from Admiral Leahy, who would have gathered it from Atherton even if he had not heard about it on the White House grapevine.

One of Leahy's confidants was William Bullitt. Bullitt was also an intimate of Henderson, Bohlen, and Durbrow, all of whom had served under him in Moscow. Bullitt had a longstanding hatred of Welles and an equal detestation of the Soviet régime. He was inclined to see Stalin's hand in every movement for social change. Mrs. Roosevelt found Bullitt "clever" but "unsteady." He disliked Russia, in part, "because he missed the atmosphere of high society there."[24] Bullitt had promoted a plan for French-German reconciliation in 1938 and 1939 to paralyze the French Left and unite Western Europe against Russia. When the French government fled Paris in 1940, he persuaded Premier Paul Reynaud to let him negotiate the surrender of Paris with the Germans.

Well aware of Bullitt's attitude toward the Soviet Union, Roosevelt had not offered him any meaningful wartime work; after the fall of France, he was sidelined. This was a considerable deflation for Bullitt after the heady sensation of intimacy with the president in the thirties, when Bullitt and Roosevelt had conversed regularly over the transatlantic phone, and he considered himself the president's principal adviser on European affairs. To go suddenly from a position of great power to one of impotence can be a shattering experience. Adolf Berle likened the sensation to hitting the pavement after a fifty-story fall. Dean Acheson compared the adjustment to a drug addict's agony of withdrawal: "Public life is not only a powerful stimulant but a habit-forming one." When the stimulation ceases, "the glands go on working for a time. This period of readjustment . . . is not altogether an easy or a happy one."[25]

Bullitt, a man easily offended, took his discharge with ill grace. Just as Loy Henderson refused to admit that the president was really against him and sought a scapegoat in Eleanor Roosevelt, Bullitt shielded his psyche from the unpleasant fact of Roosevelt's disapproval and fastened on Sumner Welles as the agent of his humiliation.

When Roosevelt sent Welles on a tour of the European capitals in February 1940 in a last-gasp search for peace, Bullitt felt betrayed. Welles, he thought, was the president's principal adviser in all areas *except* Europe. Welles had violated an agreed division of functions. Bullitt, incensed,[26] blamed Welles's overweening ambition for his subsequent decline and nursed plans for revenge.

The 1943 purge gave him the thin justification he needed to proceed. By abandoning all semblance of independence from the New Deal "proto-communists," Welles had in Bullitt's eyes betrayed the very officials who kept the American government from a complete surrender to a wholehearted pro-Soviet stance. He had become an ideological enemy as well as a personal one. One can imagine how Bullitt seethed when Leahy, Henderson and others, filled him in on what Welles had done. Now he had a cause, not merely a grudge. He could with righteousness in his heart warn various senators that Welles's supposed private indiscretions made his continuation as undersecretary an unacceptable risk. Few other accusations would as easily alarm southern senators, Hull's chief constituency. And Hull, of course, was Bullitt's ultimate audience.

The strategy worked. Hull got wind of Bullitt's charges from his friends on the Hill. It is somewhat farfetched to argue that Bullitt's rumor-mongering in itself forced Welles's dismissal. There is an unspoken mutual-protection agreement among incumbent politicians that they will not expose each other's private lives for political gain. Bullitt may have threatened to violate that agreement, but there is a question whether the press would have given him a hearing. In any case, Bullitt would have gotten nowhere had Hull not decided to use the occasion to destroy Welles. He put it up to Roosevelt. Choose one: Welles or Hull. And Roosevelt had no choice.

By cooperating in the purge, Welles destroyed his political base in the foreign service. Hull saw his opening and took advantage of it. He could now dispatch Welles without arousing any resentment among his Europeanist allies. Once Welles abandoned the Europeanists, he discarded his only shield against Hull's wrath.

Rumors abounded that Hull would seal his victory by appointing his confidant Breckinridge Long as undersecretary and elevating Dunn to an assistant secretaryship. I. F. Stone darkly hinted that Roosevelt's partiality for "the pro-Franco clique led by Dunn" stemmed from his fears of Vatican retaliation if he demonstrated excessive faith in Stalin's promises. "The bond between that clique and the White House," Stone wrote, "is the orientation towards the Vatican in European affairs which seems to be a permanent feature of Roosevelt's foreign policy, albeit largely for domestic political reasons."[27] The president, the argument went, was torn between the rival claims of Stalin and Pius XII. To hold his party together, he had to appease the pope; to keep casualties down he had to appease Stalin. He could neither resolve the conflict nor eliminate it. He had to live with it—and one consequence, as the New Dealers saw it, was a long festering war of attrition within the State Department. Each side—New Dealers and diplomats—won victories, but neither could vanquish the other. The president needed both.

ED STETTINIUS AS UNDERSECRETARY

Roosevelt named Ed Stettinius as Welles's successor. The capture of Stettinius by the Europeanists would more than compensate for the disagreeableness of the recent purge. The White House Cerberus Sumner Welles was gone. Stettinius, supposedly a Hopkins agent, soon became a mouthpiece for EUR.

Stettinius, as far as anyone could tell, had no interest in policy. His sole objective was to please as many people as possible as often as possible, and to give the illusion of efficiency in the process. As head of Lend-Lease, he had pleased Roosevelt and Hopkins with his eagerness to carry out their wishes. At the same time, his public-relations background stood him in good stead with Congress. Every congressional inquiry and complaint received prompt and courteous attention. "Public relations," Stettinius noted in one memo, "is a matter that is very close to my heart."[28] His appointment received almost unanimous acclaim on the Hill. Stettinius was a neutral medium, acceptable both to Hull and the New Dealers. No one felt threatened by him; indeed, all felt they could manipulate him. Stettinius aroused no tempers, ruffled no feathers. In the wake of the Welles imbroglio, he was exactly what the president needed.

Stettinius did not care what the output of his organization was as long as everyone was happy. These habits went back to the time he was head of U.S. Steel before the war. He did not have a desk in his office, only a table with a telephone on it. "The papers," he explained to his aide Robert Lynch, "should be with the man who is doing the job."[29] Appleby describes Stettinius's style at LendLease.

> Almost every morning . . . there was a conference of Stettinius' top flight people. It seemed to me then that Stettinius had no interest in policy—he had a great interest in getting things decided. He was almost a stage executive in that he was snapping his fingers to get things decided. He would present some problem that had been on the agenda for the morning discussion, and he'd look around the table and say, "What shall we do about this?" One man around the table might say, "Maybe we can do so and so." Stettinius would look around the table and say, "Is that agreed to?" Unless somebody spoke up fast, that was the policy.[30]

Stettinius operated on the same principles at State—please most of the people most of the time. One day the question of granting a loan to India came up for discussion. The issue was whether or not to require the British to underwrite the loan. A British guarantee had been standard procedure in the past, but by 1943, neither the British nor the Indians wanted it: the Indians were sensitive to such colonial practices, while the British were striving desperately to limit their postwar financial liabilities. Acheson, sensitive to British problems, argued this point, but on a show of hands everyone in the meeting voted to request British underwriting. And that was all that mattered to Stettinius. The ayes had it. Nothing could outrage Acheson more than such a display of stupidity.*

When the meeting ended, Acheson went up to Stettinius and said tartly, "Ed, in the State Department we don't count heads, we weigh them." Two or three weeks later, the British having refused to underwrite the loan and the Indians having refused the loan with British underwriting, the matter came up again. "This time," Appleby recalls, "all the hands were up in favor of making the loan to India on India's credit."

Once again the ayes had it.[32] Stettinius snapped his fingers. He hadn't changed his mind. He was merely the scorekeeper.

John Carter Vincent has a similar recollection. "Stettinius was very affable and would have been a good politician. He always remembered what you'd said to him the last time. I got to know him quite well. But there was always the feeling that he was the brightest pupil in the class . . . always the first one to stand up and say his piece. He didn't give the impression of really being on top of his job. . . ."[33]

A mindless man is a perfect administrator of a department one does not expect to do any thinking for the country, but, hopefully, simply to be a reliable mouthpiece for policies decided elsewhere. Roosevelt just wanted to keep the State Department out of his hair, and Stettinius seemed well-chosen for this role, being both noncontroversial and a willing servant of FDR and Hopkins. He literally rose to the top because of his incompetence. He did not rise to his own level of incompetence; he rose way above it because others saw his ascension as serving their purposes. In a hard-fought game amongst men who all outreached him in cunning and intellect, he won the prize as a compromise candidate

*MacLeish describes his "oldest and dearest friend." "A faculty of judgment lies at the core of every man. In Acheson's case it does not hinge on a sense of moral right or wrong but of intelligence or stupidity. He did not shrink from making enemies and had almost no tolerance for what he felt was inferior intelligence or stupid questioning."[31]

again and again between men whose very strength and mental power made them political burdens to FDR. Roosevelt had enough battles to fight without feeding the raging controversies in a department he considered a useless appendage anyway. If the department would just not get in his way, that would be a major achievement.

Hopkins's hope that he might run the State Department through Stettinius, as he had Lend-Lease, was somewhat naive. Hull appointed Dunn to guide the new undersecretary around—and Stettinius soon became a mouthpiece for the Europeanists. Unlike Welles, he never sent anything back to be redrafted. "Stettinius took me up when he came into the Department," Dunn recalled. "I just practically never let him out of my sight. He was grateful."[34] Roosevelt hoped that Stettinius could somehow "reorganize" the department to make it more responsive to his will, but Dunn guided the changes and made sure they were no more than cosmetic. "Stettinius," wrote Sherwood, "at Roosevelt's direction, made a determined effort to reorganize the State Department and bring it up to date. He drew up an enormous and impressive chart with myriad boxes in orderly array. But he found out that this rearrangement could produce no real change in the character of the State Department as long as the occupants of the boxes, particularly on the upper middle level of divisional chiefs, remained the same; and they did remain the same, for these were the permanent career men who knew that they would still be there when the Franklin Roosevelt Administration had been replaced by another one. . . ."[35]

Roosevelt never gave up his desire to reform the department. Hope springs eternal when frustration is endemic. Stettinius, it was true, was Roosevelt's servant, but more to the point he was everyone's servant. He aimed to please—and the foreign service officers had many more opportunities to ask his favors than did the White House. Elbridge Durbrow, who moved up a notch on the Russian desk after Henderson's transfer, tells how Stettinius was tutored.

> Stettinius was the nicest man I ever knew—pleasant, delightful, considerate—and the worst secretary of state. His whole experience was on the merchandising side of U.S. Steel and he was imbued with the philosophy that the client must be right. Whenever an ambassador came in with a request, he would say from habit, "Why, yes, we can do it." We had to send him memos telling him to hold back. That's a fine way to run a business but not foreign policy.[36]

Stettinius's habitual affability was not protective coloration. He was not so much a chameleon seeking to camouflage himself from criticism as a pond that rippled one way and then another as different people skipped stones across it. I. F. Stone characterized the new undersecretary as "a swell egg—an unfamiliar type in the State Department, where most of the officials seem to be trying hard to look like one of their own ancestral portraits." But he wisely did not see the appointment of this bland Hopkins favorite as a New Deal victory. "He is a man of good-will, but he is not forceful, shrewd or well-informed. The deft and subtle cliques in the State Department may find this big guileless boy scout easy pickings."[37]

Although Roosevelt had little hope that Stettinius could make a lasting impact on the department, he still relished the hope that he could make life less comfortable for the foreign service. He reviewed his grievances in a two-hour drive around Washington with Stettinius, Mrs. Stettinius, and Grace Tully. The old Atherton problem of "phony Englishmen" still galled the president. "He said," Stettinius noted, "he had been trying ever since he had been in Washington to reorganize our foreign service so that these professional diplomats knew something about America. He felt diplomats should be recalled and sent to Tennessee for a year, etc." Presumably, Hull would understand the value of spending time in Tennessee. Grace Tully complained about the interminable delays in getting the department to respond to Roosevelt's memos. "Mrs. Stettinius," FDR declared, "Ed is going to raise hell in the State Department when he gets there and he will do it with my blessing."[38]

Stettinius took over on September 25, 1943, but not very much happened. Roosevelt sent Hull a memo around Christmas jogging his arm. "What has happened to the plan for reorganization of the State Department?" Earlier in December, Roosevelt had offered an olive branch: Loy Henderson's rehabilitation. He cabled Hull from Tehran on December 4, asking what he thought of Henderson as Winant's assistant on the European Advisory Commission (EAC), the interallied planning body in London. He "knows extremely well the territory involved," the president flatteringly added. Hull wouldn't bite. The transfer, he replied, "might have unfortunate results." Kennan would be sent instead. "Hull knew I would be attacked bitterly if I went on the EAC," Henderson later recalled. FDR could not grease Stettinius's path with this sort of cynical gesture. Winant evidently did not get the word. "While I was in Cairo," (at the Roosevelt-Churchill conference), he cabled Hull in mid-December, "I was told that Loy Henderson would be assigned to me. I am looking forward to his early arrival." In January, Harriman joined the chorus, cabling Stettinius a request to have Henderson transferred to Moscow. Stettinius asked Dunn what to do. Same answer: he should not be sent. "Dunn was right," Henderson commented. "He was a very good friend of mine. It would have been a bad choice." Hull and Dunn protected Henderson from further exposure to the assaults of the New Deal press. He was now a Class One Officer and would return to the limelight when memories faded. In any case, they would not give Roosevelt the satisfaction of accepting his apology.[39]

Hull had given Stettinius his marching orders back in October. After placing him under Dunn's aegis and recommending Atherton and Matthews as experts on European affairs, he cautioned: "Anything you do is satisfactory, but watch out for extremists and do not bring in any leftists."[40] Stettinius could play around with Americanizing the foreign service, but Dunn was to have ultimate control. Stettinius's efforts to please Roosevelt led to some ludicrous memos. In one "private and confidential" memo to Roosevelt he announced that "refresher training courses" would begin at the earliest possible moment in the "grass roots" section of the country "in such states as Kansas and Nebraska." To cut down on effete dandies, Stettinius suggested altering the examination standards. The test was so hard that "we have been getting the academic type of fellow. Hence, we are studying the idea of shifting the emphasis to attract the strong, tougher type of individual."[41]

While the new undersecretary beguiled Roosevelt with this eyewash, Hull forestalled Stettinius's efforts to bring some genuine hardnosed business executives into the department. The Europeanists, of course, had always looked down on the bourgeoisie. "The State Department," commented Foreign Economic Administration (FEA) head Leo Crowley, who knew by firsthand experience, "has always been a place where they consider business sort of beneath them." Hull protected the Europeanists from attack by these annoying philistines. "You know," Stettinius lamented to a reporter, "the old man was sort of set and old-fashioned in many of his ways. He never liked to tinker with a lot of new ideas. There were a number of occasions when I wanted to make some improvements, or bring new people into the Department. But Mr. Hull put his foot down. He didn't like to experiment with a lot of changes."[42]

Hull had no objection, however, to tightening the grip of his own loyalists on the departmental machinery. Stettinius prepared the reorganization plan in consultation with Dunn, Assistant Secretary for Administration G. Howland Shaw, and Legal Adviser Green Hackworth. The report to Hull in early December recommended the appointment of a new assistant secretary of state for political affairs with responsibility over all the geographical offices, ARA, NEA, FE, EUR. Dunn, of course, was the candidate for this new position. Larry Duggan (ARA), Wallace Murray (NEA), and Stanley Hornbeck (FE) would no longer report directly to the undersecretary as they had under Welles. Dunn would be their new superior. And nothing could be presented to the impressionable Stettinius without first being cleared with Dunn. The Europeanists would dominate all. Also recommended was the creation of a single Office of Economic Affairs to be headed by Harry Hawkins, Hull's reliable free-trade zealot. Despite a plea from Hull and Stettinius, Roosevelt refused to make Dunn political czar of the department. But Dunn did achieve one of his main objectives—control of the geographic desks over the economic offices of the department. "The Geographic Divisions," the report read, "should be given greater importance because the Department's *No. I* job is dealing with foreign countries." The non–foreign service officers, in short, would by departmental order have to clear their cables with the relevant political desks. "The new plan," read one analysis, "recognizes the fundamental character of the decision to make the country desks the pivotal point of foreign policy." The title of political adviser was abolished and replaced by that of director. Thus, "divisions" were raised to "offices," "desks" to "divisions." The Division of European Affairs became the Office of European Affairs, Dunn the director of the Office of European Affairs, and Bohlen chief of the Division of Eastern European Affairs. This inflation of titles was more than a formality. The country desks now reported to an *area* director, not a political adviser. An area director could claim jurisdiction over *all* matters affecting his territory; a political adviser had no presumptive claim to clear economic matters. Moreover, the area directors would report directly to the undersecretary. They would not have to report to any of the assistant secretaries. This new system seems little more than an attempt to keep Acheson under control and set up an early precedent for foreign service domination of any new personnel that might enter the department in subsequent reorganizations. The United Nations planners in the department were also placed on a tight string. An Office of Special Political Affairs (SPA) appeared on Stettinius's chart. In the original plan, SPA was to report to Dunn, the new political assistant secretary. When Roosevelt scotched this idea, Dunn suddenly took a great interest in UN planning, becoming acting chief of SPA. He kept close watch over these starry-eyed oneworlders throughout the preliminary UN negotiations in 1944. As an added help, he returned Ray Murphy to grace, promoting him to special assistant to the director of the Office of European Affairs—namely, Dunn. Welles had been destroyed forever. Murphy, twice banished by Welles, returned stronger than ever.[43]

Dunn also took advantage of the shift from political advisers to area directors to move the Europeanists into control of the two offices run by outsiders—ARA and FE. Larry Duggan, Welles's protegé, resigned in July 1944 and was replaced by vintage club member Norman Armour. China hand Stanley Hornbeck, an irascible academic who had dominated FE since 1932, soon headed for the Netherlands. His successor was none other than Joseph Grew, who had been passing his time making speeches since his return from Japan after Pearl Harbor. Grew's deputy director, Joseph Ballantine, another Japanese expert, handled most of the work. "I had practically complete carte blanche," Ballantine recalls. "He left it entirely to me." Ballantine shared Grew's view that Japan should be treated leniently at the war's end, that Russia was the real danger in the Far East, communism the challenge in China. Ballantine had little use for his subordinate, John Carter Vincent, head of the Division of Chinese Affairs.[44] Vincent felt, as did most of the China hands, that rising nationalism was the predominant fact in Asian politics. Anticolonialism, not anticommunism should be the theme of postwar American foreign policy in East Asia.

Ken Landon, an officer on the Southwest Pacific Affairs desk, shared Vincent's outlook, as did his chief, Laurence Salisbury. FE, unlike EUR, was not a haven for seaboard aristocrats. The language barrier prevented that. Instead, it attracted the sons of Chinese and Japanese missionaries, who had grown up speaking an Oriental language and been immersed in the culture for many years. Some of these like Vincent, Landon, John Paton Davies, and John Stewart Service, identified with the hardships of the Chinese peasantry rather than the Western-oriented circle around Chiang Kai-shek. And they did not see every movement for social change as a threat to Western civilization. Landon was a latecomer to the department. After graduating fron Princeton Theological Seminary in 1927 at the age of twenty-four, he spent the next eleven years in Siam as a missionary, gaining in the meantime a Ph.D. in philosophy from the University of Chicago. His wife wrote *Anna and the King of Siam.* Landon served with a number of war agencies, moving to the State Department in October 1943. As an outsider, he was not trained in the habitual deference of career officers to EUR. Nor was his chief, Salisbury, who had spent the twenties in Japan and the thirties in China.

When Southwest Pacific Affairs, responsible for Siam, Indochina, Indonesia, and Burma, suddenly became a division in January 1944, Salisbury and Landon felt they had come into their own. They had memo pads printed proudly displaying the name of the new division and promptly circulated to all the offices a statement of their policy toward the Dutch Indies. This produced an "explosion" in the Division of Western European Affairs. Hornbeck recounts: "The memo dealt with a colonial dependency of a European country. In the handling of such questions it had been the practice of the American government to communicate, through the Division of Western European Affairs, with the government of the sovereign country." Dunn fired off a memo "bitterly complaining about their invasion by FE." Salisbury resigned, but Landon stayed on, becoming even more assertive. Vincent relates: "Landon turned out to be a good friend. He was of the same opinion I was—the nationalism of Southeast Asia was the important thing to handle. He was forever getting into squabbles with the European office. The European office had a condominium in those days because Southeast Asia was still made up of colonies and the European division could assert the right to have a 'say so' in any decision made with regard to Southeast Asia because of the metropolitan country's interest."

Dunn may have been doubly annoyed because he had expressly dealt with this problem in the initial planning meetings. Knowing Roosevelt's anticolonial impulses, Dunn had the following paragraph written into the minutes of a meeting with Shaw on December 2, 1943.

> It was agreed that primary responsibility for matters concerning the Far Eastern territories and possessions of European states should be visited in the respective Divisions of the Office of European Affairs since the basic principle underlying the organization of the four geographic offices involved the concept of dealing with sovereign governments. . . . There should be . . . a Division of Far Eastern Territories which would have *participating* rather than primary responsibilities in these matters.[45]

Apart from this minor rebellion, quickly quelled, the Stettinius reorganization proceeded without incident. By the fall of 1944, the Europeanists had significantly tightened their grip on the departmental machinery. Dunn, Murray, Armour, and Grew stood as the four horsemen of the service, outflanking all intruders, whether economists, UN planners, New Dealers, Welles loyalists, or FE China hands. Stettinius was a blessing in disguise. With Hull in the hospital much of the time ("No one paid much attention to Hull," Vincent found), Stettinius was de facto secretary of state throughout 1944. A Roosevelt favorite who did Dunn's bidding, he was a sheep in wolf's clothing. He roared reform but lay down quietly at Dunn's command. He was a perfect front man for the service. And with Hull increasingly absent from the department, Dunn needed a substitute shield against White House snipers.

10 | THE STATE DEPARTMENT RETREATS

THE STETTINIUS APPOINTMENT strengthened the grip of the Europeanists on the departmental machinery. Stettinius's vaunted New Deal reorganization actually benefited the service far more than had any of Welles's White-House directed shakeups. Hopkins had been stood on his head. Nonetheless, White House pressure began to tell. The urge for acceptance converted Cordell Hull into a vigorous partisan of the Grand Alliance after Welles's departure. Further down the line, Charles Bohlen, Henderson's successor, succumbed to the seductive lure of White House intimacy. He not only translated Roosevelt's orders at the Big Three conferences; he absorbed them as well. Although he could not alter the flesh in the department, Roosevelt did begin to affect the spirit—within limits. Bohlen and the Europeanists gave the president his due, but hedged their bets against the day he would no longer be in office.

Cordell Hull would always back "his boys" in political fights, but, as usual in this distinctly nonideological man, his views on policy often derived from his personal feuds. One unexpected consequence of Welles's departure was Hull's conversion in late 1943 into an acolyte at the altar of Soviet-American friendship.

As salve for his wounds, Roosevelt asked Welles to go to Moscow for a conference with Molotov and Eden in late 1943. Relations with Moscow were the key to the postwar world, Roosevelt argued. Welles could help win the war by securing Soviet agreement to stay in the struggle until the end and help secure the peace by winning Soviet consent to participation in the United Nations Organization. Hull reluctantly consented to the Welles mission, but when Pearson broadcast his charges that Welles was the victim of an anti-Soviet clique in the department, the secretary stiffened. In this context, a Welles mission of conciliation to Moscow would appear as tacit agreement with Pearson's charges and a repudiation of Hull. Hull telephoned Jimmy Byrnes, head of the White House Office of War Mobilization (OWM), and stated his case. Byrnes, a court reporter in his youth, took Hull's words down in shorthand and transcribed them for Roosevelt. "This fellow should issue a sweeping statement," Hull said, "correcting the lies that have been told by his friends about the attitude of the department as to Russia. He ought to put up to the President the danger of this stuff coming to the surface." If Welles did not repudiate Pearson, Hull implied, he could not agree to his going to Moscow. "I want it understood," Hull said, putting Roosevelt on the spot, "that I am not unqualifiedly opposed to the appointment."[1] Welles, knowing that he would have to report through Hull, considered the situation untenable. He turned down Roosevelt's offer.

The Europeanists then urged Hull to go himself. After all, he was the American foreign minister, the counterpart of Eden and Molotov. Why shouldn't he show that he could do as good a job as Welles? Hull resisted. He was no globetrotting cosmopolitan. And, what about what happened at the 1933 London Economic Conference? Could he trust "that man," as he called Roosevelt, not to undercut him? But he finally gave in. "Hull was under great pressure to do the things the European division wanted him to do," Vincent recalled. "He went to Moscow under great pressure. He didn't want to go. 'We got the old man to go to Moscow,' they told me. He was a hardheaded old hillbilly southerner, just didn't want to go to Moscow."[2] Hull was not optimistic. "Before I went," he later told a journalist, "I was sure it would fail completely."[3]

The conference was a rousing success, surprising Hull as much as anyone. Suddenly he was an international diplomat of the first water, skillfully welding the shaky coalition together and smoothing the path for the first meeting of the Big Three in November 1943, at Tehran. To cap his triumph, on the way home the Senate endorsed, 85 to 5, a resolution supporting United States membership in a postwar international organization to maintain the peace. Hull was succeeding where his hero, Woodrow Wilson, had failed. He would be the instrument of international pacification. His prestige in the Senate would convince even former isolationists to support American participation in the UN. Essential to his self-image of world peacemaker was an optimistic attitude toward Russia. With proper handling, the isolationists could be disarmed and Stalin reassured. "After Hull's trip to Moscow," Henderson ruefully recalls, "he thought he had solved everything. I warned Hull, 'Don't let them take you in.' But he fell for it."[4]

"Isolationism" had replaced "trade barriers" as the cause of war in Hull's universe. And not a moment too soon. The old formula was losing its potency. "The reciprocal trade agreements program was my policy," Hull told Appleby in 1942. "It was my policy for the prevention of this war, and I didn't get enough support in it, and see where we are now." Appleby found this analysis "pathetic." So did many others. But "isolationism" was an evil almost all recognized. Under this banner, Hull could win widespread approval and praise. Accordingly, his analysis of the cause of World War II changed. "The roar of the guns out there," he said to Stalin, "in which thousands of your men are dying is due to isolationism. We must all work together."[5]

In interviews with journalists after the Moscow Conference, Hull reiterated the necessity of bringing the feuding parties together. He told of his efforts to persuade the isolationists to grant Russia the benefit of the doubt and to persuade Stalin to be careful not to ruffle American opinion. "There are a number of things we may not like in this development of Soviet activity," he told *Time* State Department correspondent John Metcalfe, "but you can't solve that sort of thing by running to the press every time. It isn't going to help matters to keep broadcasting our differences and dislikes in newspaper headlines." Hull added that the United States had acted in good faith with Russia and that he believed that Russia, in turn, was acting in good faith with the United States. Of course, there would be Russian actions the United States would not like but "the U.S. cannot expect to run the world." He felt confident that most difficulties would be solved.

Those who insisted on resisting the spread of Russian power into Eastern Europe were akin to warmongers—or at best unrealistic. "Let me tell you a story," Hull began.

> You know, a lot of fellows have been in to see me about that feeling over Soviet policy. But there is one in particular I want to tell you about. He came in here with demand after demand that we tell the Russians to do this and that. That we stop them from doing this and that. He was awfully loud about it.
>
> So, I told him that as Secretary of State I was quite sure I could arrange for him to take a trip to Moscow, if he was really serious about his demands. I told him I would be glad to give him the opportunity to meet the Soviets eye to eye, talk to them face to face. Then, I suggested, if he was really insistent upon making his demands, he might want to take the U.S. Army and Navy along, just as a precaution. I thought he might need this support if he intended to enforce his demands.[6]

Three weeks later, on January 19, 1944, *Nation* correspondent Louis Fischer came in for an off-the-record talk with Hull. Fischer, an early supporter of the Communist experiment, recoiled in revulsion when a number of his close friends in Russia were executed during the purges. Fischer knew at first hand that terror was a major instrument of Stalin's rule—and he feared the expansion of Stalinism in Europe after the war. "Since I last saw you," he said, "you have had a very exciting experience. "Yes," Hull replied, "very exciting and very fatiguing." But it was worth it "to get to the bottom of the many separate peace stories" and discover that Moscow was "ready to cooperate in an international organization." Then Fischer bored in. "Were you able to pin them down on the Polish issue?" Hull, as before, brushed aside particular points of contention.

> All these matters take time. One must be patient. The moment anything happens I hear the charge of "unilateralism." There is no use flying off the handle. Christ, if we do that there will never be any unity. We have to consider the years of mistrust and isolation of Russia. They have been suspicious of us and we have been suspicious of them. They have not known us and we have not known them.

Fischer felt he knew them quite well and that Hull had let his "success" at Moscow go to his head. Stalin, he suggested, was manipulating Hull and Roosevelt for his advantage. He wanted to woo the Americans but also keep them off balance—a judicious mix of sweet-and-sour tactics. Tehran had been *too* friendly for his taste. It was in Russia's interest to keep alive American fears of a separate peace—ergo, the *Pravda* publication of a Cairo rumor about British negotiations with Hitler a month after Tehran. The problem was not to allay Stalin's suspicions but to comprehend his diplomatic strategy. Stalin was pulling the strings, Fischer implied, not Cordell Hull.

The secretary reacted sharply to the implication that he had been taken. "I think you're, if you'll allow me to say so, I want to be dogmatic on this. I think you're wrong. Some time ago my old friend Alf Landon came to see me, and he protested against unilateral decisions on the Baltic States and Poland." And Hull launched into the same story he had told Metcalfe—with the same punch line: ". . . but I suggested that he ought to take some of the U.S. Army and Navy with him." Evidently, whenever anyone confronted Hull with a disturbing hypothesis about Soviet behavior, he simply told this story, whether relevant or not, subtly implying that anyone who distrusted the Russians was a warmonger. Hull did not deal in fine distinctions. "All relations with Russia have to be handled with infinite care," he counseled Fischer. He was tutoring Stalin in the intricacies of American domestic politics so that the dictator would not inadvertently offend American opinion. "I . . . cabled to Moscow, this is very private, asking them not to fly off the handle when something they didn't like appeared in our press." Wendell Willkie, for instance, had just published an article questioning Russian intentions. "Maybe Willkie was thinking of the votes of the Poles and the Finns. That's politics. The Russians ought to understand that."

Fischer felt he had been filibustered. "He talked total optimism and he talked. During the 40 minutes I must have said about a hundred words. His tactics seemed to be not to let me talk."[7] Hull, it appears, had adopted not only FDR's foreign policy but his political style as well. Roosevelt habitually filibustered visitors he had to see but did not want to argue with. He simply told one gay story after another until "Pa" Watson announced that it was time for his next appointment. Hull did the same. "He was a master at handling people," Durbrow recalls. "He would talk on and on—to some it seemed mindless rambling—and then excuse himself and see them out without even letting them force on him the business they had come to transact. . . . He could be blunt or roundabout as the situation required."[8]

As 1943 turned into 1944, Hull became, of all things, a mouthpiece for the White House. Or, more accurately, he acquired the Messiah complex that made him feel, as did Roosevelt, that he could redeem Wilson's failures. He became for Roosevelt the bridge to the Senate thet Wilson had tragically lacked. "Roosevelt's concept of his dependence on Hull was justified by the enormous success of the Moscow Conference in October," Sherwood wrote, "and its consequent profound effect on Congressional opinion."[9] Hull spent his last year in office as assistant secretary of state for congressional relations.

Dunn felt the new breeze from the secretary's office and heeled over slightly. "Doc" Matthews had replaced Atherton. "Doc and Dunn," Durbrow recalls, "would sometimes get on us and say, 'God, you guys have been there too long. . . .' But we are supposed to say what we feel."[10] Even in EE itself, a lessening of vitriol was evident, particularly in the person of Henderson's successor as section chief, Charles Bohlen.

Educated at St. Paul's and Harvard, Bohlen had strong roots in the seaboard aristocracy. He was an amiable and intelligent Brahmin, thoroughly content with his comfortable social position, and, in the Grew-Phillips tradition, looking for adventure abroad. He was not like Kennan, who found an identity in the foreign service, or like Henderson, who was motivated by political conviction. Kennan idealized Old Russia and wished that fate had allowed him to be a member of "the prerevolutionary cultural intelligentsia"—"a world to which, I always thought, I could really have belonged, had circumstances permitted. . . ."[11] Although Henderson did not share Kennan's intellectual interests, he too had a sharp personal vendetta against the communists. His wife was from the Baltic states; he had been part of a Red Cross mission there in 1919; and he had been trained by Kelley in the nonrecognition catechism of the twenties. His views were as unshakable as Kennan's, his willingness to act on them as firm. Indeed, his opposition was the purest of all—a hard, bright, inalterable flame compared to the multicolored fireworks of Kennan's expressive mind. Kennan, the intellectual, seemed always, almost by temperament, to be in opposition to current policy. He measured official positions by his own consistent and intricate intellectual conceptions and usually found the government wanting. Henderson had no such analytical pretension or talent. He never swerved from total and unqualified opposition to the Soviet régime.

Bohlen had neither Henderson's intensity nor Kennan's brilliance. A Europeanist in upbringing, he chose Soviet studies because he sensed the opportunity for rapid advancement in this new career niche. The choice had nothing to do with intellectual interests or identity problems. "I am not sure why I chose Russia," Bohlen wrote. "I do not recall any deep interest in what the Bolsheviks were trying to do. . . . I did see, however, the growing importance of the Soviet Union, and realized that the United States would need experts to deal with the Communist state."[12] In other words, he just wanted to get ahead. He had become a Russian specialist in anticipation of American recognition. He would be first in line for the new openings. "Obviously," he wrote, "I was delighted with the decision to recognize the Soviet Union." Obviously, Kennan and Henderson were not.

When the New Dealers began to attack EE at the beginning of Roosevelt's second term, Bohlen had to add a new element to his calculations. He had better not identify too closely with the Kelley-Henderson position in case their days were numbered. On the other hand, he had better not go overboard in agreeing with the White House lest he jeopardize his standing in the service. One might expect that Bohlen would be steadfastly opposed to the extinction of EE in the 1937 reorganization. Instead, he found himself "pulled somewhat in both directions." On the one hand, "there was no doubt in my mind that Roosevelt was right in believing that the Soviet Union would be an important fact in the world and that a fresh view was needed in the State Department to deal with this fact. . . . After all, I represented new blood." On the other hand, "I could not but be fearful of accepting the Bolsheviks at face value. Kelley's skepticism was healthy."

At the Moscow embassy in the last years of the decade, Bohlen walked the same path of prudence. The utter lack of sources of reliable information on the internal workings of the Soviet government, of course, made caution sensible. Kelley had taught his charges not to speculate without evidence. Alexander Kirk, Bohlen's superior in Moscow, reinforced this point. "In accordance with Kirk's teachings, I did not want to make any suppositions or assumptions that would mislead officials in Washington." And besides, it was safer not to put oneself on the line. Strong opinions had been Kelley's downfall. Who could say the same might not happen to Bohlen? "There was an ever present danger of misinterpretation through oversimplification as reports moved through the State Department and White House bureaucracy."

In late 1942 Bohlen returned to the Russian desk, joining Henderson and Durbrow. "I quickly learned that the struggle over Soviet policy that I had been caught up in five years before still persisted." Bohlen's future brightened when Henderson was sent to Iraq and he became head of EE. "I was the first of the six specialists who started the Russian-language program in the late 1920's to become the head of a division of the State Department," he said proudly. Having profited from Henderson's transfer, Bohlen understandably may have been somewhat embarrassed by the circumstances of his promotion. It is not surprising that he misrepresents the facts in his memoirs. "A man of the highest character, absolutely incorruptible, [Henderson] always spoke his mind, a practice that did not make him popular. Overruled time after time, he asked in 1943 to be relieved of his duties as chief of the division, and I was appointed to succeed him."[13] Bohlen obviously knew the truth—that Henderson was forced out by the White House "over Mr. Hull's dead body," as Durbrow put it—but he chooses to disguise this fact. How would it look if he wrote: "A man of the highest character, absolutely incorruptible, Henderson was forced out by the White House because he was considered too critical of the Soviet Union. I was appointed to succeed him."

Did the White House agree to Bohlen's appointment because he was considered more tractable than Henderson, a man who would hold his tongue to maintain his popularity on the other side of Executive Avenue? Certainly, in the department, Bohlen had never disagreed significantly with Henderson. The only difference was that Henderson spoke up; Bohlen kept quiet. "Chip had the same basic pitch as Loy," Durbrow recounted, "but Loy had been saying it openly since 1939." Henderson himself viewed Bohlen's appointment with little enthusiasm. But he was better than what the White House was offering. "I recommended Bohlen to replace me, partly because an outsider was being pushed in whom I didn't trust, a Russian specialist, later a professor." Henderson had no respect for Bohlen's habit of keeping his neck deep inside his shell; of not offending the New Dealers. "Harry Hopkins shared Mrs. Roosevelt's view of the State Department. He had pets—Chip Bohlen, Doc Matthews, Llewellyn Thompson." William Bullitt, Bohlen's former boss, felt the same way. He was quite scornful of Bohlen for his "sellout."[14]

Bohlen admits that he played both sides. The basic pitch of EE did not change, but the trumpet was muted. "Like Henderson, I, too, thought that we were dealing with the Soviets on an emotional instead of a realistic basis. However, I did not feel as strongly as Henderson about changing policy," primarily because of the grim military situation. Although he felt admiration for the Russians "was blinding Americans to the dangers of the Bolshevik leaders," Bohlen "rarely tried to convince anyone. . . . During the war, there was always this ambiguity in my attitude toward the Soviet Union."

The ambiguity extended to the United Nations. Bohlen expresses both skepticism and enthusiasm in a single split-personality sentence.

"Most of us who had doubts—I was as enthusiastic as some about the United Nations as a peace-keeping mechanism—were silent because we had no hard evidence to support our instinctive feeling that trouble lay ahead."

In the White House circle Bohlen carefully suppressed his trained pessimism about the Soviet régime ("obviously Hopkins and Roosevelt had an influence on me") and embroidered his analysis with "political realities." Perhaps the idea of the UN was unrealistic, as Kennan argued, but it was "the only device that could keep the United States from slipping back into isolationism." Maybe a frank spheres-of-influence agreement with Russia would be the best guarantee of postwar peace, but it was politically impossible. "To have agreed to consign the small countries of Eastern Europe to the Soviet Union undoubtedly would have aroused fierce antagonisms among the ethnic groups in the United States . . . a loud and effective outcry from our own Poles and Czechs." Public opinion had to be pacified although the resulting foreign policy might not be "the optimum from an abstract point of view."[15] This is a startling view from a foreign service officer trained to safeguard the flame of "national interest" and deeply suspicious of the fickle breezes of public sentiment fanned by election-conscious politicians. The lure of White House intimacy induced Bohlen to forsake the trained parochialism of his chosen profession. Bohlen's professionalism was a far cry from that of General Marshall—always careful to limit his advice to military considerations alone—or of Kennan and Henderson—loyal to the truth as they saw it regardless of its political palatability. Once he had convinced Harry Hopkins of his reliability, Bohlen became part of the White House foreign office, moving into the East Wing with Hopkins in November 1944. At the Cairo Conference in November 1943, Hopkins, ever distrustful of the "anti-Soviet clique," had grilled Bohlen on his views about Russia. "My arguments must have impressed Hopkins, because we got along well after that. Within a year, he took me into the White House."[16]

Bohlen's defection from the EUR tradition should not be exaggerated. His office mate, Elbridge Durbrow, made sure he did not drift too far away from service orthodoxy. Between the Tehran Conference in December 1943 and his move to the White House a year later, Bohlen reported for work each morning to the EE office in the Executive Office Building, Room 385, which he shared with Durbrow. Although he was on call to the White House, his day-to-day job, as head of EE, was the old cable business. With Durbrow—a solid Hendersonite—at the next desk and Dunn across the hall, he could not speak as expansively as he might in the White House. Besides, Roosevelt was mortal; the service would outlive him. No point in making trouble for the future by becoming a Roosevelt ideologue *in the department.* From July 1943 to November 1944, when he moved to the White House, Bohlen's work *as EE head* reflected the standard skepticism of the Russian experts. His studied "ambiguity" was really a dichotomy—skeptical on the third floor of the EOB, trusting in the White House. Bohlen took on the coloration of his immediate environment.

As Henderson's double, Durbrow set the pace. Bohlen could not lag too far behind without suffering considerable embarrassment in front of his EE colleagues. "Our biggest problem in EE," Durbrow later recalled, "was to try to convince people that it wouldn't be all hearts and flowers, sweetness and light with our Soviet allies after the war. . . . They were bent on taking over the whole world." Durbrow was the perpetually dissatisfied housewife of detergent commercials, pointing out the stubborn stains in the freshly laundered garments hanging on the Soviet propaganda line. OWI was the worst offender. Durbrow recounts:

> OWI was very definitely pro-Soviet. Elmer Davis [director of OWI] was a fine man, high-principled, honest, but he couldn't get himself to believe they would behave as they did. They had made a film called "One Day at War" which showed the various national forces in action. This was made in the middle of the war and was almost as bad as Davies' film which we called "Submission to Moscow." The OWI film had priests and churches and bells ringing . . . troops praying at the front. It was just for the birds. It was sent by the State Department to report on it. I took extensive notes and when I returned told Jimmy and Doc, "This is for the birds." It gave completely the wrong impression about how humanitarian, religious, etc. the Soviet Union was. We got in a hell of a hassle. "Oh, you can't say that. It will hurt our Russian friends." I answered that it will also fool the American public. Davies was being a nice guy . . . support our gallant allies.[17]

When another wartime bureaucrat, Donald Nelson, head of the War Production Board, embarked on the OWI path, Durbrow lashed out again. Nelson came back from a meeting with Stalin aglow with the promise of vastly expanded postwar Soviet-American trade. "It was a fine idea," Durbrow recalled, "but it was obvious it couldn't work. They didn't have anything to exchange with us. I wrote a memo . . . fine idea but unrealistic . . . no basis from our end." He recommended "extreme caution . . . to avoid false impressions being created regarding the possibilities of postwar trade with the Soviet Union." The distance between EE and the New Deal agencies is quite evident in this episode. Henry Morgenthau's economists later recommended a $10 billion credit to Russia. Durbrow set a ceiling of $200 million.[18]

Nothing disturbed him more than the dissolution of the Comintern. Roosevelt and Hopkins might be satisfied by this apparent evidence of their success in wooing Stalin, but Durbrow felt only trepidation. The bosses were fooling themselves. Russian objectives had not changed. Their methods had just become harder to detect.

> The almost unqualified approval by the Soviet government of the Anglo-American plans regarding Italy . . . has more to it than meets the eye. Because of the methods used and the lip service paid to "democratic" ideals, it may be possible that the other really democratic elements in Italy may not fully realize, unless they are constantly on guard, the increasing control which the Communists may gain in the country until it is too late.[19]

In a long memo in February 1944, Durbrow expanded on the theme that the Grand Alliance was a grand deception. He first took a bow in the direction of the Tehran "policy of cooperation." Journalist Forrest Davis had spent a weekend with Roosevelt after Tehran and written an article for the *Saturday Evening Post* that Durbrow termed in an interview "an authentic trial balloon for FDR's Russian policy." He could not ignore it completely. "The word was passed down to us that we should read this article as guidance for the way the President was going to play the thing." Durbrow, therefore, began with a careful understatement: The Russians "apparently are not fully convinced that this policy [of cooperation] will succeed," and urged his superiors to note renewed Comintern activity throughout Europe, "which unless it is studied and correlated might not otherwise be apparent." In Eastern Europe and the Balkans Communist "elements" were allying with the strongest nationalist groups in a bid for postwar domination. By the time the victims discovered the penetration, it would be too late. "The 'front' organizations are controlled by a small percentage of Communist Party workers, while a large majority of the members often do not realize that they are members of a Communist-dominated group." Correcting another misconception, Durbrow emphasized the fanatic discipline and devotion required by the Party. One Communist was equivalent to many democrats in political weight. Do not be misled by "the often mistaken idea that the Communists cannot represent any really important force since there are so few of them." He anticipated "more or less complete Soviet hegemony" in the Balkans, Greece, and Eastern Europe if nothing were done to halt these "back-door" methods.[20]

Bohlen joined hands with Durbrow in the department to employ the EE cable-writing and memo-drafting power to stifle White House initiatives to compromise impending conflicts with Russia.

11 | THE POLISH IMBROGLIO

THE PRIME CONTENDER with EE for control of policy toward Eastern Europe, was the Foreign Nationalities Branch (FNB) of OSS, headed by DeWitt Clinton Poole, a pre-Rogers Act Russian expert.[1] FNB had a short life—it died at the age of four: b. November 1941, d. December 1945. Yet it stands as one of the most fascinating innovations in the history of American foreign policy. Poole's small unit, housed in both New York and Washington, monitored the activities of the thirty immigrant groups in the United States with an interest in the European peace settlement. At the heart of the organization lay the Ethnic Desks manned by academicians familiar with the language and politics of the various European nationalities. The branch employed twenty-six languages and worked in six different alphabets—Latin, Greek, Cyrillic, Hebrew, American, Arabic. One of Poole's assistants compared it to the Soviet Ministry of Nationalities. "The only other large country in the world," he wrote, "that possesses a citizenry of any such national variety is the USSR and there," he pointedly added, "a Ministry of Nationalities functions on a footing of equality with the other principal executive departments."[2]

Like big brother OSS, FNB sought intelligence that would contribute to the war effort. Any domestic agitation that might damage the Grand Alliance caused Poole concern. Ethnic developments that promised to tighten the coalition won his support. Not surprisingly, he concentrated his manpower on those groups "disposed by sentiment to concern themselves—often actively, sometimes passionately—with the fate of the lands whose cultures they still share in some degree." Preeminent were "the twenty million or nearly one-sixth of our people . . . recently derived from the 19 countries of Central and Eastern Europe."[3] Poole noted that the American foreign nationality groups were "not true samples of the European bodies politic." Certain groups migrated in large numbers; others stayed home. And this made a difference in how American politicians viewed events abroad. In the British Isles, to take the simplest case, native Englishmen dominated. "In the United States, the Irish element followed by the Scottish and Welsh groups, is proportionately powerful." In Poland, Poles from the center and south ruled the country between the wars, but most of the emigration to America came from the poorer north and east, the most anti-Semitic and anti-Russian area. In Yugoslavia, the Orthodox Serbs dominated, but in the United States the Catholic Croats and Slovenes were numerically the largest. "When, therefore," Poole wrote, "one views the politics of Europe reflected here . . . it is necessary to allow for some distortions . . . of numerical distribution."

Secondly, the American fragments, even if numerically representative, were out of date.

> Allowance must be made in nearly every case for a political time lag. The American foreign language group is likely to be thinking in a frame of factual and sentimental reference which has become in some degree outdated in the homeland by the passage of later events. This phenomenon, natural whenever groups of people are transplanted, has become especially marked in the United States since free immigration ceased about 1920.[4]

When the reagent of academic analysis was added to this complex solution, two political facts precipitated out. The American nationality groups were (1) disproportionately Catholic and (2) disproportionately conservative compared to their former countrymen still in Europe. They were grist for the restorationist ambitions of the prewar *cordon sanitaire* régimes. "The exiled governments sit in London," noted one FNB memo," but the only free constituencies which they still possess are for the most part in the United States." American relations with Russia could only suffer from this situation.

Examining the ethnic underpinnings of the debate on the future western frontiers of Russia, the same analyst noted that "this question touches the political quick of not less than thirteen foreign nationality groups . . . 5% of the total population." Only one million, the Czechs and Carpatho-Russians, could be considered friendly to Russia. The other six million were distinctly hostile. And to them could be added five million Germans, 327,000 Greeks, and the bulk of the 400,000 Yugoslavs. Catholic Croats and Slovenes outnumbered the Slavophile Serbs eight to one.

The conclusion was clear. If, for instance, the United States recognized Russian sovereignty over the Baltic states, "the chorus of protest which might be expected from these three groups would doubtless be swelled by voices of fear and misgiving from most of the other groups which have been mentioned and which all together make up a considerable fraction of the American population." The writer saw the same political potential the Republicans observed. Most of these ethnic groups were concentrated in large cities in congressional districts "where voting strength and foreign national sentiments are pretty solidly identical." They would not lack "convinced spokesman in Congress." Large numbers were Roman Catholics. For Poles and Lithuanians, in particular, "national sentiment and religious sensitivity" reinforced one another.[5]

Poole carefully distinguished his work from that of the FBI. He sought intelligence, not indictments. "It is essential at all times to have regular contact, other than crass police surveillance, with movements in opposition which may someday become governments. . . . It is not a police operation and cannot properly be left to the FBI. It is a political operation. . . ."[6]

FNB diverged from the FBI not only in method but also in ideology. The communist-hating FBI maintained a strong underground affiliation with leading Catholic prelates, exchanging information on the red network. The FBI, as a police organization, drew heavily on Irish Catholic neighborhoods. FNB, manned by Jewish and Protestant academics, was mainly concerned with the Vatican International and anticommunist foreign agents. Pledged to further the war effort, FNB wrote extensive reports on Catholic and Polish agitation against the alliance with Russia. Poole encouraged dissident Catholics hostile to Polish landlordism and Vatican ambitions just as Hoover sought renegade Communists to criticize the Party.

The high point of Poole's effort to undermine the appeal of anti-

Russian Poles to the American public was the Orlemanski mission. Father Stanislaus Orlemanski, a Polish Catholic priest from Springfield, Massachusetts, became Poole's vehicle for convincing the American public that Stalin's intentions toward Poland were benign. When Poole first talked with Orlemanski in New York on February 11, 1944, he was fascinated by this rough-hewn outspoken cleric. "Orlemanski's thinking," he wrote, "is based on an intensive Americanism." He did not like "this damned clique"—the Polish government-in-exile and a portion of the Catholic hierarchy—that sought to mobilize American Poles for foreign purposes. Also, Orlemanski's family came from German Poland. "As long as the world exists, a Pole will never be a brother to the German," he wrote. "In contrast to the Orlemanskis," Poole commented, "most Americans of Polish extraction came from the part of Poland which was formerly Russian, and thus brought with them a tradition of anti-Russianism." As a western Pole, Orlemanski hated Germany more than Russia. As a patriotic American—"well-known as a baseball player" in his youth—he wanted to support the president. He resented a letter sent to the Polish churches, including his own, by a Polish consul, suggesting masses be held in protest against "the brutal force of Russia." "Why," he asked, "should a Consul of Poland, a foreigner, not an American citizen, tell American churches what to do?" He saved his greatest anger for Polish clerics who toured the United States lecturing on Russian atrocities and conferring with the Polish-American clergy on how to fight the spread of Russian influence. "Those foreign rats come in here and dare to preach against me right in my own country!"

He did not want to see a restored Poland run by the same landlords and clergy who had "held the people down" in the past. The heart of the problem was his own church. Poole reports:

> It was the Catholic clergy, above all, Father Orlemanski asserted . . . who . . . had been stirring up the Polish-Americans into an anti-Russian fervor, and this during the very time when the President of the United States was endeavoring to work out some sort of friendly cooperation with Russia. The fact was, Orlemanski said, that in the campaign against Soviet Russia, we were confronted not so much by a Polish as by a Catholic phenomenon. It was the priests, he went on, who feared and hated the Russians not only as Communists and atheists but as those who would do away in Poland and elsewhere with priestly power and it was the priests who exercised the real control over the thinking of Polish-Americans.

Only Roosevelt himself could change this by a forthright stand *against* the government-in-exile. This would not lose him votes. The president, Orlemanski implied, exaggerated the power of the clergy to lead their flock in opposition to an "authoritative" presidential policy. "As Poles and Catholics the Polish Americans wanted to believe what their Polish and Catholic authorities told them; as Americans they wanted to follow their President." If the clergy remained "intransigent," they would find themselves "deserted." Roosevelt, of course, would never take such a chance. He feared the Church too much. The conservatives had to be wooed; they could not be met head on.[7]

Orlemanski asked Poole's help in arranging for him to go to Russia. If he could talk to Stalin, he was sure he could solve the Polish-Soviet dispute and discredit the Pilsudskites. Poole formally discouraged him, but he steered him in the right direction. The State Department clearly would be no help. Orlemanski did write a letter to Hull but received no answer. Instead, he went to the Soviet consulate general in New York to ask for a passport because Poole "told me I couldn't get there unless they wanted me." This move broke the ice. Both Stalin and Roosevelt were looking for an opportunity to pacify Catholic opinion. Stalin reportedly asked Roosevelt to grant Orlemanski a passport. The president overrode EE and Mrs. Shipley in the passport office. He was characteristically disingenuous when asked by reporters how Orlemanski got his passport. Did he have advance knowledge of the trip, one reporter asked.

> THE PRESIDENT: No. We are sending people abroad all the time. You can apply to go over. And you would be surprised that a lady over in the State Department—I can't think what her name is—
>
> Voices: (interjecting) Mrs. [Ruth] Shipley.
>
> THE PRESIDENT: She's grand. A regular "ogre." She's a wonderful "ogre."
>
> Well, if you can get by Mrs. Shipley, it means that you have conformed, you have lived up to the law, and everything else. And then, apparently, these two people got over. I think Mrs. Shipley was satisfied with the reasons they gave for going over. There are people going over all the time. Why, all of you could get over, if your excuse was good enough. Think of that! (laughter) There are only a few of you that I wouldn't allow to go over. (more laughter)[8]

When his protegé returned from Moscow with signed undertakings from Stalin guaranteeing religious toleration and national independence for Poland, Poole was ecstatic. He waxed rhapsodic in urging the president and the State Department to follow through on Orlemanski's initiative. He glorified the priest, praising his "missionary zeal and two-fisted drive" in service of "an American-style Poland."

Determined not to let the chance for a reconciliation between Rome and Moscow die from indifference, Poole offered to arrange a "discreet meeting" with Orlemanski for the president or Hull. "It is difficult to escape the impression," he wrote, "that Stalin intended serious commitments respecting both (1) Vatican relations and (2) the Russian-Polish problem." He urged "action perhaps at the highest level." By the nature of his job, Poole, perhaps more than any other wartime bureaucrat, understood the domestic consequences for American foreign policy of a failure to reconcile Rome and Moscow. "To fail to make something of the opportunity which appears to present itself might be to miss a fine chance in great matters. . . . It might mean not only an opportunity missed but a set-back to postwar adjustment."[9]

After submitting his memo to the White House and the State Department, Poole began a telephone campaign to jog the reluctant Russian experts into action. Bohlen, however, fell back on technicalities to deflect the pressure. There were "plenty of regular channels open without attempting to use an irregular one." The State Department should keep "wholly out of this."[10] Durbrow respected Poole but felt he had gone a little soft. "Poole was an old Russian hand and realistic," he recalled, "but he would say, 'Durby, let's go easy, you can't tell. . . .' "[11]

Roosevelt, however, wanted to encourage Stalin's peaceable gesture toward Rome. He suggested to Hull that they adopt Poole's suggestion and arrange an "off-the-record" talk with Orlemanski. Bohlen drafted the reply that went to the White House under Hull's signature. First, he advanced the technical arguments for doing nothing. Poole's memo did not disclose any new information unavailable through "official channels." (Bohlen's irritation at Poole's poaching is evident.) And, besides, anything Orlemanski had to say was already in Poole's account. This was hardly persuasive. Roosevelt was not looking for information but for favorable reverberations in Moscow. Second, Bohlen noted the political arguments. He airily dismissed "the somewhat vague indications of a slightly modified Soviet attitude towards Poland" and emphasized the "unfortunate publicity" likely to arise from a meeting with the renegade priest. Polish-American and Catholic circles would blast the president for flirtation with the dupe of the Kremlin. Bohlen knew how to play on Roosevelt's most sensitive nerve. Did the president really want to "involve this government in an attempt to settle the merits of the Polish-Soviet dispute? . . ." Surely, this was "highly undesirable." Unstated implication—especially five months before an election.[12]

This memo was the epitaph for the Orlemanski mission and Poole's effort to gain a share of the foreign policy business for FNB.

EE foot-dragging plus election-year timidity effectively killed Poole's initiative—despite FDR's sympathy. The president, however, still liked the idea, even if he could not act on it himself. "Have you seen Orlemanski?" he asked Polish Prime Minister Mikolajczyk in mid-June, two weeks after Hull's memo. Mikolajczyk had not. Orlemanski was eager to come to Washington to see Hull and himself, the president said. As a goad to Mikolajczyk, Roosevelt incorrectly added that plans were being made for such a conference. Then, in what may rank as the most extravagant statement of his presidency, Roosevelt said that Stalin's pledge not to interfere with religion indicated that he might favor a reunion of the Russian Orthodox and Roman Catholic churches under the leadership of the pope! Mikolajczyk must have considered the president a simpleton or suspected he was being taken for one himself. Roosevelt, however ineptly, was trying to get Orlemanski an audience in Polish circles.[13]

The Orlemanski incident was merely one episode in a running skirmish between the Europeanists and the New Dealers, including Roosevelt, over Polish policy. Although the disagreement never broke into the press, Poland was a subdued 1944 equivalent of the Darlan deal within the government. The war in Europe blanketed the press, but behind the scenes the New Dealers continued to tussle with EUR. Dunn, Durbrow, and Bohlen, despite contrary tuggings from Hopkins and Hull, were the lineal descendants of Gibson, Lane, and Moffat in their steadfast support of the Pilsudskite remnant that dominated the Polish government-in-exile in London.

The rivalry between Poole and EE had first boiled over when Poole prepared an opinion poll to measure Polish-American interest in foreign policy and the impact of government-in-exile propaganda on whatever opinion did exist. OWI willingly distributed the questionnaire. Poole hoped it would demonstrate that the Polish voter paid little attention to the issue and that foreign propaganda was responsible for whatever discontent did exist. The survey, he hoped, would help persuade the public opinion–conscious White House that the Polish problem was better handled by cracking down on the government-in-exile than by running scared before the artfully generated phantom of an aroused Polish electorate. Durbrow had the survey stopped.[14]

The New Dealers, however, did not moderate their campaign against the London Poles. An OSS memo in January 1944 described the political complexion of the government-in-exile in less than flattering terms, as did an OWI memo of the same date, which spoke favorably of the Russian-backed Union of Polish Patriots in Moscow.[15] Adam Kulikowski, a board member of the Union for Democratic Action (UDA), wrote the OWI report. UDA embraced the *Nation* and *New Republic* constituencies and had reprinted Mowrer's address on "Our State Department and North Africa." Kulikowski's OWI superior was Alan Cranston, "a big, shy, gawky, ex-newspaperman," according to White House staffer Jonathan Daniels. Daniels occasionally sat with Cranston and others on the Interdepartmental Committee for Foreign Nationality Problems, chaired by Adolf Berle, and he and Cranston became quite friendly. Cranston irreverently explained to Daniels that the purpose of the committee was to find a job for Berle, "the most intelligent jack-ass" in Washington.[16] Cranston fed Daniels OWI memos on Poland for delivery to the White House.

Daniels had joined the White House staff in late 1942 partly as a favor from the president to his old World War I boss, former Secretary of the Navy Josephus Daniels. His son Jonathan wanted something more exciting than the pointless civil defense job he had drawn in the wartime sweepstakes. He moved over to the White House in late 1942 as one of Roosevelt's personal aides with a "passion for anonymity." He had no particular area of responsibility but was available to carry out any *ad hoc* assignments for Roosevelt that required loyalty, discretion, and a nose for political enemies. He was a presidential antenna probing the subterranean currents of electoral and bureaucratic politics, looking for shoals upon which an unwary president might run aground. Daniels brought with him a keen journalistic mind and a dedication to New Deal liberalism; he was a true southern progressive from North Carolina. From his father, he absorbed a mild suspicion of those State Department "reactionaries." As ambassador to Mexico in the 1930s, Josephus Daniels had fought for a sympathetic American stance toward the oil-confiscating Cardenas régime. Like Ambassador Claude Bowers in Spain, he viewed the reformers as overseas New Dealers, marching to the same drum as Roosevelt. "The old career people in the State Department never liked Bowers," Josephus Daniels wrote to his son.

"They would like to get him out of Chile [his current post] as they did out of Spain."[17] Daniels became a political handyman—tracing leaks, keeping tabs on anti-Roosevelt insurgents in the South, holding the hands of congressmen who wanted to see more of the president (including Lyndon Johnson), maintaining liaison with the Democratic National Committee, holding strategy meetings with the New Deal brain trust,[18] on "what to do to prevent the Republicans from taking over in '44," conferring with the congressional leadership on Roosevelt's strength in the country, rooting out Willkie's influence in OWI, and, in general, offering an avenue for *sub rosa* approaches to the president.[19]

Any issue that might have serious electoral consequences for Roosevelt was a potential magnet for Daniels's attention. By the spring of 1943, he was seriously concerned with efforts by the London Poles to arouse Polish-Americans against Roosevelt's Russian policy. His information came from the OWI/OSS (FNB) memos that portrayed the London Poles as a narrow clique of anti-Russian reactionaries, willing to plunge the United States into war with Russia to preserve their feudal estates in Galicia and the Ukraine—and willing to finance anti-Roosevelt activities if the president resisted their demands. "Both the big war politics of now and the big enough politics of 1944 both need care on the Polish-American scene," he wrote to Presidential Secretary Marvin McIntyre on May 8, 1943. In mid-June, 1943, Daniels encountered Polish ambassador Ciechanowski at a Washington dinner party. "Bald, Roman-faced, looking very much like Joe Davies whose mission to Moscow he definitely does not like," Ciechanowski quickly confirmed Daniels's prejudice against the government-in-exile. Daniels baited him, asking a question about the big "feudal" estates in eastern Poland. "Soviet lies," said Ciechanowski. At the dinner also was Arthur Bliss Lane. "A puffy creature of no great intelligence, but what he has of a very conservative kind," noted Daniels.[20]

Joe Davies, meanwhile, through his conversations at the Soviet embassy, was passing similar impressions along to Harry Hopkins. The Russians will not tolerate a Polish government which is "innately and secretly hostile," he wrote. "They had had a bitter experience once with the 'Colonels' Government' dominated by the great landowners and business interests of Eastern Poland—when in 1939 because of their bitter hostility to the Soviets the Polish government refused ever again to having the Red Army come through their country to the Germany boundary to help the Poles resist an impending invasion by Germany. With that kind of a government they will have 'nothing to do.' "[21]

Hopkins had his own theme to add to the chorus of condemnation. Ambassador Ciechanowski, "richly financed by the large Polish landlords," was spending close to a million dollars a year on expensive propaganda booklets critical of U.S. policy, he told Davies. The distribution of these in the United States is a "violation of diplomatic proprieties." The Polish government is again "putting its foot into it," Hopkins ruefully added.[22]

It is not surprising that FDR responded to the OSS/OWI analysis of the Polish situation and the parallel urgings of Daniels, Hopkins, and Davies to hold the emigré government at arm's length and send out a tentative feeler to the Union of Polish Patriots in Moscow. It made sense to encourage those Polish spokesmen who supported the Grand Alliance, seemed most New Dealish, and wished Roosevelt a long term in office. The London Poles, it appeared, were anti-Soviet, anti-Roosevelt, and proto-Hooverite in ideology. Better to unload them—but carefully, delicately, so as not to create a Catholic uproar. He must somehow support the Moscow Poles without attacking the London Poles. A telegram of greetings from Wanda Wassilewska gave him the innocent opportunity he needed. "Will you acknowledge the enclosed telegram from Wanda Wassilewska, President of the Union of Polish Patriots in the USSR?" he blandly requested in a memo to Hull.

Welles referred the memo to Atherton for the drafting of a reply. Atherton refused. A reply would be "improper" and "lead to misinterpretation." It might imply a lessening of the American commitment to the London Poles. Welles agreed, and Atherton drafted a memo to Roosevelt explaining why "no reply has been drafted."[23] The president did not press the issue. Perhaps he wanted to nudge the London Poles toward compromise but did not want to be the target of criticism when the letter of acknowledgment was released. The London Poles would get the message as would Stalin, but Hull and the department would be the lightning rod for any domestic criticism (exactly the same tactic as his referral of reporters to Mrs. Shipley for information on Orlemanski's passport). When Hull refused to play the part of potential scapegoat, Roosevelt backed off. His sensitivity to Catholic opinion had not lessened.[24]

The Europeanists parried Roosevelt's thrust and tried to deflect him into greater support of the London Poles.

In January 1944, Soviet armies crossed the Riga Line, prompting increased State Department urging that Roosevelt overtly reinforce his formal recognition of the government-in-exile. Request after request went to the White House imploring the president to meet with Mikolajczyk. Stettinius dutifully carried these requests across West Executive Avenue, but the president would not budge. He did not want to commit himself further to the London Poles. Quite the opposite. But he could not, of course, say this publicly.

He temporized. "The President does not feel the Polish Prime Minister should come now," Stettinius noted after a cabinet meeting on February 11, 1944. "There is nothing he could say to him." H. Freeman Matthews, Atherton's replacement as Dunn's first deputy, countered with the suggestion that Roosevelt see Polish ambassador Ciechanowski instead—to offer some heartening words he might carry to Mikolajczyk in London. Bohlen chimed in with a memo to Stettinius suggesting calling in Ciechanowski to allay fears that we were "abandoning Poland." He offered some encouraging words as a draft text. Stettinius took these with him to the next cabinet meeting on February 18. Roosevelt again was unmovable, "definitely opposed" to seeing Ciechanowski. Stettinius read Bohlen's statement but to no avail. He then fell back to the third trench, saying it was "essential" that he at least meet with the Polish ambassador in the State Department and be authorized to make some statement to him. Roosevelt consented, said the draft was satisfactory for this purpose, and then ticked off three points it would be useful for Ciechanowski to consider: (1) It is not a good start for the days ahead for any country to make too much of an issue about a border question. (2) Perhaps the Poles did not fully realize the suspicion with which the Russians had looked upon the present refugee government. (3) It would be constructive for the present Polish government to make clear to the world its intention to retire once hostilities ceased and let free elections determine who ruled postwar Poland.

These were hardly encouraging words. They, indeed, understated Roosevelt's own hostility toward the London Poles. If the State Department could push, he could push back. But gently. He did not instruct Stettinius to pass on the three points, merely "thought it would be a good idea to get this across. . . ." When Stettinius saw Ciechanowski later in the afternoon with an EUR amanuensis present, he conveniently muted Roosevelt's words and made a show of reading the "authorized message" drafted in the State Department. "The Ambassador was most appreciative," Stettinius noted. "He was deeply touched and seemed to feel that this message was almost as satisfactory as if he had seen the President personally." Indeed, it was better. Stettinius, as the EUR mouthpiece, sang more sweetly than the more acid Roosevelt. EUR persistence had partially blunted Roosevelt's effort to dissociate himself from the London Poles.[25]

Meanwhile Daniels had picked up two more White House allies—David Niles and Isador Lubin. Niles, a Frankfurter favorite from Boston, was Roosevelt's ethnic expert, a one-man FNB. Lubin had been recruited by Niles from the Labor Department to give Roosevelt his own data base on war production. The president had been impressed by Churchill's map room and set up one of his own. He also liked "the Prof," Professor F. A. Lindemann, later Lord Cherwell, who served as Churchill's personal figures man. He wanted to have his own and instructed Harry Hopkins to find one. At Hopkins's request, Niles recruited Lubin, then commissioner of labor statistics. An astute and greatly respected second-leveler, Lubin was a thorough New Dealer, especially close to Labor Secretary Frances Perkins. Under Hopkins's direction, Lubin helped Roosevelt keep his own tabs on the mobilization effort and gathered data on munitions assignment. (Hopkins was chairman of the Munitions Assignment Board.) Lubin's range extended to helping Hopkins oversee the implementation of all allocation decisions, monitoring War Production Board indicators, Office of Price Administration (OPA) statistics, and other numerical arcana. He also researched and verified statistics cited in Roosevelt's speeches.

Lubin became involved in the Polish question when a friend in the labor movement passed along a series of articles written in the Polish press by right-wing intellectual Ignacy Matuszewski. A typical quote from one of the articles read: "Four percent of Lend-Lease to Russia is the work of American Poles; Russia is set to destroy Poland; therefore the American Poles on the production lines work and sweat only to enslave their relatives and destroy their homeland." Lubin sent the articles to the only State Department official he fully trusted, fellow member of the Frankfurter circle Dean Acheson. "I don't know whether anything can be done about this," Lubin noted, "but I thought it might interest you to know what is going on." The articles reportedly were having "a serious effect on the morale of Polish workmen." At the same time, Daniels, armed with Lubin's memo, went searching in the State Department's FBI liaison office for information on Polish activities in the United States. A month later, Daniels, Niles, and Lubin briefed Roosevelt on the situation after a press conference. "The President was disturbed by things I told him," Daniels noted, "and by things Dave Niles and Lubin told him, about the activities of the Polish government in Washington in propaganda in the U.S." Another White House aide,

Lauchlin Currie, added his own tidbit. The Polish government was drawing all of its money from the Treasury in cash, generally in twenty-dollar bills. One of those present suggested the money be traced. Roosevelt agreed. "Here is something you ought to write if I should pop off," Roosevelt said to Daniels. With this odd introduction, the president stated his disagreement with the Poles on the border issue. He felt "very strongly that Stalin had been most generous in his offers. . . ."[26]

Roosevelt did finally give in to State Department pleadings and scheduled a meeting with Mikolajczyk for early June. But he also asked Daniels and Lubin to supply him with some inflammatory Polish propaganda pamphlets "as a basis for discussion" with the Polish prime minister. On the eve of Mikolajczyk's arrival, memos from Daniels, Niles, and Lubin all crossed the president's desk. Daniels's briefing vibrated with invective. "The European Poles are reactionary ultra-nationalist colonels and politicians who hope to influence American and Polish foreign policy by propaganda, pressure, and the threat of winning Polish-American voters from their traditional Democratic voting habits." Daniels took a good New Deal swipe at this retrograde group. "Obviously, these European Poles seek a Poland not only shaped in terms of old boundaries but also in terms of old economic and social patterns." Right-wing American Poles, many "anti-Administration Republicans who hope to swing some votes to the Republican camp by agitating the Polish boundary issue," were allied with the Polish Information Center in New York. The Information Center, an agency of the government-in-exile, was using $12 million in presidential funds, authorized for anti-Nazi activities in Poland, to print and distribute anti-Soviet propaganda. "Certainly any connection between U.S. funds for Poland and the use of such funds for anti-Administration propaganda in the United States deserves attention," Daniels concluded.

Lubin made the same points in a covering memo for the pamphlets Roosevelt had requested. Niles, reporting on the Polish-American Congress, convened in Buffalo to back the London government, noted "a terrific resentment against the Administration," but reassured Roosevelt that "we pulled some of the fangs out of it." Jangling the president's most sensitive nerve, he noted that "the official Catholic Church is taking a very positive position in the matter and through its affiliated bodies is urging the Poles to take off the gloves." The Association of Catholic Trade Unions, a potential anti-Roosevelt catalyst in the labor movement, "is most militant, urging the Poles at the instigation of the Clergy, to be more aggressive. . . ."[27] Niles also mentioned, a sure alarm bell, that the organizers of the Congress were all Republicans.

When Mikolajczyk arrived, Roosevelt did not equivocate. He all but insisted that the Poles accede to Stalin's demands to modify the Polish-Soviet frontier line and purge anti-Soviet officials from the government-in-exile. "When a thing becomes unavoidable," he said in election-year cryptography, "one should adapt oneself to it." And then, more directly, "there are four times more Russians than Poles. [Russia] could swallow up Poland if she did not reach an agreement on her terms."[28]

Roosevelt sent Mikolajczyk to Moscow to negotiate directly with Stalin and the Lublin Committee. In early August, Stalin cabled Roosevelt that talks had occurred but no agreement had been reached. He then tested Roosevelt's willingness to abandon the London Poles. Would the president support the Lublin Committee's offer of the foreign affairs portfolio to Professor Oscar Lange? Lange, a University of Chicago economist, had accompanied Orlemanski on his trip to Moscow. Less flamboyant and more sophisticated than Orlemanski, Lange, nonetheless, was equally unsympathetic to the government-in-exile. Bohlen drafted a reply pointing out that the United States could not take such a move without strengthening the claim of the Lublin Committee to be the legitimate government of Poland. The cable went out as drafted, but a few days later, while he was at Quebec for a conference with Churchill, Roosevelt once again tried indirectly to recognize the Lublin Committee. Stettinius received a curious presidential message through the Map Room: "I think the gist of our telegram to Marshal Stalin ought to be got in some way to the Polish Committee of National Liberation. How to do it, I don't know." As before, Roosevelt did not *order* the department to add the Lublin Committee to its list of addresses. He merely scratched his head and asked Ed Stettinius if he might be able to think of some way. The responsibility—and the repercussions—were in State's hands. It was less than two months until the election. Roosevelt wanted to say, "Tell Harriman to open quiet talks with the Lublin Committee." But Stettinius did not get the point. He, as always, sent the message to the relevant desk officer. Durbrow stopped it cold, noting quite obviously (though rather beside the point) that Stalin would let the Lublin Committee know what was going on. And, more important, to follow Roosevelt's suggestion would convey the impression that Harriman was dealing officially with the Polish Committee of National Liberation. (This, of course, was precisely what Roosevelt wanted.) Stettinius, unable to penetrate beneath the literal meaning of Roosevelt's message, endorsed Durbrow's rebuttal. The department, during Stettinius's tenure, could always stymie Roosevelt when he wanted to do something but could not afford to take the responsibility for it. Ed just couldn't take a hint.[29]

The Moscow deliberations came to a head in late October, climaxed with an impassioned appeal from Mikolajczyk that Roosevelt intercede to prevent the city of Lwow and the East Galician oil fields from becoming part of the Ukraine. He would try to persuade the government-in-exile to accept the Curzon line if Stalin would make this concession. Durbrow drafted the kind of reply Mikolajczyk wanted. "I fought like hell for Lwow," he later recalled. But Roosevelt threw the draft away and sent a noncomittal acknowledgment instead. "Crisp and short," he told Stettinius. Dunn took alarm, worried that the Poles would feel Roosevelt was giving them the "brush off." But the president refused to carry a brief for the government-in-exile, despite continued EE urgings for a more encouraging stance.[30]

As soon as the election had passed, Roosevelt apparently contemplated drastic action against the London Poles. The Polish ambassador and his staff had been "caught cold" by the authorities agitating among Polish-Americans and conducting "subversive activities," White House Press Secretary Steve Early told his good friend, Joe Davies. Ciechanowski's recall was "in the works," merely a matter of time. The Palace Guard and the OWI/OSS (FNB) memo writers had apparently triumphed over EE.[31] But the recall, for as yet undiscovered reasons, never took place.

At the same time, however, the White House moved once again to break up the annoying State Department "clique" that on occasion strangled the president's most delicate (and therefore most vulnerable) initiatives.

12 | THE DECEMBER 1944 REORGANIZATION

DAVIES HAD LOST no opportunity in the months since the Henderson-Atherton purge to point out to Roosevelt and Hopkins that little had changed in the department. Although Bohlen catered to the White House, Davies received reports from the Soviet embassy of his and Durbrow's hostility to the régime on day-to-day EE business. "The Soviet Foreign Office believed," he told Hopkins in September 1943, "that there were powerful forces in the State Department which never lost an opportunity to disparage and fight the Soviets (to wit, the Polish situation . . .)." A week later, Davies was in Mexico City sounding out Soviet ambassador Oumansky on Russian grievances. Roosevelt and Hopkins, ever mindful of the Nazi-Soviet pact, still feared a separate peace. What if Stalin should feel that Roosevelt had as little regard for an alliance with Russia in 1943 as Chamberlain had had in 1939? As evidence of lack of "good faith" Oumansky cited "subordinates in the State Department . . . openly critical and hostile to an ally, the Soviet Union." Davies reported to Roosevelt on his talk a few days later. The president was "particularly concerned," Davies noted, "over Oumansky's statement of the indiscretion of career men in the Diplomatic Service in voicing their hostility to an ally." In a memo to Roosevelt in

May 1944, Davies accused EUR of undermining Hull's confidence in Stalin by portraying Soviet recognition of the post-Mussolini Badoglio régime as "unilateral." All the blessings of Hull's trip to Moscow might be dissipated by this unfair construction. In fact, Davies explained, Stalin had moved as rapidly as possible to recognize the Anglo-American-endorsed government to demonstrate solidarity with his allies and "kill the bogey" that he wished to communize Italy.

> [The Russians] have complete confidence in you and Cordell since Moscow. But they are definitely of the opinion that there are those in the Department who either openly or quietly are constantly resolving doubts as to the good faith of the Soviets against their fighting ally because of prejudice and hostility. Whether they exaggerate this situation or not, it is a fact that has serious weight with the Soviet Foreign Office in my opinion. That is one of the factors which threatens future cooperation in post war reconstruction.

The Russians were not easy to please. They apparently wished Roosevelt to reconstruct not only the Polish government but his own as well.[1]

Davies had Bohlen and Durbrow in mind. At the same time he was composing his memo of complaint to Roosevelt, his wife, Marjorie Merriweather Post, informed Henry Wallace at a party that Bohlen was "one of Bill Bullitt's boys . . . all of them looked down on the Russians, suspect them . . . make every possible difficulty." Wallace, upon meeting Bohlen, came to the same conclusion. He found him "definitely anti-Russian in his attitude."[2]

When Cordell Hull resigned in November 1944, Roosevelt mounted a last attempt to remake the State Department in his image. He appointed the faithful Stettinius secretary of state and gave him authority, working with Hopkins, to reorganize the State Department to get rid of the "reactionaries." Stettinius at once asked Joe Davies to be undersecretary and planned the creation of two new assistant secretaryships to be occupied by New Dealers Ben Cohen and Archibald MacLeish. But the plan failed. Davies wanted to help. "Little men, who got into the saddle by fishing in the troubled waters of the Hull-Welles quarrel, are shrewd and persistent," he noted, and wished he could aid the inexperienced Stettinius in thwarting their designs. But his doctors vetoed any work that required "persistent confining effort." He had turned down Roosevelt's offer of the Paris embassy a month before for the same reason and would also refuse the London embassy in January.[3]

Davies's appointment, no doubt, would have created an explosion in the department, and may have been tendered with the knowledge that it would be refused. The actual choice was a triumph for the Europeanists—Joseph Grew. John Carter Vincent recalls:

> Stettinius' influence was exerted primarily through his choice of undersecretary of state. In Grew he had a man who would allow him to forget about the State Department. Here was a man who had been associated with the State Department for the past forty years in every field, Europe, Far East, and what not. In fact, it was such a logical choice that when people were betting around the State Department who it would be I said, "There isn't any bet at all. It's got to be Grew if Stettinius is to operate at all with his lack of knowledge of what's going on."[4]

Even more dismaying to the New Dealers was the promotion of Jimmy Dunn to assistant secretary of state for political affairs, in charge of all the world except Latin America. Dunn's dream job, vetoed by Roosevelt the previous January, now became a reality. Hull traded on his political leverage in the Senate to force the appointment. Roosevelt, fearful of a repeat of the 1919 League of Nations struggle, tried to dissuade Hull from resigning, even going out to the hospital to plead with him. Hull was adamant. Would he at least stay through inauguration? "Sentimentally, I want him to finish out his three terms," Roosevelt told Stettinius. "No." Roosevelt still resisted, sending Stettinius back for yet another bedside plea. Casting about, he told the oblivious Stettinius in deadpan that no hasty decisions should be made. "Are we going to send him a bill [for the hospital]—there are a lot of angles." Even if Hull resigned, Roosevelt said, "we still might get him to preside at the UN Conference" in order to ensure Senate ratification. The secretary, Roosevelt felt, "had a better standing in the country" than Roosevelt himself.

Until the last moment, Dunn was not slated for promotion. During a hospital visit the afternoon of November 20, Hull had asked Stettinius "whether or not [Dunn] had his feelings hurt that something hadn't been done for him." Stettinius assured him that Dunn "understood why he hadn't been made an Assistant Secretary." At noon the next day, Stettinius told Roosevelt of Hull's concern and presented him a list of new appointments to approve, including Dunn as assistant secretary. In deference to Hull, Roosevelt lifted his veto. "While he had some question about Dunn in the past," Stettinius noted, "Roosevelt felt he was now entitled to be Assistant Secretary." But the president did not really know what he was signing. "I did not cover the matter of Dunn being an Assistant Secretary of all political matters, exclusive of Latin America," Stettinius confided to his diary. Dunn had worked his quiet charm on Stettinius as he had previously on Hull. The new secretary, supposedly Hopkins's plaything, was misleading the White House for Dunn's benefit. Foreign service wooing of Stettinius and Hull's indirect pressure on Roosevelt had turned the tide. "Pa" Watson, Roosevelt's appointments secretary and political intimate, reminded Stettinius on the way out that on election eve Dunn's wife had attended a Republican party. But he supposed that Dunn himself was reliable. "I'm sure of it," Stettinius said. "I put in Jimmie just to make Cordell feel good," Roosevelt explained to a dismayed Henry Wallace. He implied that he did not really trust Dunn and that he would "bear watching."

Dunn's appointment forced Ben Cohen off the list. Roosevelt had initially warned Stettinius that Hull "wouldn't like Cohen and MacLeish," and Stettinius himself knew of the unpopularity within EUR of the idea of appointing Cohen. MacLeish would be a gadfly, but Cohen was an effective operator. Insulted at being offered the post of assistant legal adviser, aide to the musty and conservative Green Hackworth, Cohen decided to leave the government altogether, resigning from his post of general counsel to domestic mobilizer Jimmy Byrnes. A long personal talk with Roosevelt partially dissuaded him. The president, rather unbelievably, told him that he had promised the Congress not to fill the job Cohen really wanted—State Department counselor. Only when the liberal afternoon daily *PM* portrayed Cohen's tendered resignation as a matter of personal pique did he feel he had to stay on.

Acheson barely survived. With no forewarning, Grew informed him of the changes, including the appointment of foreign trade expert Will Clayton to his current job as assistant secretary for economic affairs. There was only one post left, Grew said, "with the solemn and portentous look of an eminent physician about to impart grim news"—assistant secretary for congressional relations. "The offer carried with it," Acheson recalls, "the distinct impression that it was expected to be declined." But Acheson disappointed Grew and accepted, less enthralled with the idea of leaving the department during a "general housecleaning" than with the job itself. He had no illusions, however, about who would be running the department and planned accordingly. The liberal press revealed his intentions. "Able Dean Acheson will resign as Assistant Secretary of State around March 1," wrote Drew

Pearson. "He didn't want to get out with the Berle-Long-Shaw general exodus, but can't stand the gaff much longer than this winter." I. F. Stone made the same prediction. "Acheson, a corporation lawyer by trade but too liberal-minded for the Department, is expected to leave in March."[5] While waiting, Acheson found himself relocated from his prestigious corner office to a smaller one with windows facing the White House. Down the hall in corner office 200 sat Jimmy Dunn, who had leapfrogged over Acheson not only in accommodations but also in seniority. As senior (and sole surviving) assistant secretary, Acheson by tradition should have been acting secretary in the absence of Stettinius and Grew. This problem would not have arisen at all had Acheson taken the hint and resigned. Grew, however, was not easily discouraged. He convinced Stettinius that Dunn's line authority over the political desks made him the wiser choice. Grew did not want it generally known that he had conspired to downgrade Acheson. When speaking with UN planner John Ross, he said, contrary to his advice to Stettinius, that he did favor naming Acheson first assistant secretary because of seniority. "But," he added disingenuously, "if it has already been settled that Dunn gets this position, Stettinius should be careful to inform Acheson beforehand."[6]

The dismissals were as instructive as the appointments. The two assistant secretaries who had interested themselves in European politics—Adolf Berle and Breckinridge Long—were fired. No longer would these outsiders "interfere" with the service monopoly of advice on European politics. Berle, who felt his abrupt discharge was "brutal," accepted a respectable exile as ambassador to Brazil. His departure was the only point of agreement for the foreign service and the Frankfurter circle in the entire reorganization. Both groups detested him. On the right, Bullitt considered Berle "a shifty, smart, little person. Clever little Adolf! . . ." In the department, Dunn and Acheson were both glad to see him go. MacLeish reminisced in an interview:

> There was a violent lack of love between Acheson and Berle. Acheson would not have stayed if Berle were around. You say that you have an intimation that some of the geographic officers were happy to see Berle go. That's putting it mildly. Acheson had contempt for Berle. He was a pipsqueak, a little squirt, vindictive, played politics under the rug. I don't think the president liked him either but that's a pure guess. His appointment to Rio was recognized by everyone as exile.

Felix Frankfurter, pleased at MacLeish's appointment as assistant secretary for cultural affairs and Acheson's retention, had no use for Berle. "There is not one iota of doubt," he confided to his diary, "that Berle is almost pathologically anti-British and anti-Russian, and his anti-semitism is thrown in, as it were, for good measure, though probably derived through certain personal hostilities and jealousies."[7]

Apart from removal of this universal irritant, the reorganization was a one-sided victory for the foreign service. Hull and Dunn had stymied the president's attempt to remake the department. And so, as before, he would have to continue handling foreign policy in the White House.

Stettinius certainly was not expected to dominate the department—quite the contrary. Berle, boiling mad at his firing, asked Roosevelt how he could make such an appointment. "A Secretary of State should be able to read and write and talk," he said to Roosevelt. "He may not be able to do all of these, but Stettinius can't do any of them." "I know that, Adolf," said FDR. "But I was being pressed to take two men who would have upset the postwar agreements in the Senate—Wallace and Byrnes. So I just stuck Stettinius in there to stop it. I realize that I'll have to do the work now, but I had no choice." The usual chorus of insider disbelief accompanied this latest Stettinius elevation. "Stettinius was secretary of state but he never was," commented MacLeish. "It was a matter of common discussion at the time." Economist Willard Thorpe, Clayton's deputy, offered this thumbnail impression.

> My impression of Stettinius was that he was a handsome, frank man. You went in to see him with a proposal, he would say, "That's wonderful. We must do it." And then nothing whatsoever would happen. I suspect that he had very little real impact upon the department. I've always been amused by the fact that as far as I could tell the most important thing which he did in connection with the United Nations Conference, which came to dominate his interest, was to decide what color the backdrop should be, what kind of blue. He was a person, of course, with lovely silver white hair. I always had the feeling that since he was going to be in front of that curtain a good deal, this became the controlling factor in this very important aspect of United Nations life. So, I would write him off as far as you can in terms of his importance in the picture.

Henry Wallace was also amused at Stettinius's passion for décor. People tackle a job at a level they can understand. Stettinius, evidently, confused reorganization with redecorating. He had the cosmetic sensibility of a public-relations executive—packaging was all. "Stettinius insists on a State Department barbershop and cars for assistant secretaries with a Cadillac for himself," Henry Wallace noted. "The State Department is being modified over to resemble the high command of GM."[8]

The liberals might laugh at Stettinius's superficiality, but they were shocked at the political complexion of his subordinates. "The New Dealers," wrote Arthur Krock, "are happy only with Acheson and MacLeish." In Stone's words: "Not one of the new men is faintly progressive except MacLeish, who like Acheson will have a job of explaining to do." As assistant secretary for congressional relations, Acheson "will find himself apologizing for much with which he will disagree."[9] The ideological scars of Spain and Vichy were ripped open by the new appointments. Those who felt that Roosevelt would force Dunn and Grew to carry out a liberal foreign policy, Stone wrote, "display remarkably short memories. They can usefully recall what happened during the Spanish civil war and again during the North African invasion. They cannot ask us to accept these appointments on faith and then at some future date complain of a new Darlanism." Stone concentrated his attack on Dunn: "Dunn has the proud and supercilious look of a Spanish hidalgo . . . the face of a snob firmly shut against the world. . . . [His] pro-Franco views are notorious. 'I can't see how the Spanish war had any effect on the present European war,' he told a *PM* interviewer in 1941. Former Ambassador Dodd seems to have thought him an ignoramus."[10]

Eleanor Roosevelt, who shared Stone's distaste for the diplomats, as well as his suspicion of undue papal influence in the department, was "alarmed and outraged" at Dunn's appointment. She wrote a forceful and petulant letter to Franklin.

> It does make me rather nervous for you to say that you do not care what Jimmy Dunne thinks because he will do what you tell him to do and that for three years you have carried the State Department and you expect to go on doing it. I am quite sure that Jimmy Dunne is clever enough to tell you that he will do what you want and to allow his subordinates to accomplish things which will get by and which will pretty well come up in the long time results to what he actually wants to do.
>
> In addition, it seems to me pretty poor administration to have a man in whom you know you cannot put any trust, to carry out the things which you tell him to do. The reason I feel we cannot trust Dunne is that we know

> he backed Franco and his regime in Spain. We know that he is arguing . . . in favor of using German industrialists to rehabilitate Germany. . . . The fine Catholic hand is visible in Europe and in our State Department.[11]

Echoing the *New Republic* and the *Nation,* or perhaps inspiring them, she concluded: "I can hardly see that the set-up will be very much different from what it might have been under Dewey." Stone wrote the same. "If only some way could be found to make a place in this constellation for John Foster Dulles, Wall Street would have no cause to regret the failure to elect Dewey."[12]

Henry Morgenthau reinforced Eleanor's plea, dragging in Robert Murphy for good measure. The previous September, Morgenthau had protested Roosevelt's choice of Murphy for a top job in Germany. "Why pick Robert Murphy for this job?" he asked. "In the minds of the people it connoted Darlan and everything that goes with it." Mrs. Roosevelt, who was present, had interjected that with the attitude of the pope, it was a mistake to send a Catholic to Germany. Pearson noted that Murphy wanted to keep Germany as a "bulwark against Bolshevism," the same theory held by Dunn.[13] Morgenthau literally had the last word. After dinner on April 11, 1945, he and the president settled down for a talk about Germany at Warm Springs. It was the last political conversation of Roosevelt's life. Morgenthau began to complain about Murphy. "Well, what's the matter with Murphy?" Roosevelt said. "Murphy was too anxious to collaborate [with Vichy]," Morgenthau answered. "Mr. President, I was in your office when you appointed him, and Hull forced him down your throat." Morgenthau's account, dictated before he went to bed, continues, anti-Catholic, anti–foreign service as usual.

> The President thought it was a mistake at this time to send a Catholic to Germany. I said, "Caffery [Ambassador to France] is a Catholic, too." and he said, "Yes, but he is in Paris." I said, "Yes, but Caffery and Murphy work pretty closely together."
>
> Then the President said, "Well, what have you got in mind?" I said, "In order to break the State Department crowd headed by Jimmy Dunn . . . my suggestion is that you make Claude Bowers political adviser to Eisenhower and send Murphy to Chile."
>
> . . . I criticized Dunn, and the President said that at the first meeting at Quebec, Dunn was good, and I said, "I think Dunn is terrible."[14]

Roosevelt himself, though he defended his actions against the strident complaints of his wife and Morgenthau, shared their apprehensions. He refused to approve a press release on the new slate because MacLeish's name had been omitted. He grumbled to his press secretary, William D. Hassett, that "Archie was the only liberal in the bunch, which is top heavy with Old Dealers." This was not done for effect, since Hassett was no liberal. When a group of Senate liberals tried to block approval of the new slate, Roosevelt had them in for a talk and praised their efforts. Dunn, he said, was Hull's personal choice. He implied that a request for Dunn's promotion had been made when Hull resigned. The fight against the new State Department executives "was a very healthy thing," he said, "and will put them on guard for the future."

A few weeks later when Stettinius suggested Dunn as one of Roosevelt's advisers at Yalta, the president made his feelings clear. He refused to take him, saying, "He'll sabotage everything."[15] Dunn's version of the story is more muted: "Stettinius told me this: he proposed me and Mr. Roosevelt said, 'He has too much rank. I don't want anybody as high as that.' " Stettinius then suggested Alger Hiss because the UN would be discussed at Yalta, and Roosevelt agreed. Hiss went to Yalta and Dunn stayed home, a clear indication of Roosevelt's sympathies. Although the foreign service had thwarted his reorganization, he still had the alternative of making foreign policy without the diplomats and boosting the apostles of international cooperation for good measure.[16]

Roosevelt faced, however, one insoluble problem: mortality. His failure to reform the State Department guaranteed that New Deal foreign policy would not outlive him. When the wartime agencies dissolved and Roosevelt's personal diplomatic apparatus dispersed, the foreign service picked up the threads of American diplomacy.

IV
DEATH AND TRANSFIGURATION

★ ★ ★ ★ ★ ★ ★ ★ ★

I want lots of action, new blood, that's what we need around here.

—ED STETTINIUS

13 | THE YALTA DECLARATION ON LIBERATED EUROPE

THOUGHTS OF AN imminent succession were not far from the minds of most Washington insiders in the winter of 1945. The last time Dunn saw Roosevelt alive the president was considering a telegram about Poland. "He was seeing the paper but not reading it . . . picking out something to show he was alert. He was in no shape to do anything." MacLeish saw it too. "Do you think as often as I do," he later wrote to Jonathan Daniels, "of that afternoon in March when he came in through the door of the Oval Room with the cold spring light on his face and death in his eyes? I shall never forget it." Though he portrays it otherwise in his memoirs, Truman knew he was waiting for his cue. He was sitting in Congressman Sam Rayburn's office just starting to take a drink when he got word to go to the White House immediately. "He knew and I knew," Rayburn later recalled, "though we didn't say so." Roosevelt also knew. In January 1945, Frances Perkins told Henry Wallace of her most recent talk with the president. "He was in a pitiable state," she said, "appalled at the magnitude of the tasks ahead of him and not knowing whether he had the strength to see himself through."[1]

Having strengthened their hold over the department in the December 1944 reorganization, the Europeanists next sought to make State a real power in foreign policy. The political questions surfacing in the wake of military victory required expertise about international politics. As the White House foreign office withered and the army increasingly sought guidance on political problems, the Europeanists filled the vacuum. As Roosevelt's grip weakened, they moved in successfully to secure a presidential mandate for a primary State Department role in managing relations with Russia. The process began, ironically enough, with a long memo written by Adolf Berle in late September 1944.

Berle addressed himself to the question of the American role in postwar Europe. He assumed that Europe would be divided into Russian and British spheres of influence. The Russians, Berle anticipated, would seek to extend their sphere south to the Persian Gulf and west to Cairo, including Turkey, Iraq, and the Levant. The British, of course, would strongly resist, seeing "a threat to the empire lifeline" that would reduce Britain from a world power to merely "a strong Atlantic power." Since Britain would be "unlikely to recede in face of Soviet desires," the clash between these rival imperialisms in the eastern Mediterranean could become "the breeding ground of a third world war." In these circumstances, Berle argued, the United States could not remain aloof. EUR's wartime policy of "giving all possible aid to the Army" was no longer adequate. It may have hastened the defeat of Germany for the United States not to "become involved in the internal political affairs of southeastern Europe," but the continuation of this policy might simply allow postwar Anglo-Soviet conflicts in this area to provoke yet another world war. "Power politics," Berle warned, "is continuing between these countries today on the pattern made nauseatingly familiar by the Axis in 1935–39."

What could the United States do to prevent this competition from sparking a world conflagration? Given the traditional disinterest of the United States in the politics of Eastern Europe, the Balkans, and the Near East, and the obvious unwillingness to send American troops into these regions, the United States could best calm the situation, Berle argued, by scrupulously avoiding taking sides between the two antagonists and instructing American representatives "to resolve differences between the major contending forces." The particular alignment that would result was a matter of little concern. A Soviet sphere of influence along the lines of the Good Neighbor policy "would be no threat to anyone," Britain included. A year and a half earlier, Berle had elaborated on this idea to a *Time* reporter. "I'd like to see a whole group of contented little states, friendly to the Soviet Union as the states of

Central America are friendly to us. They would not be buffer states any more than Guatemala is a buffer. But they would be in Russia's orbit and they would know they were and they would learn to welcome a Soviet desire to establish a base at some convenient point as Latin Americans have learned to welcome the establishment of a U.S. base in their territory. A base means a lot of sailors spending money; it's good for trade; they don't think any more about it." A benign form of British imperialism could also be tolerated. As long as neither power sought a "closed zone" completely excluding the other, accommodation could be realized. "In this case it would make relatively little difference to us . . . who had the dominant position." To attain "a modification of the ruthlessness of British commercialism and the ruthlessness of Soviet nationalism," American representatives should be instructed to mediate. To maintain American credibility with both contenders, the United States should dissociate itself from any unilateral actions taken by Russia or Britain in these sensitive areas. Except where American troops were in occupation, the United States should withdraw from all civil affairs and military government commissions. It would be best to "play out," for there would be "no point in prolonged argument with allies when their views will not change and we are unwilling to use force."[2]

Berle's suggestion that the State Department emerge from the army's shadow and take the initiative in defining American interests abroad received warm approval in a meeting of the State Department Policy Committee, called to consider his proposal. EE chief Charles Bohlen, led the discussion. He acknowledged the United States' "traditional stand as observers in that part of the world" and agreed that maybe it would be better "to take a positive position and then seek Russian and British support for that." He suggested, in particular, that the Russians might welcome a "comprehensive" American plan for resolving tensions in Europe. Berle endorsed the idea, saying he hoped they would accept a "generalized good neighbor policy" but that if Britain and Russia "play power politics, we have to decide what to do."

A subcommittee of the Policy Committee was appointed to draw up a plan to present to the Soviet Union. It included Berle and three foreign service veterans with recent experience in all the major regions of the world except Europe. Joseph Grew was an expert on Japan, Wallace Murray on the Near East, and Norman Armour on Latin America. On November 8, 1944, two days after Roosevelt's reelection, the results of the subcommittee's deliberations were forwarded to the president under the title: "United States Interest and Policy in Eastern and

Southeastern Europe and the Near East." Berle's hand was evident in the drafting. The operative sentence read: "This government should assert the independent interest of the United States . . . in favor of equitable arrangements designed to attain general peace and security on a basis of good neighborship and should not assume that the American interest requires it at this time to identify its interests with those of either the Soviet Union or Great Britain." Then, in a list of points that foreshadowed the Yalta Declaration on Liberated Europe, the department endorsed the "general principles" of national sovereignty, nonexclusionary trade policies, free press access, and the protection of American economic interests and philanthropic and educational activities.[3]

Missing from this memorandum, however, was Berle's desire that the United States actively mediate between Russia and Britain and his proposal that the United States not make strong unilateral representations to either of the two powers. Nor did the memorandum suggest that United States interests per se in these areas were minimal. The tone of the document, despite the vague phraseology, suggested a vigorous espousal of *American* interests in the political conditions of these areas, regardless of the wishes of Britain or Russia, and quite separate from any attempt to mediate between them. The foreign service officers, it appears, had chipped away at Berle's argument, retaining the plea for a positive American role but redefining it to allow an independent American negotiating stance rather than a position of disinterested arbitration. There was no hint of "playing out" the American presence or avoiding "prolonged argument with allies."

That the American role might be more combative than conciliatory and more anti-Russian than anti-British became evident later in the month. On November 16, Murray sent a letter to Leland Morris, ambassador to Iran and an old foreign service colleague. Murray alerted Morris to the new policy and mildly rebuked him for encouraging the Iranian government to take a measured stance in response to Russian requests for an oil concession. Morris hastened to assure Murray that he was prepared to oppose uncompromisingly all Russian initiatives. "You seem to have understood that I was recommending a policy of conciliation with the Russians for fear that a vigorous and open policy of objection to their methods might cause perturbations in our relations with the Soviets," he wrote. This impression, he assured Murray, was "entirely erroneous." To the contrary, Morris supported strong "representations" to the Russians and repeated his worry that Murray might be under some "misapprehension" as to his attitude. He offered this credo for dealing with America's ally: "We should neither be silent nor timid in our relationship with the Russians on matters of general policy. They are roughnecks and only understand crude and open language." He plaintively added: "I hope the foregoing will serve to clear up any divergence of understanding."[4]

Morris was clearly concerned that his colleagues in the department might consider him too friendly to Russia. Murray's answer served to allay his fears. His original letter was not a rebuke but merely "to let you know how some of us were thinking here in the Department." Murray explained:

> This seemed especially advisable in this case, since our views and our action in the oil controversy represented a new departure in our relations with the Russians—a kind of "trail blazing." We were fortunate to have Mr. Harriman here at that time to support our idea of speaking to the Russians in all frankness. Otherwise it is probable that we would have been talked down by the doubting Thomases.[5]

Or, Murray might have added, by the "doubting Franklins," for the foreign service initiative clearly ran counter to President Roosevelt's policy of seeking accommodation with the Russians rather than making formal "representations" or adopting "crude and open language."

Berle had left Washington to chair the Chicago Civil Aviation Conference that opened November 1. The policy memo, in whose drafting he participated, had reached Roosevelt a week later. Under the guise of standing aloof from imperial quarrels in the Mideast, it permitted the "independent interest of the United States in favor of equitable arrangements" to become a license for an assertive policy of obstructing all Russian initiatives in the countries bordering the Soviet Union. With Harriman's encouragement, the foreign service officers on the geographic desks drafted instructions for him on this new basis. Berle, had he cared to object, was in Chicago. After the December reorganization, he was gone for good. Although no friend of the Soviet régime, Berle's views accurately reflected those of the president: the United States should seek to conciliate Britain and Russia, moderating their quarrels in the interest of a general European settlement. The elders of the foreign service instead converted Berle's initiative into a license to draft instructions to American representatives overseas urging vigorous opposition to Russian overtures. "Mediation" gave way to "representation." While Roosevelt prepared to sail for Yalta, bent on the reconciliation of differences with Russia, the foreign service began a campaign to eliminate Soviet influence in the countries bordering Russia.

Old service stalwarts were assigned to the key capitals in Eastern Europe, the Balkans, and the Near East. Wallace Murray, a vigorous anticommunist and the head of NEA, replaced the slightly suspect Leland Morris as ambassador to Iran. Murray had been chief of NEA since 1929. His appointment as ambassador, therefore, was not a routine transfer. The heaviest guns in the service were being moved up to the borders of the Soviet Union. In neighboring Turkey, where the sensitive Straits question was a certain postwar issue, Ambassador Laurence Steinhardt, a nonservice appointee, was replaced by veteran club member Leland Harrison (Eton and Harvard), ambassador to Switzerland since 1937. Steinhardt was sent to Czechoslovakia, a country of little interest to the service because of President Edward Benes's friendliness to Russia. In France was Jefferson Caffery, in Germany Robert Murphy. Although the New Dealers wanted Murphy out and Roosevelt had actually planned to replace Caffery, neither moved. The appointment of Richard Patterson as ambassador to Yugoslavia in September 1944 had been a setback for the service. "Patterson is a silver-haired former director of RKO Radio Pictures and hails from Omaha," a *Time* correspondent wrote. "He . . . charmingly stated to me that he knew nothing about Yugoslavia." Fearful of Russian influence in the Adriatic, the service wanted an effective representative in Belgrade. The consensus was that Kennan should replace Patterson and Reber take Kennan's spot as counselor in Moscow. But Patterson, most likely a larger contributor, stayed on.[6]

To Poland went Arthur Bliss Lane, now fifty-one. Lane tried to relive the Blue Palace days of 1919 in a Poland that was rapidly eradicating the social basis of the old régime. A cable from *Time*'s Warsaw correspondent, John Scott, in January 1946—a few months after Lane's arrival—captured the spirit of his mission.

> Watching the confused scene from Warsaw's sole intact hotel, the Polonia, sit several score diplomats. They eat better than they could in almost any other European post today, occasionally go to an extremely primitive but spirited performance of an opera or ballet held in makeshift quarters, and talk to each other and with small circles of English- and French-speaking Poles who hover around the hotel, and most of whom have little sympathy for the present government or even for nationalization-advocating Mikolajczyk. Some diplomats get out into the countryside and into other circles

> of Polish society, but many remain cut off by the language barrier, by banditry on the streets which keeps them in after office hours, and in some cases by a fundamentally hostile attitude toward Poland's provisional government and everything it stands for.[7]

Presenting a demand that American businessmen be permitted to visit their properties prior to nationalization, Lane became so carried away that he left the impression that he had delivered an American protest against nationalization. Lane told one correspondent that it was impossible to maintain business or social relations of any kind with Soviet diplomats in Warsaw, "so we just ignore them." Two days later the same correspondent was invited to lunch by the British embassy and found that his fellow guests were two secretaries of the Soviet embassy.[8]

In the aftermath of a pogrom in Kielce in the summer of 1946 that left forty-one Jews dead, Lane called in the foreign correspondents in Warsaw and suggested that they seek a statement from the Polish Roman Catholic primate, Augustus Cardinal Hlond. The cardinal, Lane said, "was ready to talk" to the correspondents. Hlond sounded like a Gibson in ecclesiastical dress; he said the things Lane wanted to say but could not utter openly. Poland's rising anti-Semitism, Cardinal Hlond explained, was "to a great degree due to Jews who today occupy leading positions in Poland's government and endeavor to introduce a governmental structure that a majority of the people do not want." The cardinal offered a personal opinion that the killings "did not occur for racial reasons." *New York Times* correspondent Bill Lawrence later recalled: "I was outraged by him, especially by his declaration that only recently he had refused a request by American Jews to issue an appeal against anti-semitism with the explanation that he did not feel the facts justified such a proclamation from the Church."[9]

In the war-torn Balkan countries of Bulgaria and Rumania were Maynard Barnes and Burton Berry. Barnes, a Balkan expert, had assisted Grew at the Lausanne Conference in 1923 and risen through the ranks. At forty-seven, he was being given his first ambassadorial assignment. Berry, four years younger, had served in NEA capitals and occasionally in Italy for seventeen years.

Lane's misrepresentations paled in comparison with the campaign Barnes undertook to create a Soviet-American confrontation in the Balkans. The United States had scant historic interest in Bulgaria: Roosevelt had stated time and again that he had no interest in the area. "It appears that it is the President's desire," Berle told a meeting of the

Policy Committee two days after the Normandy landings, "that this government not become deeply involved in Balkan politics."[10] Yet even before Yalta, Barnes began to beseech the State Department to oppose the growth of Soviet influence in Bulgaria. On December 7, 1944, he cabled that "advocates of democracy" within Bulgaria were near despair at American indifference to Soviet designs. Continued "cooperation" with Russia, he warned would "harm our position . . . with sane and sober opinion in the country."[11]

Although Barnes's telegrams repeatedly contrasted struggling democratic elements with ruthless communist minorities controlled by Moscow, he presented a less ideological view of Bulgarian politics in a letter to Matthews that did not go through official channels. First of all, he wrote, the move to the left was distinctly Bulgarian in origin. "As I see matters here, we are now going through the 1944 Bulgarian version of what began to happen in Russia in November 1917; or, to put it another way, September 9, 1944 in Bulgaria picked up the threads of the Stambuliisky regime, broken by the *coup d'etat* of June 1923." The *coup d'état* in 1923 was a military overthrow of a radical peasant-based régime. The Bulgarian communists, remembering the murderous 1923 coup, were determined not to become so vulnerable to a right-wing takeover in the future. The Russians agreed with this analysis, but the impetus was domestic. "Our Bulgarian Communists are seeking only, in fact, to assure for themselves the advantages and security that the bourgeois system in Bulgaria has in the past conferred upon those who now constitute the hated and dreadful 'fascists.' "[12] Once the communists had guaranteed their own security, Barnes implied, they might become more tolerant of their political opponents.

Barnes's private analysis indicated that it was not so much democracy that was at issue in Bulgaria as which faction in a winner-take-all political system could impose its will on the others. Democracy American-style, in fact, was unknown in the vendetta politics of the Balkans. Elections were purely cosmetic. Whoever ran the elections won them. The only loyal opponent was a dead one. Yet in cables to the department that would be read in the White House, Barnes portrayed the communists extirpating "democracy" in Bulgaria. An extensive purge of the old régime in the spring of 1945, revenging two decades of right-wing rule, left thousands dead. Barnes concluded that "the Communists are determined to eliminate all potential democratic opposition." And, he added, pinning responsibility on the Russians: "Democratic opinion here continues to ask 'why have we been delivered over to the Russians by the Anglo-Saxon powers?' " The Pladne Agrarians, however, Barnes's favorite "democrats," joined the purge which had the support of all groups excluded from power between the wars. And, as Barnes had written to Matthews, the initiative was Bulgarian, not Russian.[13] Berry's reports from Rumania were similar in tone and substance.[14]

From the liberated capitals of Eastern Europe and the Balkans, a steady stream of cables began to flow into the State Department documenting Russian outrages. Most of these protests invoked the Declaration on Liberated Europe, an idealistic statement about democracy and national sovereignty that had been added to the Yalta communiqué on the initiative of the career diplomats. Drafted by Dunn and Matthews, the declaration embodied the principles of the October policy statement and served the same purpose—offering the diplomats a rationale for urging strenuous protests against Soviet activities in Eastern Europe and the Near East. In this case, however, the mandate was signed and publicly issued by Churchill, Stalin, and Roosevelt. It was Dunn's finest hour.

Roosevelt had not liked the Declaration on Liberated Europe as drafted but was persuaded to present a modified version to Churchill and Stalin for the salutary effect it would have on the American debate over participation in the UN. This statement provided assurance, as the State Department briefing book put it, that the world organization would not "merely underwrite a system of unilateral grabbing." For if this were to occur, the Senate, disgusted at the resurgence of "power politics" in Europe, might repudiate international collaboration and retreat into sullen isolation. In drafting this rationale, Dunn had turned his oversight of the UN planners to good purpose.[15] The issue was settled when Stalin enthusiastically embraced the declaration, pleased with the phrase that committed the allies "to destroy the last vestiges of Nazism and fascism." He might have been more cautious had he realized that by embracing this American proposal, he gave the State Department a perfect vehicle for opposing Russian influence in Eastern Europe.

Lord Gladwyn, Dunn's counterpart in the upper reaches of the British Foreign Office, recounts the history of the declaration. During the interallied postwar planning sessions, Dunn and Gladwyn had become good friends. As Gladwyn recalls, they "saw eye to eye on most outstanding problems." Gladwyn's memoirs offer at one remove an insight into Dunn's thinking on dealing with Russia after the war.

Gladwyn, from the British side, pushed for adoption of Dunn's original language, which "would have been a document obliging all the allies to see that, among other things, free elections were held in countries 'liberated' by them and to make it in some way legally incumbent on them to do so." But Roosevelt and Hopkins were not interested in contesting a Soviet sphere of influence in Eastern Europe. They forced modifications. "The final version," Gladwyn notes, "merely said that the three would 'assist' the liberated peoples to do such things and would 'consult together' when necessary." Gladwyn recalled Hopkins's stubborness on this point. "I remember an agitated discussion in the Livadia with Harry Hopkins (in bed), in the presence of Jimmy Burns [*sic*], in which I attempted to resist any whittling down of the original text by Hopkins. In the event it *was* whittled down, but not, perhaps, irremediably."

Gladwyn envisioned considerable leeway for an activist State Department to find the Soviet Union guilty of bad faith, even within the scaled down terms of the final declaration.

> It seemed to me at this time that the signature of the Declaration on Liberated Europe even if it did not result in our inserting pro-Western elements into the governments of the "liberated" states of Eastern Europe, would at least give us an excellent bargaining counter in the event of its effective repudiation by our allies . . . the signed text, after all, morally committed the Russians to the holding of "free elections" in the countries "liberated."

Although Gladwyn realized that a loose formulation served British interests (did Churchill want "free" elections in Greece?), he hoped that a one-sided dramatization of Soviet bad faith would win public support for a reversal of the policy of collaboration. "And as I always thought, its possible violation by the Russians would give us an excuse for not withdrawing to our [occupation] zone unless we wanted to." This was precisely the line that Grew took in May 1945, in urging Truman to refuse to withdraw American forces from territories that fell in the occupation zone allotted to Russia. The Europeanists did not wait till the allied armies met, however, to begin wielding the Yalta Declaration.[16]

Soon after the Crimea conference, Grew had a memo drafted for Roosevelt's signature assigning responsibility for "the speedy and effective implementation" of the Yalta agreements to the State Department.

Grew explained to Secretary of State Stettinius: "We think that this is the time for the State Department to consolidate the preeminent position which you have achieved for it." One of Stettinius's aides advised him, "Mr. Dunn, Mr. Matthews, and Chip Bohlen attach a great deal of importance to this, as I believe Mr. Grew also does." Stettinius dutifully signed and Bohlen, the White House liaison officer, got Roosevelt's consent.[17]

The Europeanists had gained a presidential mandate to interpret the Yalta agreements for the American government. Overshadowed by the military and left idle in the backwash of Roosevelt's personal diplomacy during the war, the foreign service now had seized the lead in defining postwar American foreign policy. During the October meeting to discuss Berle's memo, Bohlen had commented that "the Soviets because of their lack of qualified personnel in the field of foreign affairs do not often draw up long range plans in regard to foreign policy but rather tend to act on an *ad hoc* basis." They would, however, he added, "often accept comprehensive plans presented to them by others." The Declaration on Liberated Europe was the "comprehensive plan" finally evolved by the diplomats. It was now to become the instrument for dramatizing Russian "bad faith" to the American public. To Roosevelt, Yalta symbolized Great Power collaboration. The offer of the State Department to ensure "speedy and effective implementation" of the Yalta agreements may have appeared to him as a welcome gesture on the part of the department in support of his approach to postwar problems. If so, he was mistaken. The career diplomats, convinced that the Soviet régime was untrustworthy and unfit to be an ally of the United States, sought evidence to sustain their beliefs. By laying their hostile preconceptions alongside the idealistic standards of the Declaration on Liberated Europe, they generated a persuasive argument for abandoning Roosevelt's policy of standing aloof from Balkan quarrels.

The Declaration on Liberated Europe gave Barnes the hook he needed to force American involvement on the side of the Bulgarian faction he preferred. Rebuked for pressing for greater involvement by the United States in opposition to Russian wishes, Barnes denied the charge and counterattacked. "I think the time is rapidly approaching when, even in little Bulgaria, we and the British shall be compelled openly to test Russian honesty, or completely to lose face ourselves as a courageous people, fighting for the ideals that we express in such documents as the Crimean Declaration."[18]

On March 1, the department received its mandate to "implement" the Crimea accords. A day later Barnes cabled that "the Agrarians are most anxious for signs from us and the British that it really was intended at Yalta to assure elections in ex-satellite countries that would permit the democratic elements of each country freely to express their will." Grew and Dunn orchestrated the response, supporting Barnes's assertion of American interest but cautioning him not to overplay his hand. Barnes, not one for restraint, quickly informed the Bulgarian foreign minister that he "had perceived in communication received from Washington since the Yalta Conference a more direct interest on the part of the Department in Bulgarian affairs than had formerly been the case."[19]

Throughout the spring and summer of 1945, conflicts over adherence to the Yalta Declaration were the central motif of American-Soviet relations. So many representations were urged on the Moscow embassy that Harriman, pleased at the general tenor of the reports, had to set priorities. He decided, for instance, that Poland would make a better "test case" than Rumania. There were simply too many protests being generated by energetic foreign service officers for him to service them all.

14 | THE EUROPEANISTS CONSOLIDATE THEIR GRIP

THE YALTA DECLARATION put the Europeanists back into the foreign policy business, but it did not end their internal problems. The residue of twelve years of Rooseveltian diplomacy remained to be removed. The UN planners had to be contained, Will Clayton's economists neutralized, Bohlen and Matthews reeducated, Acheson and MacLeish disarmed, and the China hands discredited. Roosevelt's departure made the housecleaning considerably easier. What could not be eliminated was carefully circumscribed. Stettinius's "new blood" ran in carefully segregated capillaries, never staining the cable traffic.

THE UN PLANNERS

The UN office—the Office of Special Political Affairs—was developing an uncomfortable degree of autonomy within the department in early 1945. Although Dunn took a leading role in UN planning to keep things under control, the possibility existed that an ambitious SPA director could turn the office from a technical to a policy-making division, especially if a supportive secretary of state were in office—a Stettinius with brains. After all, it was as director of international conferences that

Dunn had first won Hull's favor in 1933. The UN was a continuous international conference. Whoever managed the arrangements for this perpetual negotiation would sit aside a vital crossroads of memo and cable traffic. It bore watching.

The occupants of SPA were themselves suspect in foreign service eyes because American-Soviet cooperation was a necessity if their jobs were to be important. The UN planners saw the UN as the culmination of their vision of an international cooperative order and readily recognized that an emphasis on Russian bad faith could destroy their painfully constructed machinery for collective security. The leader of this nucleus of non–foreign service international organization zealots was the Brookings economist Leo Pasvolsky. "This round-eyed, round-tummied, little owl-like man," as David Lilienthal described him, was a native White Russian who conversed volubly in Russian with Andrei Gromyko, his Soviet counterpart in the Dumbarton Oaks negotiations.[1] Pasvolsky's deputy, Alger Hiss, offers this recent description: "Leo Pasvolsky, a White Russian, and no liberal, but a sophisticated European, saw that the Soviet Union would not accept a re-establishment of the cordon sanitaire and would, on the contrary, insist on hegemony in Eastern Europe. His field of responsibility was the UN: he did believe that coordination of major policy within the UN with Russia was possible and desirable."[2] In a draft of suggested remarks for Truman's Navy Day speech in October 1945, Pasvolsky offered these pacifying words: "There are no conflicts of interest among the victorious powers so deep rooted that they cannot be resolved. . . . For our part we seek to understand the legitimate urge toward security that motivates other nations, and to understand their special problems as well."[3] In the interests of American-Soviet collaboration, Pasvolsky was willing to concede the Russians a sphere of influence in Eastern Europe. Even more important, he accepted Soviet aims as "legitimate" and capable of reconciliation with American desires through give-and-take negotiation. Where the foreign offices had failed, the UN would succeed.

Until the UN was established, however, Pasvolsky's influence on American policy would be minimal. As Alger Hiss described it: "He had no responsibility for the day to day decisions made by the European Division in its administration of our relations with the Soviet Union. He wasn't consulted and was not even aware of the detailed actions that developed and fixed our Russian policy. And he had no personal influence with the European desk officers and, indeed, little in the way of personal relations with them."[4]

Nevertheless, some young foreign service officers thought about switching over to SPA. That might be where the action would be in the future. And Alger Hiss himself, not lacking in ambition, had also seen an opportunity for himself in this new unit, as did Adlai Stevenson. The 1944 reorganization had helped to contain SPA, but no one could be sure of the future.

CLAYTON'S ECONOMISTS

Equally disturbing was the outlook of the new assistant secretary of state for economic affairs, international cotton trader Will Clayton. Clayton cherished a one-world vision of international amity through economic cooperation and trade. In contrast to the Europeanists, he considered the Soviet Union a potential partner, not an inevitable adversary. Clayton's chief experience with the Bolshevik régime was a mammoth World War I cotton sale for which the Soviets had paid in full. "You don't understand the Russians," he told a less optimistic colleague in mid-1945. "I've dealt with them over the years. They've always paid their bills." Raymond Vernon, who worked for Clayton, offered this sketch in an interview.

> I had very strong impressions of Clayton. In terms of moral values he was a New England WASP of about 1910, decent, courageous, reliable, trustworthy. He was old-fashioned and gracious, very much like Cordell Hull, and he had been conditioned by the fact that he was a senior partner in Anderson Clayton. Since Anderson Clayton was a world trader in commodities, his perception of heaven was a world without trade barriers. . . . After he left [the government] he joined Clarence Streit's Union Now and did a lot of writing on world government. The quality of the man, this kind of strong, fresh, naive, uncomplex decency shines through. There's nothing disingenuous about the writings. . . . The simple unadorned Will Clayton approach said: "Trade makes friends. This is a brave new world. Let's open up all the borders."
>
> Q: Then, he had hopes for a one-world vision way beyond the point that a lot of other people did?
>
> A: Oh, yes, very much so. He had Cordell Hull's vision there.
>
> Q: And he had hoped to incorporate the Soviet Union in that, too?
>
> A: Yes. As a matter of fact there's a famous memo in the State Department which he wrote in, I think, May '47, in which he said: "Now

there will be a temptation to sell this Marshall Plan on the grounds that it's a counter to the Soviet menace. We must resist this temptation at all costs. We have to sell it on its own merits as a contribution to the growth and well-being of Europe. On this basis the Soviet Union has to be invited in."

Q: Why did he resist the idea of selling it on the basis of anticommunism? It certainly would be easier to put through the Congress on that basis, as the Truman Doctrine was.

A: Yes, but in his view it would corrupt the whole program in substance and in its objective as far as he was concerned.[5]

Because free trade with Eastern Europe and Russia depended on amicable American-Soviet relations, Clayton sternly opposed the toe-to-toe bargaining favored by the Europeanists. He opposed legislation that would restrict trade with Russia, pumped for substantial loans to *all* war-torn nations to enable them to restore their trading ability, and sought to prevent the establishment of "closed blocs"—East or West—that would choke the flow of trade.[6]

The staff of economists under Clayton shared his outlook. This galaxy of future notables included, among others, John Kenneth Galbraith, George McGhee, Charles Kindleberger, and Walt Rostow. From OSS, FEA, and other wartime agencies, young economists, excited at their first governmental experience, flocked to Clayton for a postsurrender opportunity to continue making policy. A *Time* dispatch during the first week of January 1945, lamenting Ben Cohen's exclusion from the new State Department, noted "one bright spot in the picture . . . for the liberals," namely, the appointment by Clayton of "two New Deal professors to be his assistants in handling the economic affairs of the State Department . . . Ed Mason, Harvard economist . . . formerly with OSS, and Emille Despres [*sic*], who did some work with Leon Henderson and later worked for OSS."[7]

If the economists saw a test looming for American foreign policy, it was not with the Russians but with their own textbooks. They were enchanted at the idea of trying out their theories on the real world. "They were fresh creative kids," Vernon recalls, "excited about a piece of machinery they got hold of. That's the dominant ethos. Close to the throttles of power with the opportunity to do something that in the public eye was more creative than destructive. Close to the mainstream of history and knowing it. Everything else was less important than that. Ideology wasn't terribly important." The economists certainly had no animus against Russia, if indeed they ever thought much about the question. Clayton's deputy, Willard Thorp, reminisced:

> Most of the people on the economic side who were busy trying to develop economic policies and so forth were not inclined to be strongly anti-Russian. . . . I think, in general, most of the economists were one-world people. I would not say that there were many of them who had spent a great deal of time abroad. I don't have a sense of being able to define them in ideological terms. They weren't thinking in terms of defending the world against communism. To an economist, of course, the economic side of communism is a matter of interest and concern but not something to hate, and, therefore, it depended upon the degree to which the individual was concerned with human rights, with aggression, and so forth. . . . Undoubtedly there were some with strong feelings on one side and some with strong feelings on the other side. But by and large this issue was not central to the problems we were working on.[8]

One might think a little experience negotiating with the Russians would quickly dispel the stardust. But such was not the case. Thorp, who handled the day-to-day negotiations during 1945 and 1946, was more bemused than outraged. He overlooked the idiosyncracies and sought bases for agreement. "We disagreed on a good many things," he related, "but as far as one could tell from the discussions and debates, it was not a matter of hostility." Before 1947, he found, "the disagreement was not so much out-and-out hostility as what one would expect as disagreement." Cultural differences and incongruities in language often created the appearance of enmity where none existed. Thorp became an expert in untangling these snarls. Lend-Lease was one.

> In Lend-Lease the kind of difficulty was this: the Lend-Lease agreement said that a recipient would not have to pay for anything that was used up during the war. We worked out the residual lives of trucks and drilling rigs and all sorts of things and said that they ought to pay us for the life that was left in them. The Russians said, "No, this was already used up." It turns out that in the Russian accounting procedure in the government a thing disappears when it is delivered to its final user and, therefore, you got a real difference in accounting technique and concept. This is the thing that makes it very hard to understand [each other].

Thorp caught two language snafus that threatened disagreement in negotiations over reparations and access to Trieste. In the reparations case, the initial draft of the treaty, agreed to by both the Russians and the Americans, had in its English version the phrase "manufactured and mining products." In the final session with all countries present, one representative asked whether sulphur was a mining product. Thorp said, "Yes." The Russian said, "No." It turned out that the Russian word for "mining" meant that one had to go down into a hole in the ground. Sulphur is open pit and therefore not "mining" in the Russian language. "We finally worked it out," Thorp commented, "and you will find a very curious phrase, something like 'products of the soil' because there was no real disagreement about this." In the Trieste matter, the Russians at first refused to allow private planes to fly into Trieste. Since they had no word for private planes, the translator had used instead the Russian word for "commercial airlines." The Americans, reading the English-language version, thought the Russians were reneging on a settled point when the Soviet representative claimed: "There's nothing about private planes, only commercial airlines." Thorp unscrambled this one also. "These are just the kind of things," he commented, "that can be very upsetting if you don't catch them."

Even when the Russians, as they frequently did, resorted to insult and invective, Thorp did not take alarm. This was merely their style of negotiation. If the Americans took offense, it was not the fault of the Russians but of their own ethnocentrism which blinded them to cultural traits different from their own.

> There are such different national styles and Americans don't realize this. When a Japanese says, "I think you're right but in one small aspect I'd like to suggest that it be modified," and when a Russian says, "Anyone who makes a statement like that ought to be hung, drawn, and quartered. He's a traitor to mankind,"—they're both saying the same thing. This is a difference in forensic manners. The Russian forensic manners are, by and large, very hard for an American to take. I think this has something to do with the reaction towards them.

There is not a trace of Bohlen's superciliousness in Thorp's detached analysis. Unlike the Europeanists, he did not consider Russian customs inferior to Anglo-Saxon, merely different. And this distinction guided his negotiating strategy. He didn't respond to "insult," he merely ignored it. Does harsh language necessarily mean the Russians are unwilling to negotiate or compromise, he was asked. "Not a bit." Furthermore, Thorp added, American language stiffened, not in response to

Soviet provocation, but to meet the expectations of a radio audience unschooled in Russian culture.

> I think our negotiating techniques with the Russians changed drastically the first time the Security Council of the UN was put on the air. Up to that time the Russians very frequently would say very insulting things. I remember they explained to me once publicly in the UN that we had bombed our own properties in Rumania so that we could recover damages. In that case I merely said, "This has nothing to do with the subject we are discussing." . . . As soon as something went on the air, on television, then if the Russians came through with this kind of charge, the American representative had to answer in kind. He couldn't give a soft answer or the American people would be very unhappy about it. These meetings came to be broadcast back when Senator Austin was our representative. I think if one examined it, one would find a complete change in Austin's style of debating and it is logical that it should be so.

Thorp's nonapocalyptic attitude offered scope for imaginative responses to Soviet unpleasantness. The Europeanists welcomed confrontation; he sought to sidestep it. "The question came up in the secretary's meeting once that the Russians had just restricted the travel of Americans to 25 miles from the center of Moscow. What should we do to the Russians? I argued that we should compel every Russian to travel 10,000 miles a year in the United States. I got nowhere with this."

Inevitably, the economists came into conflict with the Europeanists. In Vernon's eyes, the difference was simply a matter of perspective.

> Well, you've read Kennan's book. Kennan's is an approach based in history, based on an intimate knowledge of some aspects of the culture of the Czars and the Soviet Union after that. It's a cultural approach and an historical approach. The economists were *wunderkinde.* The world for them started around 1940. Nothing that happened before that had much relevance. They couldn't be bothered less with studying Soviet culture or imperial Czarist culture before that and if they did they couldn't conceive how it might have any relevance. And they were busy fashioning a brave new world. These two strands of perception obviously clashed.

The Europeanists and the economists both had a lifetime of experience —one in salons, the other in seminars. And both sought to mold the postwar world to their own preconceptions. EUR girded for a climactic struggle with demonic communism; Clayton's entourage sought to unite mankind under the aegis of Adam Smith. The economists suspected the geographic offices of supporting the notorious political "interference" that had historically blocked their ideal of "peace through trade." And the political offices returned the suspicion. "The political people," Thorp noted, "had a feeling that the central issues in foreign relations are the national security. . . . All these other activities—cultural relations, economic relations, and what not—have to be done but are not central. If anything, they can cause trouble."

One of the biggest uproars was over Japan. The economists backed the textbook anticartel position whereas the political desks wished to retain the *zaibatsu* to speed the recovery of Japan as an anticommunist bulwark. "The economists were trying to protect their antimonopoly position," Vernon explained, "while the politicians were trying to protect their growth position. Oh, God, it was brutal." Joseph Ballantine, a Japanese expert who succeeded Grew as FE head in the December reorganization, took part in the early stages of this fight.

> We had a complete impasse with the economic officers of the State Department. They wanted a Morgenthau peace. Turning Germany and Japan into goat pastures was uppermost in the minds of the so-called liberals in the State Department who had been brought in; people who had no experience in Japan and the Far East and knew nothing about the country. They wanted complete decentralization in Japan.

Ballantine singled out Willard Thorp and the "young economists who had Ph.D.'s in economics but had never been to Japan."[9]

The political desks won this fight, and, in general, managed to dominate the economic offices. Thorp describes what happened when one ambitious economist, Walt Rostow, tried to expand into the political area.

> I set up a little unit to deal with Germany, having raised several times in the secretary's meeting the fact that the department had to deal with the problem of Germany separate from Europe in general and got nowhere, and therefore I set up an *economic* unit on Germany. We set up the unit with Ken Galbraith, Walt Rostow, and Emile Despres. Shortly after Rostow came into the department he wrote a memorandum that had to do with solving the German-Polish border and the Poland-Russia border problem as it had developed at that time and circulated it throughout the department. Whereupon the political characters landed on me at great length:

> "By what right did someone in the economic branch not merely have a political solution but circulate it throughout the department?"

The economists presented a more immediate problem than the UN planners. Clayton was a more imposing figure than Leo Pasvolsky. And he was encamped in Room 300, Dunn's old office—an alien occupant of the formerly sacrosanct command post of EUR. The UN planners, at least, were down on the first floor, or even in the Siberia of overflow offices in other buildings. Loans and reconstruction were immediate business; UN meetings, apart from the heralded founding conference at San Francisco, a distant prospect and a ho-hum "League of Notions" one at that. The ideology of the economists upset the Europeanists. The tension surfaced in a *Fortune* article a year later.

> The political offices of the department are engaged in running warfare with the economic staff headed by Assistant Secretary Will Clayton. The Foreign Service men in the European and Near East and African offices are generally committed to the idea of two blocs in the world—the Russian and the non-Russian. They think in terms of "containing" Russia by a series of firm stands on specific points: Iran, Trieste, and so on. Mr. Clayton's men are more interested in exploring the possibilities of collaboration with Russia on a variety of economic problems that cut across political boundaries. Mr. Byrnes may soon have to negotiate some sort of peace between these two factions.[10]

Henderson's Return

To contain these apostles of global harmony required a vigorous effort on the part of the foreign service stalwarts. Furthermore, someone had to keep an eye on Stettinius and the UN crew in San Francisco. A few days after Roosevelt's death, Dunn left for San Francisco to be at Stettinius's side during the conference. To replace him as top political officer in the department beneath Grew, William Phillips responded to the importunities of his friends for help in their hour of difficulty and took over as head of EUR. During April, May, and June, Grew and Phillips ran the department while Dunn oversaw the road show in San Francisco.[11]

To complete the reunion, Loy Henderson returned from Iraq in late March to become head of the Division of Near Eastern and African Affairs, responsible for Greece, Turkey, and Iran—all looming arenas of confrontation with Russia. The service elders had discreetly reassigned Henderson from EE. In so doing they placed him astride the cable traffic to and from Athens, Ankara, and Tehran. Henderson had every reason to seek to vindicate the views for which he had been banished. A highly principled man of fierce conviction, he did not shrink from open battle with the "leftists" in the economic and UN offices. He, more than any other individual, mobilized the foreign service to do battle with the suspect newcomers. He urged an unrelenting anti-Soviet stand on his superiors at the same time he worked with Dunn—and Ray Murphy—to rid the department of undesirables. Within NEA, he had a group of loyal assistants, especially J. Lampton Berry, who aided the cause. Turkish desk officer G. Lewis Jones, convinced that Russia would sooner or later move to take over the Straits, coined the slogan that Turkey was "the Beachhead of the Western World." Henderson agreed.[12] Wallace Murray had left him a solid base from which to operate.

Except for EUR, however, the department seemed to Henderson, a dismaying assemblage of naiveté and doctrinaire leftism. And even some of the more trustworthy spirits in the geographic offices were becoming demoralized. "In 1945 the department was a dismal place," Henderson recalled.

> There was a fine group of men in NEA but a lot of new people had been brought into the department during the past year and a half. They opened new offices. There was an atmosphere of timidity in the geographic bureaus who had been pushed to one side by the up and coming New Dealers. The new people felt the "old fogeys" should be pushed out. People were afraid to speak up. The economists and the left wingers didn't understand the real problems in dealing with the Russians. They saw a bright era of international cooperation . . . will work out unless old-fashioned diplomats oppose us.
>
> Economic problems were no longer handled in the geographic offices. The economic people were the most naive group about Russia. "Handle everything so that the Soviet Union is not offended. Work with them carefully and we'll have perfect relations." Anyone who knew anything about Russia knew we couldn't possibly team up with them. . . . After V-E Day, one group doing economic warfare in Latin America wanted to ruin any traders with Germany, vendetta even after the war was over . . . and confiscate every German embassy in the world. I had to fight against that.
>
> FE was a maverick and part of the time ARA wasn't with us.[13]

Furthermore, the elders of the service could not count on the undivided loyalty of two of the most prominent officers of the younger generation—"Chip" Bohlen and "Doc" Matthews, both of whom, Henderson felt, had succumbed to White House blandishments. Matthews had succeeded Atherton as head of EUR at the same time Bohlen replaced Henderson. A loyal junior Europeanist, he too had played the White House game, becoming Harry Hopkins's chief adviser on France. The new head of the Russian desk, Llewylyn Thompson, also left something to be desired as a cold warrior. Matthews must have raised a few eyebrows when he reported that "the general atmosphere" at Yalta was "extremely good and it was clear that the Russians genuinely wish to reach an agreement . . . this includes Poland. . . ."[14] Matthews had been at Yalta, as well as Hiss.

The younger generation, though more in favor at the White House, did not have seniority in the department, where Grew, Dunn, and Henderson still ruled. Henderson, though least in formal authority, was the most energetic. Grew, aging and partly deaf, lacked force. He ably represented his subordinates, but he did not command. Phillips was temporary. Dunn, though a masterful operator, was not a zealous ideologue. He had distinguished himself by an uncanny ability to become a trusted and indispensable aide to incoming secretaries of state. He was a classic insider, a careful technician, but if a liberal secretary arrived, he might find a way to go along. Henderson, indifferent to approval, loyal only to his beliefs, spearheaded the drive to neutralize the invaders. Raymond Thurston, Henderson's choice to organize the India desk in NEA, returned to the department from overseas in mid-1945. "When I returned," he recalled, "there was an atmosphere of distrust within the department involving certain people who were liberal or naive about the Soviet Union. Henderson in this battle played an important role. He felt the Soviet Union was expansionist, perhaps the scars of 1943 . . . Henderson's revenge. [He was] certainly one of the cold warriors."[15]

Henderson's first counterblow was to disband part of the elaborate committee system set up by Stettinius. In good consensus style, Stettinius had established layers of committees to vet every issue before a decision was reached. Young officers like Charles Yost saw the committee secretariat as a potential position of great power, controlling the briefing memos and directives that flowed in and out of these meetings. Dunn had told Stettinius that he thought these gabfests useless, but the machinery came into existence nonetheless. Henderson was dismayed at the opportunity this arrangement gave the new offices to butt into business traditionally the monopoly of the geographic offices.

> Stettinius tried to organize the department . . . tried to shift responsibility to committees. I, to my dismay, was elected chairman of the Committee of Directors, one level below the assistant secretaries. Over twenty-two directors of offices in the department were supposed to have a discussion once a week . . . to comment on each other's problems. They had secretaries to pass decisions up to the assistant secretaries.
>
> I engaged in all kinds of fights . . . geographic people lining up against other people. Inexperienced men wanted to give their views on problems of the geographic bureaus. They had no idea of what was going on. It was a mockery.

Henderson torpedoed the meetings by nominating a chairman with no interest in presiding over the weekly marathon. "It got so bad I got a resolution through to get a member of the assistant secretaries' committee to be chairmen of *our* group. This resulted in no more meetings."[16]

THE FRANKFURTERITE REMNANT

At the assistant secretary level, Grew, Phillips, and Dunn had their hands full fending off Acheson and MacLeish. Neither was fully satisfied with the policy of obdurate nonrecognition of new governments in the Soviet sphere of influence. Acheson asked Phillips one day what was being done about recognizing the new Albanian government. He had heard "favorable reports" about it and suggested that Phillips talk to Roy Hendrickson of the United Nations Relief and Rehabilitation Administration (UNRRA) "who had just returned from Albania." MacLeish plaintively asked Dunn whether he was satisfied with the reporting being done by the department's representatives in Rumania. He said that "in reading their reports he had wondered whether they were aware of any constructive developments which might have occurred such as land reforms." Dunn replied that he was satisfied with the quality of the reporting and that he thought it had been "very restrained." End of discussion. Another day MacLeish complained that the department had been too eager to turn the question of Anglo-American versus Yugoslav occupation of Trieste into a confrontation with Moscow. He asked mildly whether "there had been sufficient consultation with the Soviet Union on the matter." Grew and Phillips said there had been. MacLeish used his mandate as interpreter of public opinion to press a step further. "The charge would be made," he said, "that the United States was fighting to preserve the old frontiers of Europe. . . . An incident involving us directly in a conflict with the Soviet Union would be very unpopular." Grew replied that ignoring the situation would be worse.[17]

MacLeish, however, was very limited in what he could do. He peppered Grew with memos on the friendliness of the American people toward Russia, the unpopularity of anti-Soviet actions, and the protests of liberal journalists such as Walter Lippmann and Raymond Swing against the stiffening of American policy. He also drafted conciliatory statements for public distribution, "to get rid of the sense that there is an unbridgeable chasm between Stalin and us." Letters to the department from private citizens landed on MacLeish's desk. He relayed to Grew concern about hostile American statements directed at Russia. These worries indicated, he noted, "what a great many serious, concerned, and anxious American citizens have in mind." His draft replies downplayed indications of Soviet-American conflict. "I feel very strongly," he wrote in one reply, "that the United States and the U.S.S.R. must, and can, live and work together, and that there are no reasons on either side, except fear and suspicion, for their failure to do so." Replies drafted in the geographic offices that did not endorse this outlook ran into his editor's pencil.[18] But he could not touch a single cable. Nor could Acheson, the harmless liaison with Congress.

MacLeish and Acheson could, however, exert leverage over statements prepared for presidential utterance by invoking the "necessities" of public and congressional opinion. Grew's campaign to preserve the Japanese emperor as an anchor against radicalism in postwar Japan drew an angry response from these two antifascists. "Acheson advocated a harder line toward the Japanese emperor than most people did," recalled John Carter Vincent. "I felt there was no need to get rid of the emperor as long as we clipped his wings. Acheson wanted to get rid of the bastard."[19]

FE

A more serious worry for Grew was the China division of the Office of Far Eastern Affairs. These "mavericks," as Henderson termed them, were more interested in fighting colonialism in Asia than communism. Before he retired, Grew wanted to weaken the influence of the liberal China hands and cement the control of the Japanese specialists in FE.

The differences were basic. "The China hands," recalls John Carter Vincent, head of the China division within FE at this time, "could make a better case for China than China could for itself, and the Japan hands could make a better case for Japan than Japan could for itself. No question about it, we were partisans. It got into your blood." The hostility preceded the war. "I hated the Japanese," Vincent said, "more because of the 1930s wrangle than the war itself, which seemed a much more forthright business. I was in Manchuria when the Japanese came in."[20]

Throughout the Roosevelt years until early 1944, the China crowd controlled FE through the dominating presence of Political Adviser Stanley Hornbeck. In early 1944, Hornbeck was kicked upstairs to be special assistant to Hull by a squeeze play from above and below. The young China experts, tired of his autocratic habits and his undying affection for Chiang Kai-shek, revolted. Larry Salisbury and Ed Stanton, two junior members of FE, wrote Stettinius a letter refusing to serve any longer under Hornbeck. Vincent added an oblique endorsement of their position. "Hornbeck was irascible and pigheaded," Vincent later recalled. "He antagonized people in any meeting. By 1944 he had sold his soul to Chiang Kai-shek. No one thought of getting rid of him till his underlings protested." And then everyone thought of it. The revolt against Hornbeck made him appear suspect to the consensus-minded Stettinius. And with Dunn at Stettinius's side and Grew looking for a job, Hornbeck was not likely to last long.

Grew hated this righteous academic. He believed that Hornbeck's prejudice against Japan had prevented a last-minute reconciliation in 1941 to avert war—and the failure of Grew's ten-year mission in Tokyo. He attributed his homebound voyage of failure after Pearl Harbor as much to Hornbeck as to the Japanese.[21] Hornbeck returned the feeling. The two men felt, in Vincent's words, a "hearty dislike" for each other. When his doom was certain, Hornbeck recommended that Alger Hiss, his assistant since 1938, succeed him as head of FE. If not Hiss, he preferred Vincent, but not Grew, who, he advised Stettinius, had too much prestige to take a job as office head. Grew's appointment was a slap to Hornbeck.

The 1944 replacement of Hornbeck with Grew and Grew's deputy Joseph Ballantine meant the ascendancy of the Japanese hands in FE just as postwar issues in Asia were coming to the fore. The young China experts had rid themselves of Hornbeck only to fall under the sway of the rival Japanese experts. "Grew wanted to get back into a controlling position," Vincent recalled. "He wanted to be active again and probably wished to come in because the conservative crowd saw there would be a contest over Japan at the end of the war. Grew wanted to keep the emperor from being a war criminal."

The Japanese hands were in the EUR mold—at home in polite society and at perpetual war with radicalism. The China hands welcomed a new order in Asia, an end to imperialism and autocracy. The ideological split reinforced the differences in national loyalties: liberal China hands versus conservative Japanese hands. With Grew as undersecretary and Dunn as assistant secretary for FE as well as EUR and NEA, the China hands were squelched. Vincent recommended, for instance, that OWI Far Eastern specialist Owen Lattimore be a consultant to FE. "Grew nearly hit the ceiling," Ballantine recalled. "He squashed that."[22] But Grew could not eliminate the White House liberals—Harry Hopkins's and Roosevelt's free-lance China expert, Lauchlin Currie. When Grew became under secretary, Ballantine became FE head. At that time the American ambassador to China, Clarence Gauss, resigned. Grew asked Ballantine to succeed him. A Japanese expert as ambassador to China! Grew was sealing all avenues. Ballantine was wary, "afraid of—Currie, Hopkins and all that crowd. I knew that they would have no use for me and there'd be some undercutting me all the time in Washington." Stettinius, as advised by Grew, sent in Ballantine's name. "A few days later word came back from the White House: nothing doing. Naturally I wasn't surprised at all."[23]

Eugene Dooman, a member of Grew's staff in Tokyo, came into Dunn's office as a special assistant for Far Eastern affairs. He spoke for Dunn in interdepartmental meetings with the Pentagon on Asian questions. Dooman's fellow Japanese hands loved him. His mind was "outstanding in its quality of penetration, knowledge and understanding of Japanese character," commented Ballantine.[24] Vincent had a somewhat different opinion. "Dooman was psychologically diseased. He loved to know the names of the big boys, Baron Shinewawa and the like. He was an ultraconservative, suspicious, anticommunist and had the FBI outlook on anybody who adopted an attitude not openly condemnatory of Russia itself. He further fortified the Japanese approach to problems. Dooman fitted perfectly into Dunn's scheme of things."

The discovery that young China hand John Stewart Service had leaked memos critical of Chiang Kai-shek to the left-wing journal *Amerasia* offered Grew an unexpected opportunity to destroy the liberal China faction once and for all. Service, along with John Paton Davies,

John K. Emmerson, and Raymond P. Ludden, had filed reports from China during the war critical of the Nationalist government and favorable to the Communists. Although Service met privately with Harry Hopkins, there was no hope of seeing the liberal view prevail in FE during the Grew-Dunn-Ballantine-Dooman régime. Ballantine supported Service's right to report as he saw fit, though he considered his views "inexperienced." But he could not abide Service's attempt to outflank him by leaking his reports to *Amerasia*. "When they came back to Washington, and when they found that they were overruled in their ideas, instead of saying either, 'Aye aye Sir, at your orders' or resigning, they started to build a fire under their superior officers by going outside. . . . I think that that was insubordination. It was Service and Davies that were responsible there."[25]

After a nine-week FBI investigation, the evidence for "illegal possession of government documents" was presented to the attorney general. Prosecution appeared imminent. But someone in the White House asked for a postponement to avoid upsetting the founding conference of the UN at San Francisco. The incident inevitably would be portrayed as Soviet espionage, although no evidence at all of espionage existed—merely heavy leakage to a radical periodical. Service later said he believed it to be the custom in the foreign service to let reputable journalists have "background" and "reportorial" materials of this sort. Adolf Berle, for instance, had provided most of the information to Joseph Alsop for his book *American White Paper,* a contemporary look at internal debates in the department in the Munich period. The leak was an accepted part of governmental politics in Washington. Although the Soviet Union benefited occasionally from the sympathy of a disgruntled insider, the British were regularly privy to internal U.S. government communications legally forbidden to them. Since both were allies of the United States, this was business as usual.

To ignore, chastise, or prosecute was a matter of discretion, a political decision, and Grew wished to go the limit in order to discredit his opponents in FE. He went straight to Truman with news of the postponement, where he put a legalistic face on the issues. The new president called the FBI and ordered the investigation resumed. Anxious not to have his vendetta backfire, Grew demanded assurances from the FBI, which he received, that the case was airtight. Then he authorized the arrests. On the morning of June 6, 1945, Service and five others were arrested. Later that day Dooman gloated to Vincent, "We're going to get bigger fish than that. Isn't it too bad about John Service?"[26] The

Amerasia case, however sensational it appeared, was merely another episode in the continuing campaign by the Europeanists to rid the department of unwelcome opinion.

INDOCHINA

If the China experts were at a disadvantage, the Division of Southeast Asian Affairs (SEA) under Vincent was even more severely handicapped. Only Roosevelt's steadfast opposition to the return of the French to Indochina had given these anticolonial zealots a lever to overcome Dunn's hostility. Similarly for British, Dutch, and Portuguese possessions in Southeast Asia. After the Salisbury-Landon notepad fiasco of early 1944, Vincent had brought in Abbott Low Moffat to head SEA. He had nothing in common ideologically with his cousin, Jay Pierrepont Moffat, save his name. This Moffat felt that EUR was as blind to the postwar realities in Southeast Asia as the French or Dutch colonialist who expected to take up just where he had been when so rudely interrupted by the Japanese. The European condominium in Asia was ending, Moffat felt. The psychological effect of seeing Europeans driven from the area by the Japanese could not be reversed. SEA, in short, should no longer be a stepchild to EUR but a full-fledged member of the foreign service family. Moffat wanted to remove the requirement of prior consultation with EUR on all colonial matters—a requirement Dunn had etched into the January 1944 reorganization directive.

Moffat's frustration was acute. Any information he received on French preparations to return to Indochina went into a memo for the White House. Since these were simple factual statements, EUR had to concur. About every third memorandum would produce a reaction; the president would endorse it with a statement that this must stop, or that the American military must scrupulously avoid aiding the French. These FDR gibes were relayed to the military, but with little effect. The French found ways to circumvent Roosevelt's desires. Beyond this small satisfaction, Moffat was completely stymied. Any effort to reform American policy toward colonial dependencies was blocked by EUR. There was no interest topside in a Declaration on Liberated Asia. "Why are you fussing about Indonesia?" an exasperated Dunn asked Moffat one day. "It's only a Dutch colony."

Less than a week after Roosevelt's death, Dunn decided to end the fuss once and for all. Grew called Moffat in at five P.M. on a Friday afternoon and handed him a draft memorandum for Truman on Indochina that had been prepared in EUR. Dunn had asked, Grew explained, that Moffat add his initials so the memo could be considered at the Policy Committee meeting the next morning. Moffat read it over, profoundly shocked. The memo mentioned nothing of Roosevelt's desire to exclude the French; it gave no facts about the Indochina situation; it stated merely that in the opinion of the department the time had come to give assistance to the French for their expected military efforts for the recovery of Indochina.

This memo, Moffat felt, was the acme of disloyalty; mentally he used the word "treason." EUR was capitalizing on Truman's ignorance to sabotage his promise to carry out Roosevelt's policies. Moffat protested. Grew could hardly dispute his interpretation, for he knew Roosevelt's views as well as Moffat. At a minimum Truman should at least be told that the proposal represented a complete nullification of Roosevelt's wishes, Moffat argued, and set to work to prepare a rebuttal.

When he handed Moffat the EUR memo, Grew mentioned that Dunn was pressing for SEA and FE concurrence in time for next day's Policy Committee meeting so that he could secure Stettinius's approval before both left for San Francisco and the opening of the UN Conference. Moffat feared Dunn's ability to rush his paper through the Policy Committee in the face of an opposing FE memorandum and deliberately delayed completion of the SEA paper until his nemesis was safely across the continent.

Grew brought the matter up at a Policy Committee meeting on April 22, 1945. EUR and FE had prepared conflicting memos on Indochina. Grew agreed with FE. The EUR proposal to return to the *status quo ante* with no commitments from France was inadequate. But Grew asked for only lip service. In view of the French record in colonial administration, "assurances of progressive policy were desirable." Dunn's view, he added, is that it was "necessary to propitiate the French." Grew asked the new EUR head, William Phillips, to reconcile the two positions.[27]

Phillips, who had spent part of the war years as Roosevelt's personal representative in New Delhi, knew that Asian nationalism was not simply Japanese propaganda. He had lost his job as political adviser to Eisenhower in London when Drew Pearson leaked a memo of his in the summer of 1944 critical of British policy in India. With Dunn out of the picture, Moffat had a fighting chance to win at least part of what he sought. Phillips appointed his old protegé from his days in Italy, Sam Reber, to represent EUR; Moffat represented FE. Both agreed to compromise: Reber relinquished the EUR prerogative to set policy by fiat; Moffat bent his ideals in the interest of a single departmental policy toward Indochina. When Moffat's staff saw the compromise paper, they accused him of being a traitor to all that they stood for. But the reaction in EUR was even more dramatic.

Although Phillips was in charge of EUR, he felt obligated to consult Dunn, who had sponsored the original paper, and secure his approval. Dunn wired a blistering reply from San Francisco flatly repudiating the compromise policy statement and adding that he had arranged a meeting between Stettinius and the head of the French delegation and "had" the secretary tell the French representative that the United States recognized French sovereignty over Indochina. This was more than even the French themselves claimed, since three of the five units in Indochina were protectorates, not colonies. Dunn wanted to send an unambiguous message back to Washington. With this blast, the compromise statement died and with it all efforts to draft a policy paper on Indochina. Moffat retreated to guerrilla warfare.[28]

UN planners. Economists. New Dealers. FE renegades. Grew, Dunn, and Henderson felt they had to fight these new internal threats with one hand while tutoring Stettinius with the other. One newcomer, however, was received with joy—Harry Truman.

15 | TRUMAN

ROOSEVELT COULD LIVE without the State Department; Truman could not. The new president was ignorant of European politics and needed the expertise the foreign service could provide. It was also his temperament to support his subordinates and respect their ideas. A man of few fixed purposes, trained in the up-and-down loyalty of machine politics, the new president was a bureaucrat's delight. Grew marveled at one encounter with the new president in early May: "When I saw him today I had fourteen problems to take up with him and got through them in less than fifteen minutes with a clear directive on every one of them." After years of Rooseveltian persecution, redemption was at hand. "His mind," as Grew put it, "was always open."[1]

The abortive State Department reorganization of 1944, a historical curiosity while Roosevelt lived, became quite significant once he died. Freed of the onus of Roosevelt's distrust and with a clear channel to Truman through Acting Secretary of State Joseph Grew, the foreign service converted its control of the cable traffic to overseas embassies into a presumption that the content of official cables reflected an objective view of reality in postwar Europe. The cables almost uniformly portrayed communism on the march throughout Europe, directed by Moscow and intent on subjugating the entire continent. Arriving daily in the State Department, these reports were transmitted to the White

House where President Truman, eager for information on foreign affairs, read them closely, "I've read conference records til my eyes are sore," Truman told George Allen. "Stalin is not keeping his bargain."[2]

Truman's celebrated shouting match with Molotov on April 23 did not arise from personal hostility to Russia. He simply took the approach that his tutors recommended. Leahy and Bohlen showed him certain "insulting" telegrams from Stalin that required a firm rebuke. Truman became aroused at Stalin's rudeness. He may have felt ill equipped to handle foreign affairs, but he did understand bad manners. The Russians were "like people from across the tracks whose manners were very bad," Truman told Wallace. They were "like bulls in a china shop," he said to another visitor. "We've got to teach them how to behave." International politics became a school of etiquette.[3] The Soviets "best understood 'the tough method,' " Truman explained to a shaken Joe Davies. That was why he had been so uncompromising.

Truman readily accepted the legalistic phraseology of the Yalta Declaration. He signed each indictment that Grew brought in. His first impulse was to leave Balkan disagreements to the British and the Russians, the policy favored by Roosevelt. Grew convinced him that it would be better to leave representatives on the Allied Control Commissions in Bulgaria and Rumania to defend American interests.[4] Fashioned by Dunn and Matthews, rejected by Roosevelt and Hopkins, the Yalta Declaration pitched the problem of American-Soviet relations at a level Truman could understand. "I said to you this morning when we first met," he told Molotov, "that what we wanted was that you live up to your Yalta agreement as to Poland. We will live up to ours strictly. . . . There is no use discussing that further."[5]

Truman was nervous at the idea of meeting Stalin and Churchill at Potsdam. He did not feel equal to a spontaneous discussion on the organization of postwar Europe with these two seasoned statesmen. "Truman was defensive and sensitive at Potsdam that he would be slighted," commented John Carter Vincent. He came into the conference "preceded by a wedge of Secret Service people. Churchill and Stalin just strolled in by themselves."[6] To compensate for his felt inadequacy, Truman studied hard what he was told to read and then eagerly recited it when his turn came. "He had a way of learning his book. He did his homework," commented Jimmy Dunn. "He was almost too impetuous in Potsdam. Often they had to stop him. He was not used to waiting for the translation when someone spoke in English."[7] Davies reveals what Truman was so eager to recite. "He had a habit of reading provisions of the UN Charter, the Yalta agreement, etc., and saying the language was clear and should be abided by."[8]

James F. Byrnes, who accompanied Truman to Potsdam as secretary of state, offered Drew Pearson this account:

> At Potsdam . . . Truman got very snappy with Stalin. During the first thirty minutes of his conference, long before Stalin had a chance to get recalcitrant and while he was in a very benign mood, Truman got up and made a speech as if he were lecturing a schoolroom. The substance of it was: "I expect this and this to be done and I don't expect to stay here all summer."[9]

Apart from the convenience of the Yalta Declaration for Truman, he wished to establish a reputation as a vigorous executive. The easiest way, when uncertain as to what to do, is to agree with everyone. Anyone who walks into the Oval Office can make a plausible case for his request. "Truman was exceedingly eager to agree with everything I said," Henry Wallace noted after his first meeting with Truman. "He also seemed eager to make decisions of every kind with the greatest promptness. Everything he said was decisive. It almost seemed as though he was eager to decide in advance of thinking."[10] Budget Director Harold Smith managed to rationalize the situation. "The President's reactions were positive and highly intelligent," he recorded after his first meeting. "While he agreed with nearly all of our propositions, I did not feel that I was selling him a bill of goods."[11] Paul Appleby, at this time assistant director of the Bureau of the Budget, saw the inevitable result. "When we talked to the new President," Appleby recalls, "and recommended anything he said, 'I agree with you 100 percent. You're absolutely right.' Instead of that building us up, it pulled our punch, because we thought he must be saying the same thing to all the Cabinet members and we were afraid we would meet ourselves coming back if we relied on it too much."[12]

Henry Morgenthau seized the first opportunity to warn Truman about Robert Murphy and the Dunn clique and ran into the same kneejerk agreeableness.

> I said Robert Murphy was a mistake as political adviser to Eisenhower. He jumped out of his chair and grabbed me by the hand, shook it and said, "I agree with you." He said, "I know Robert Murphy: You don't have to tell me about him." Then I said, "Well, the suggestion I made to President Roosevelt was that he swap Claude Bowers for Robert Murphy," and he said, "That's wonderful." . . . I said, "What we want to do is break this little

> State Department clique and Claude Bowers can do it." He said, "That's wonderful. I think that's fine."[13]

Hopkins and Davies also cautioned Truman that the foreign service had a "hostile and prejudiced" view of Russia, but it was difficult to make an occasional visit carry the weight of a steady succession of official cables based on an apparent expert knowledge of European politics.

Cables required responses, and, more often than not, the response was drafted in Washington by other foreign service officers. The draft cable would then be sent down the hall or across the street to the White House to be approved, revised, or rejected. No matter what the result in any one case, the foreign service set the bounds within which the debate was conducted. It was not difficult for top officials to accept as reality the "facts" they read daily in incoming cables and outgoing drafts prepared for their signatures. Truman did not have a White House Situation Room, a CIA, or a politico-military office at the Pentagon to provide him with information on Soviet activities. The State Department, a stone's throw across Executive Avenue, was the prime source of official expertise on foreign policy—and the only one with daily actionable business from the countries liberated by the Red Army.

Truman's predilection for working through channels—in part a response to the complexity of the job he inherited—increased this natural tendency and made the foreign service, in effect, his foreign policy staff. Roosevelt's personal foreign policy apparatus of Harry Hopkins, Joe Davies, and others was disbanded. It was too "messy" for the new and inexperienced president to manage. The Map Room dissolved. When Budget Director Harold Smith asked Truman what he wanted to do about a project being handled by one of Roosevelt's free-lance operators, Truman replied forcefully that he wanted "to clean up all of this sort of thing; that if the Departments of the Government cannot do this kind of work we ought to get Departments that will be able to do it." No more tolerance of Roosevelt's lax administrative methods. By relying on the cabinet departments and demanding information in channels—and a minimum of that—Truman became beholden to the permanent government. "In the old days," Drew Pearson wrote at the end of 1945, "Mrs. Roosevelt and a score of close White House friends had access to Mr. Roosevelt's work basket. They dropped in memoranda large and small for the chief to read. . . . Today only Matt Connelly, Truman's secretary, can drop things into the basket. Official papers are kept at a minimum."[14]

As significant as Truman's reliance on the State Department was his distaste for the FDR liberals. As a junior senator in the 1930s, he had been infuriated by the arrogant and cavalier attitude of the Corcoran crowd. The very mention of the New Deal zealots—Corcoran, Wallace, Morgenthau, Hopkins—sent him headlong into invective. It was an allergic reaction; he would even condemn one liberal to another. "Morgenthau," he told Jonathan Daniels, "didn't know shit from apple butter." To Morgenthau he excoriated Wallace.

> . . . he talked in a very belittling manner about Wallace. He used some very foul language which indicated he didn't think Wallace knew what he was talking about. As a matter of fact, he used a word I never heard before—he said, "Wallace is nothing but a cat bastard." He became quite excited about him.

Truman's guidelines for a new assistant postmaster general in 1945 were simple: "There are just two things I want you to do. Never talk to Drew Pearson and stay away from Tom Corcoran." Later in his presidency, Truman reversed a contract decision by his secretary of the interior simply because Corcoran had represented the winning party.[15]

Truman, of course, had defeated Wallace for the 1944 vice-presidential nomination. Despite his initial reluctance, once Roosevelt had asked him to undertake it, he went all out after it. During May and June 1944, just prior to the convention, Robert Hannegan, chairman of the Democratic National Committee and Truman's most ardent supporter, arranged a quiet speaking tour for Truman. In the estimation of Senator Claude Pepper, a Wallace backer, "Truman and Hannegan were working a very astute game during the two months just prior to the convention."[16] Ed Pauley, California oil magnate, worked closely with Hannegan. His concern about Wallace's nomination driving big contributors out of the party may have weighed with Hannegan—and with Roosevelt.

The Claude Pepper-Joe Guffey-Eleanor Roosevelt-Drew Pearson liberals backing Wallace as well as the Corcoran-Ickes group behind Supreme Court Justice William Douglas won Truman's renewed enmity. He could scarcely suffer their presence, let alone follow their advice. CIO Chief Phillip Murray at one point in the struggle told Truman that Wallace could not be stopped, despite Roosevelt's private choice of Truman. "I know what you want me to do," Truman said, "and I'm not going to do it. There's no use talking about it. I'm not going to withdraw." After Truman became president, Murray called on him to pay his respects. Truman at once lit into him: "Do you remember that night at the Blackstone Hotel when you told me I couldn't win? You never expected me to be President, did you? But here I am. I made it in spite of you." Truman never let Murray forget the Chicago incident. And he never gave up his grudge against the liberals. Truman treated Eleanor Roosevelt and Henry Wallace with forebearance. He felt a complicated sense of obligation and embarrassment concerning Wallace, the man who would have been president, and Mrs. Roosevelt, whose husband's death had elevated Truman. His consideration, however, was mainly political. He explained to Byrnes in the fall of 1945 that "there were two persons he had to have on his political team: Secretary Wallace and Mrs. Eleanor Roosevelt—Mr. Wallace because of his influence with labor and Mrs. Roosevelt because of her influence with the Negro voter." By appointing Mrs. Roosevelt to the UN, Truman added, he would ensure Roosevelt support for his renomination in 1948.[17]

The New Deal liberals, drawn to Washington by Roosevelt's inspiration, packed their bags. "When Truman came in," I. F. Stone recalled, "the devoted New Dealers left the government." Stone ran into Harry Dexter White, Morgenthau's top aide during the Roosevelt years, in the spring of 1946. "Harry," Stone said, "the whole atmosphere is very different under Truman. What the hell has happened to the atmosphere?" "When you go in to see Truman with a new idea that excites you," White replied, "the President lets you do whatever the hell you damn please. When you leave you feel flat. When you would do the same with FDR, he would often say no. But even though you'd lost, when you left you somehow felt inspired to be working in his administration." Stone, recorder of the liberal pulsebeat, summed it up. "Roosevelt brought ebullient, devoted, and zealous people to Washington. When Truman came in, the guys in government changed. The government changed from zealots and idealists to big funny guys who told jokes and didn't give a damn. People lost heart."[18]

As important as Roosevelt's death and Truman's enmity in hastening the liberal exodus was the end of the war. Many of the wartime recruits packed into OWI, OSS, FEA, and Lend-Lease returned to civilian life after the defeat of Germany. Lawyers, academics, businessmen who had come to Washington to make the Grand Alliance a reality, supporting Russia with goods, propaganda, and intelligence, returned to more lucrative pastures in private life.

Jewish liberals who had backed Russia the strongest because they hated Hitler the most, lost much of their ardor for an alliance with Russia after Hitler's death. Palestine, refuge for the survivors of the holocaust, took priority. England became the new enemy; Russia largely irrelevant. I. F. Stone arrived in Palestine November 2, 1945. In the spring of 1946 he traveled from Poland to Palestine through the British blockade with illegal immigrants. He witnessed the Arab attack of 1948. Two books issued from his pen in the immediate postwar years, both on Israel.[19] Unlike others, the Jews did not turn against Russia; they merely turned away.

The liberals turned the government back to the permanent bureaucrats whose experience of Russia predated the antifascist alliance. The few who stayed, seeking a permanent career in Washington, were rooted out, assimilated, or neutralized by the end of 1946. The economists, UN planners, and New Dealers who bedeviled Grew, Dunn, and Henderson were the deposit of the liberal wave that receded after the defeat of Germany. They were the remains of the past, not an augury of the future. In every case, the liberal remnant fought less hard to win a dominant position than the permanent bureaucrats did to eradicate them. Simple territoriality. The invaders could always retreat to universities, law firms—their native habitat. The Europeanists had no professional existence apart from the department.

The greatest irony of all is that Franklin Roosevelt himself, the liberals' inspiration, contributed to their demise by choosing Truman as his successor. The choice was deliberate. Republican Joseph Baldwin in his last conversation with Roosevelt asked him why he picked Truman over Wallace. Roosevelt explained:

> Well, of course you can't let friendship impair your judgment. I am not sure that I'll be able to finish this term. You know your history and your politics, and when you have made as much progress as we have made in the last few years, you have to digest it—and it's time to call a halt. I want someone to succeed me who is definitely center or a little right of center. Mr. Truman has proven what he is through his record. That is why I want him to succeed me.

Some months later, after Truman had become president, Baldwin visited him in the Oval Office and told him what Roosevelt had said.

> "I think you're the only man, except myself, who knows that," Truman said. "Come to the window with me." They walked to the French windows

of the Oval Office and Truman pointed to the rose garden. He said, "Do you see that wooden bench?"

"Yes, sir."

"That's where he told me that."[20]

Roosevelt chose Truman for the same reason that he kept Hull—the trauma of Woodrow Wilson. Truman was very much like Hull—unintellectual, combative, liberal-hating, a strong nationalist, a vague internationalist. Truman could get Dumbarton Oaks through the Senate; Wallace could not. Hull had not succeeded Roosevelt in 1940, but one term later Truman, the functional equivalent, did. He could legitimize what Wallace would contaminate. Roosevelt's dependence on Hull protected the foreign service so that it could live to flourish another day after its great nemesis had passed on. Since Roosevelt chose a healthier version of Hull as his successor, it is not surprising that the Europeanists returned to the limelight under Truman. With embassies reopening, the liberals departing, and Truman signing, salvation had arrived.

The respite, however, was short-lived. Truman, heeding the advice of leading congressional Democrats, appointed a new Secretary of State who chose, like Roosevelt, to operate without the assistance of the foreign service.

16 | FDR'S GHOST HAUNTS STATE

JIMMY BYRNES, LIKE Henry Wallace, felt he had Roosevelt's private endorsement for the vice-presidential nomination in 1944. When Roosevelt picked Truman, Byrnes left the convention in a fury, blaming Roosevelt for betraying him. Byrnes was "browned off" at the president, noted FDR speechwriter Sam Rosenman.

Byrnes, smarting from his humiliation in Chicago, had hoped to be appointed by Roosevelt as Hull's successor. As a southern Democrat with great respect among congressional conservatives, he seemed the spitting image of Hull. Indeed, this is probably why Roosevelt, apart from assuaging his hurt, invited Byrnes to go to Yalta. The president warned Stettinius of Byrnes's enmity. Robert Lynch, personal aide to Stettinius, relates:

> When Stettinius was first made secretary of state, Roosevelt said to him, "Ed, I don't know that you're ever going to be happy over the fact that I'm making you Secretary of State, but," he said, "when you do, you're going to make the greatest enemy that you've made in your life. And if you're wise and you're smart, you'll always be alert to the fact that you have that enemy." He said, "Jimmy Byrnes wants to be Secretary of State more than anything else in the world, and when I appoint you as Secretary of State and not him, he's going to hate your guts. And he's going to crucify

> you if he ever can, because," he said, "he's that kind of fellow. He's nothing but a cocky bantam rooster. He has no international experience, and I would be remiss if I made him Secretary of State."[1]

Stettinius laconically noted in an interview that when he mentioned Byrnes, Roosevelt said, "Jimmy knows nothing about foreign affairs although he is a wonderful man."

Byrnes's disposition was not improved by his treatment at Yalta. Stettinius remembers: "Byrnes was not invited to the first plenary session at Yalta. He actually came to the door and looked in and wasn't invited in so he walked away in a huff. No one had noticed him. There was a fight that night in the inner family [those on the battleship—Hopkins, Leahy, Byrnes] about the President snubbing Jim." Lynch recalls Stettinius's displeasure at Byrnes's presence—as well as that of Ed Flynn, democratic boss of the Bronx. "Stettinius was furious about it because everybody, all our ambassadors, everybody couldn't see how these two guys without any international experience could use political judgment on an international thing of this kind."[2]

When Roosevelt died, Stettinius knew that his days were numbered, but he bridled at the idea of Byrnes' replacing him. "It's just a bunch of politicians trying to throw me out," he grumbled to George Allen, Truman's envoy to San Francisco to give him the news. "You're talking to a man that's fired secretaries of state," Allen boasted in an interview. "Stettinius at first refused to resign. . . . He talked about all the work he had done setting up the UN."

Truman had sound reasons for appointing Byrnes. The succession at that time ran through the cabinet rather than the Congress. Were Truman disabled, the secretary of state—namely, Ed Stettinius—would become president. Truman had greatly respected Byrnes for a decade in the Senate and felt warmly enough toward him to support him for vice-president at the opening of the 1944 convention. Truman's sense of obligation, Byrnes's recognized competence, and his reputation as a Senate leader (critical for ratification of the peace treaties) all argued for the appointment. Nonetheless, Truman delayed making the change until the UN Conference ended in June.[3]

Byrnes passed the time getting reacquainted with the White House offices and devising strategems to discredit Stettinius. The ultimate disagreement on which the success of the UN Conference hinged was the question of extending the veto to include discussions as well as votes in the Security Council. The Russians wished to be able to veto even the discussion of touchy matters. Stettinius felt American public opinion would never abide a constitutional restraint on "free speech." Ultimately, the Russians gave in, after Harry Hopkins appealed directly to Stalin in Moscow. Prior to Hopkins's breakthrough, however, the conference was stalemated. In the midst of this, Truman telephoned Stettinius from Washington. "Byrnes has an idea for handling this veto power," he said. "I haven't had time to ponder over it. That's your job. But I've asked him to get in touch with you and submit the idea to you. Then you evaluate it and decide what you want to do." Byrnes's message came over the TELEX: If it's necessary, give in on the question of the veto power. Stettinius was taking a nap when his secretary brought the message in. He took one look and called in Lynch. "Bob, can you imagine what would happen to me if I followed this advice?" "This is his way of tripping you up," Lynch said, "because the quicker he trips you up the quicker he gets out here as Secretary of State. Let me leak it to the press and say this came from Jimmy Byrnes to the Secretary of State. We can crucify him." Stettinius restrained him. "If I have to resort to this sort of subterfuge, I'd rather not be Secretary of State." Byrnes advanced the same suggestion to Hull, who also did not think much of it. After Hopkins's success, Stettinius and Hull enjoyed a congratulatory phone call.

> Hull: Well you should feel much better now, Ed.
>
> Stettinius: We've had a hell of a time.
>
> Hull: I compliment you on the patience. That's the main thing, patience.
>
> Stettinius: You taught us patience and we're carrying it out. Of course, I am awfully glad that one that came from the White House last night was given consideration in time to kill.
>
> Hull: They brought it up to me here this morning.[4]

Three weeks after this abortive effort at sabotage, the San Francisco Conference ended, and Byrnes at last achieved his ambition. On July 3, 1945, Truman appointed him secretary of state.

Byrnes was a man of many hates. Stettinius was merely the latest addition to his list of enemies. "I would rather have any twelve other senators opposing me than having Jimmy Byrnes opposing me," said Paul Appleby. "He's tireless, he's shrewd, and he's vindictive."[5] Triumphant at last, Byrnes gave his anger free rein, snubbing all those he disliked.

High on Byrnes's list of accumulated resentments were the FDR liberals. In particular, his arrival signaled doom for Treasury Secretary Henry Morgenthau. As domestic mobilizer during the war, Byrnes had clashed with Morgenthau over tax policy. In a September 1943 cabinet meeting, Byrnes had flatly announced that he would take no orders from Morgenthau. He could get along with other cabinet officers, he said, but not Morgenthau. Roosevelt insisted that Byrnes let Treasury take the lead. "I am the boss," he declared, pounding the table. "I think you and I agree on this," Morgenthau said soothingly to Byrnes. "I wouldn't agree with you," Byrnes snapped, "on anything."[6] Paul Appleby saw more than a jurisdictional clash in Byrnes's anger. The Spartanburg Democrat, he felt, was an anti-Semite. During his days as assistant to Henry Wallace in Agriculture, one of Appleby's subordinates, Milton Eisenhower, developed a plan to move a regional agricultural office from Spartanburg to Atlanta. Appleby took Eisenhower with him to convince Byrnes to agree to the transfer. Senator John Bankhead, a friend of Appleby's, talked to him afterward.

> "You made a mistake in taking Eisenhower over to see [Byrnes]," Bankhead said. "You know, he hates the Jews."
>
> Appleby said, "Well, you know Eisenhower isn't a Jew."
>
> "Byrnes thinks he is," Bankhead replied, "and that's enough as far as he is concerned."

Ben Cohen's presence on Byrnes's staff did not alter Appleby's opinion.

> I used to talk with Ben Cohen when Ben was working with Byrnes. . . . I just said that I was convinced that Byrnes was bad on the Jewish question. I said to Ben, "I think he just has you around as a hostage to the Jews to buy something there." Ben, a very gentle, fine person, would never believe any such thing.[7]

The prospect of Byrnes's appointment as secretary of state greatly alarmed Morgenthau. On the train back to Washington after Roosevelt's funeral, he made his views clear to Robert Hannegan, knowing that Hannegan had Truman's ear. "Maybe I will be cutting my throat with what I am going to say now. . . . I don't like Byrnes and I don't get along with him. . . . I think Truman would make a great mistake if he made Byrnes Secretary of State . . . he just can't play on anybody's team."[8] On June 1, Morgenthau made the same plea directly to Truman. The president was evasive; Morgenthau's days were numbered. When Truman and Byrnes left for Potsdam at the end of June, their border-state colleague Fred Vinson became the new secretary of the treasury.[9]

Any New Deal thrust that the Treasury might have applied to Truman's evolving foreign policy was weakened considerably by Morgenthau's departure. A strong secretary of the treasury, even someone other than the Germanophobe Morgenthau, might on fiscal grounds alone have opposed a view of the world that implied rising military expenditures. Vinson, however, had scant interest in foreign affairs. During negotiations on the establishment of the International Monetary Fund, he answered one of Keynes's dazzling arguments with the skeptical comment, "Mebbe so, Lord Keynes, mebbe so, but that's not the way folks see it back home in Kentucky." Lacking Morgenthau's driving concern with foreign affairs, Vinson did not feel snubbed when Truman turned to others for advice on foreign policy. Furthermore, the Treasury was a way station for Vinson, who for a while eyed the 1948 Democratic presidential nomination until he was elevated to the Supreme Court.

By contrast, the Treasury post was the pinnacle of Morgenthau's career. He had a personal stake in its influence and energetically sought to extend his reach. When John Snyder, a Missouri banker and longtime friend of Truman, took over, Treasury influence in foreign policy continued to wane. Although Snyder was concerned that the size of the military budget might force deficit financing, he never translated that worry into a plea for caution in confronting the Russians. He had no image of American foreign policy to back up his demand for a budget surplus. When the Treasury bureaucrats in Britain forced the Foreign Office and the services to withdraw from Greece and Turkey, there was no comparable fiscal voice in the American government urging that the United States save its money also. Snyder did grumble about the costs of the Marshall Plan, but his aloofness from the foreign policy process made his opposition ineffectual.[10]

Next after the Roosevelt liberals on Byrnes's list of enemies was Truman himself. Byrnes did not consider himself in the least subordinate to his accidental superior. Truman owed him the job; he owed Truman nothing. Indeed, as Byrnes saw it, he deserved to be president and Truman still a largely inconsequential senator. "Byrnes greatly resented Truman," Joseph Alsop recalled. "He had been top dog in the Senate since the year one. Truman was a very junior senator. It was like the top dog boy in school serving under a second former. Byrnes effectively tried to close Truman out of the whole process . . . become a secondary president for foreign affairs." Initially, this attitude caused no problems. Truman was relieved to have the responsible cabinet officer monopolize foreign affairs. He "was going to center responsibility in his Cabinet officers, and if they could not discharge their responsibilities he would get persons who could," Truman told Harold Smith. "He said this," Smith noted, "with a good deal of determination and vehemence." Truman preferred handling domestic problems. On the day of his departure for Potsdam, Harold Smith noticed that "he seemed concerned that he was having to spend so much time on international matters." Potsdam made Truman so uncomfortable that he vowed never again to attend an overseas summit. He never did.[11] Not until complaints about Byrnes's administration of the department and souring relationships with congressional leaders reached Truman did he consider that the secretary of state might be ignoring him—and to his detriment. For the time being he was glad to have foreign affairs out of sight and out of mind. "Matters of foreign policy," noted the Alsops, "are left wholly to Byrnes."[12]

In addition to Truman and the liberals, Byrnes had no use for the foreign service. "Hell," he said at the London Conference of Foreign Ministers in September, "I may tell the President sometime what happened but I'm never going to tell the State Department about it." Ben Cohen, his closest aide, describes Byrnes's unilateral method of operation.

> Byrnes had never headed a bureaucracy before and was unaware of the problem of maintaining morale by giving the appearance that decisions were arrived at through a concert of opinion rather than his notions alone. He was careless in reporting back to Truman, though he never intended it as a slight. It was his operating style as a senator to hold things in his own hands rather than to act as a chief of staff or simply an advocate for his subordinates.[13]

Equally alarming to the Europeanists as their loss of influence was Byrnes's attitude on negotiating with Russia. The new secretary saw himself as Roosevelt's heir, maintaining close relations with Russia as the foundation of postwar American foreign policy. That Truman actually sat in the White House was a bizarre historical accident. As Roosevelt reincarnate, Byrnes intended to project an image of leadership that would overshadow Truman and elevate himself to the stature of historical greatness. He would be the great peacemaker, creating harmony out of conflicting national interests. His senatorial reflexes reinforced this ambition. "Though he was by nature a conservative," Cohen recalls, "his entire professional bent as senator and then as head of the domestic side of the war effort was to seek an accommodation of opposing views, to achieve a settlement that everyone could live with." Byrnes, a veteran horse trader—Stalin called him the most honest horse thief he had ever met—planned to bargain hard with Molotov and then make a deal. "I know how to deal with the Russians," he told reporters over bourbon and branch water. "It's just like the U.S. Senate. You build a post office in their state, and they'll build a post office in our state."[14]

Like Roosevelt, Byrnes relied primarily on a small circle of personal aides, loyal to him alone, identified with his purposes, and inexperienced in foreign affairs. New Dealer Ben Cohen became his Harry Hopkins. "Ben Cohen would have been a rabbi in Eastern Europe in the old days," said I. F. Stone. "He was sage, wise, and gentle."[15] Cohen's philosophy was to err on the side of trust, to use every opportunity possible to work out a peaceful solution rather than to take an aggressive and uncompromising stand. Cohen encouraged Byrnes to seek "avenues of accommodation." He immediately set himself against the Europeanists' policy of refusing recognition to the new states in Eastern Europe because their governments were not "democratic." He asked Assistant Chief of EUR John Hickerson why the State Department was withholding recognition of the new Austrian régime, which even critics of the Soviet Union conceded was democratic. "Well, we might get something better," Hickerson said. "Yes," Cohen replied, "and we might get something worse."

Cohen began to doubt the reliability of foreign service reporting from Eastern Europe. And so did Byrnes. "The Eastern European situation worked out as follows," Cohen recalled.

> Representatives of the opposition parties would naturally flock to the American embassy as their only hope for sustenance. Our ambassadors, hostile to Russian influence, would welcome and succor them, even if in some cases they had very little popular base, though in some cases, of course, they did. Byrnes, Lane, and Berry saw themselves as champions of the opposition parties and played very close to them, sending cables that painted all Russian action in the most negative light. They could see nothing of value whatsoever to the Eastern European countries in Russian occupation and fought against every manifestation of Soviet influence.

When Barnes protested indignantly against Cohen's suggestion that he be a little more tolerant of the Soviet presence, Cohen rejoined, "I am trying to keep the iron curtain from dropping even faster than it already is. The more we push the more the Russians will push back. A hardline policy can get us nowhere."

Although Byrnes reprimanded Barnes and even suggested his recall (Matthews stopped it), the Europeanists' uncompromising stance hindered his peacemaking efforts. The opposition parties, encouraged by the American ambassador, forged links to opposition groups in the United States, the kind of activity that the Foreign Nationalities Branch of OSS had monitored until it was disbanded at the end of the war. Senator Arthur Vandenberg, for instance, the foremost Republican voice in foreign affairs, met privately with exiled Polish diplomats. He promised them support in opposing Byrnes's "appeasement" policy if they would lobby Polish Catholics in the United States to vote Republican in 1948. "The exiled political groups," Cohen relates, "or those with ties to the West would activate their supporters in this country to pressure the State Department and the Congress. The overall result was severely to limit the freedom of maneuver of the secretary of state in working out agreements with the Russians."[16]

Durbrow, for instance, considered Cohen a suspect member of "the accommodationist school." He recalled one conversation.

> "Now listen, Durby, they can't be that bad."
> "I'm sorry, Mr. Cohen, but that's the way they operate."
> "But they signed the Declaration on Liberated Europe . . . will live up to it soon."
> "But look what they are doing today."[17]

Cohen felt that it was not in his own interest to defy the State Department-Pentagon-Congress conservatives beyond a certain point. The bureaucrats could be sidestepped, outmanuevered, bypassed, Cohen felt, but direct confrontation could be dangerous.

> I floated the idea of giving the Russians greater participation in the Straits regime if they would recede on their request for a base in Tripolitania. We had the Panama Canal, the British Suez. Was not Russia a great power, too? The military submitted a paper saying that the existing situation was "vital to American security." I had Byrnes ask the military in what way it was "vital"? They, in turn, said that their stand was based upon policy guidance

> from the State Department. They had asked the State Department to back them up, give reasons supporting their stand. In effect, they said, "It is vital because your people say it is."
>
> In such a situation my inclination was to drop the matter. The military and the diplomats considered themselves the anointed guardians of the nation's security. I did not wish to be misunderstood, a distinct possibility as Oppenheimer discovered.[18]

Although Byrnes's arrival severely reduced the Europeanists' influence in American foreign policy, they were able to limit Cohen's accommodationist initiatives. The creation of the State-War-Navy Coordinating Committee (SWNCC) in early 1945 gave the professional soldiers and diplomats a forum for welding a common stand on foreign policy issues. This day-to-day committee work on the entire spectrum of foreign policy issues inevitably had an effect on the overworked and inexperienced circle around Byrnes. Byrnes might scorn the bureaucrats, but he needed their expertise simply to handle the myriad details of negotiating the European peace treaties. Close at his side directing the flow of bureaucratic paper was Jimmy Dunn, who adopted Byrnes as he had Hull and Stettinius before him.

When Byrnes arrived on July 3, Dunn went to see him. "I see everybody going out the window," Dunn said, commenting on a number of resignations. "I'm perfectly willing to go out the window. We have a lot of things to do here preparing for Potsdam and handling other matters. If you wish me to, I will stay on but only if you want me to." Byrnes was pleased at this show of consideration. "Well, I would be perfectly delighted if you would," he said. The July 4th weekend was at hand. Dunn went to Byrnes's longtime secretary, Cassie Connor, and said, "I'm not going away for the weekend. I'll be down at the department every day because there is so much to be done." When Byrnes heard this, he called in Dunn. "You go up there with your family," he said. "You deserve a vacation like everybody else." "No sir," Dunn said. "I'm not going." Dunn reminisced: "Poor man, he was completely alone. The secretary of state can't do everything. No secretary of state sees more than 20 percent of what goes on in the State Department—and some don't even see that much."[19]

Dunn's management of the Stettinius-Byrnes transition, though useful, did not fully protect the diplomats. They suffered a further setback when Byrnes appointed Dean Acheson to succeed Grew as undersecretary. Cohen and Acheson, both of whom had been sidetracked in the December 1944 reorganization, had now returned in September 1945 to occupy the two most powerful posts in the department below that of secretary of state.

The choice for Grew's successor had narrowed down to Dunn and Acheson. The circle of decision included Byrnes, Cohen, and two confidants of Byrnes, Donald Russell and Walter Brown. Brown and Cohen pushed for Acheson as a counterbalance to the stiff conservative State Department bureaucrats; Hull, whom Byrnes talked to frequently, backed Dunn. Byrnes, who had his own suspicions of the foreign service officers, chose Acheson. Brown and Cohen prevailed over the absent Hull. When Byrnes had his first talk with Acheson, whom he had known casually as a State Department lawyer, he was put off by Acheson's vigorous presentation of how he intended to reform the department—he felt Acheson had too many ideas and might be a rival for influence in the department. Cohen and Brown had to calm down and reassure him before he would agree to go ahead with the appointment.[20] Acheson himself was pleased with this initial conversation. "Byrnes seems to understand that the past 4 1/2 years had not been too agreeable," he wrote to Frankfurter.[21]

I. F. Stone was delighted at Acheson's appointment. "To be succeeded by Acheson," he wrote, "must be a bitter pill for Grew, as for the whole inside clique in the State Department. For Acheson has been in the minority on issues other than that of the Japanese Emperor. He has been pro-De Gaulle, anti-Franco, strongly opposed to the admission of Argentina to the United Nations, and friendly to the Soviet Union." Stone liked Acheson's friends as well as his policies. "Within the department, Acheson's closest alliance has been with MacLeish and, among the new men brought in by Byrnes, with Benjamin V. Cohen. Cohen and Acheson laid the groundwork for the destroyers-for-bases deal with England, and have long been close friends." Acheson was "by far the best choice for Under-Secretary," Stone concluded.[22]

The *New Republic* was equally pleased, hoping to see the promise of the December 1944 reorganization at last brought to fulfillment. "This [reorganization] promises to be much more thorough and to mean a great deal more than the reorganization last December by Roosevelt and Stettinius." Conservatives condemned Acheson as a leftist Frankfurter liberal. "His whole intellectual background," wrote Benjamin Stolberg in the *American Mercury,* "ever since the days when he joined the Frankfurter circle in Cambridge, predisposes him toward that wing of our liberal tradition which got lost on the totalitarian left. . . . The ground which he has stood on during his five years in the State Department is that of Soviet appeasement. . . . He is sensitive to the pseudo-liberal opinions of *PM,* the *Nation,* and the *New Republic.*"[23]

Acheson was determined to end the Europeanists' domination of the department and to make all "lines of command" run through his office. Ben Cohen's presence at Byrnes's side as State Department counselor would prevent end-runs to the secretary. No Sumner Welles nightmares of divided authority. And it was clear Acheson would not be a puppet of EUR like Stettinius. "Strong men at the top," he has written, "can accomplish a lot even with poor organization, but weakness at the top cannot be overcome even by the best." "Byrnes required a highly competent and experienced undersecretary," John Carter Vincent recalled. "For the first time Acheson had a chance to do what he wanted."[24]

Byrnes's assurance that Dunn would have no hand in running the department pleased Acheson. His nemesis would be overseas as technical adviser during the peace treaty negotiations. When this assignment ended in 1946, Dunn went to Rome as ambassador, safely out of Acheson's hair. "Dunn and Acheson had no use for each other whatsoever," Vincent reminisced. "Acheson thought Dunn and most foreign service types to be stuffed shirts. Acheson didn't like polished diplomats. He felt that there was too much of this phony side . . . felt Dunn pretentious. Dunn felt that Dean took a very dim view of the type of diplomat that Dunn was. Dunn was nothing like as bright and clever a man as Acheson was."

The Japanese hands—Ballantine, Dooman, Earle Dickover—resigned *en bloc* when Acheson replaced Grew. With FE cleansed of them, Acheson installed liberal China expert John Carter Vincent, his close friend, as office chief. Because of Acheson's favor, Vincent catapulted to the top over people with greater seniority. Vincent was astounded: "It looked like I was going to take everybody's place." Donald Russell, Byrnes's Spartanburg law partner and the new assistant secretary of state for administration, may have also played a hand in Vincent's promotion. Vincent was also from South Carolina; Byrnes knew his brother in Spartanburg. "I got to know Don Russell quite well at Potsdam," Vincent related: "We talked about FE affairs. Russell took a hearty dislike to Dooman at Potsdam. But it would have been inconceivable to put a Japanese expert at the head of the Far Eastern office at that time."[25]

James C. Dunn, January 1946. SAM SHERE, *Life* MAGAZINE © TIME, INC.

Stettinius's new team, December 1944. Left to right: Will Clayton, Dean Acheson, Joseph Grew, Edward Stettinius, Archibald MacLeish, Nelson Rockefeller, James Dunn. UNIVERSITY OF VIRGINIA LIBRARY, EDWARD STETTINIUS PAPERS

Loy Henderson as minister to Iraq, September 1943. EDWARD CLARK, *Life* MAGAZINE © TIME, INC.

Dean Acheson, undersecretary of state, 1947. WIDE WORLD PHOTOS

Secretary of State Byrnes (left), President Truman, and Admiral William Leahy at sea on the way to Potsdam, June 1945. U.S. NAVY, COURTESY HARRY S. TRUMAN LIBRARY

James Dunn, Byrnes, and Ben Cohen at Paris Conference of Foreign Ministers, August 1946. RALPH MORSE, *Life* MAGAZINE © TIME, INC.

Next, in alliance with the Bureau of the Budget and its new assistant director, Paul Appleby, Acheson announced a plan to transfer the Research and Analysis (R & A) branch of OSS to the State Department. The Bureau of the Budget reorganization plan for the State Department established the research offices of OSS as the intelligence arm of the State Department. Truman concurred because the word "reorganization" had favorable connotations to him, implying efficiency and taut administration. "I got the distinct impression," Harold Smith noted, "that he would sign Executive Orders as quickly as we sent them to him."[26] At Acheson's insistence Alfred McCormack, a dynamic and abrasive (like Acheson) lawyer with experience in Pentagon intelligence during the war, came into the department as special assistant to the secretary of state for research and intelligence.

The OSS academics tended to emphasize the possibilities for amelioration of international tensions. This group included a number of members of the intellectual migration from Hitler's Germany, prominent among them the towering Marxist intellectual, Franz Neumann, and his closest friend, Herbert Marcuse. Because of their intimate knowledge of European politics and society, Neumann and Marcuse tended to set the intellectual tone in the R & A branch. As social democrats they were far more sympathetic to the Left than was the average foreign service officer. More antifascist than anticommunist, they did not like the emerging Christian Democracy of Adenauer's Germany and insisted that the only hope for progressive régimes on both sides of the Iron Curtain was a mutual recognition of spheres of influence. Their nominal superior, thirty-year-old H. Stuart Hughes, argued that ideological barrages against the pro-Soviet régimes in Eastern Europe simply led the Russians to tighten their grip.[27]

In a December 1945 memo to Bohlen, the chief of the R & A Russian division, Geroid T. Robinson, presented a similar analysis of Soviet foreign policy strikingly different from that offered by EE. Since the Soviet Union was "too weak now to have wide freedom of action," the "initiative is in the hands of the United States." If the United States sought compromise, the Russians would probably respond in kind. On the other hand, if the United States exerted "all pressure short of war," the Soviet Union would be encouraged to adopt a counterpolicy of revolutionary expansion. "It is by no means certain," Robinson wrote, "that Soviet intentions are set irrevocably in the pattern of expansion facilitated by revolution. . . . Marxist ideology does not by any means prescribe overt conflict at all times and in all places." Furthermore, "it is by no means to be expected that in the future the foreign policy of the Soviet leaders will be determined entirely by Marxian theory."[28]

On October 27, Acheson called a meeting of the heads of the geographic offices—Henderson, Hickerson, Vincent, Spruille Braden—to introduce McCormack and announce the establishment of an office of Research and Intelligence (ORI). "In the future," Acheson said, according to Henderson's recollection, "the geographic bureaus won't be called on to do any research at all. All dispatches and telegrams will go to ORI. You won't have to read this stuff. They will work out policies and factual situations and you people will become the operating division to carry out these policies."[29] Acheson pointed to a 6-inch-thick book on his desk. "It's all in here, what this office is, what it is to do, and what its powers are to be." Braden found his attitude almost threatening. He remembers Acheson saying, "This is decided upon. If you have any objections, they'll be thrown out by the Secretary. But if you insist on objecting, then you'll have to fight it out with him and God help you."

Hickerson withheld comment because his chief, Matthews, was in Europe. Vincent, according to Henderson, "said it was wonderful. He would never say 'no' to Acheson." Braden raised hell. The new office would simply duplicate what the geographic divisions were already doing and "create confusion." Henderson's reaction was less vehement, but he supported Braden. "I know the men in the field," he said. "I like to know who writes the dispatches in order to judge them. We have experience and can judge these." After the meeting, Acheson said to Henderson. "You let me down." "I had no advance warning," Henderson responded. "Such a move would be catastrophic. You can't separate policy from operations, make believe the government is a machine with no personalities."

The Europeanists were horrified at the individuals Acheson planned to place in charge of the departmental cable process. "Some Pentagon people told me," Henderson related, "that they received orders during the war that no memo should contain any suggestion of possible bad faith by the Soviet Union. No memo should say the Soviet Union can't be trusted. This was Colonel Alfred McCormack's order." Henderson saw the New Dealers behind this attempted internal revolution. "McCormack was carrying out the line he thought the White House wanted. Hopkins still had a lot of influence. . . . Acheson was being pushed by strong left-wing New Dealers to do this . . . pushed by some people outside the department. . . . Acheson was very loyal to Frankfurter . . . didn't want to oppose him."[30]

In the eyes of the Europeanists, the Acheson plan would reduce them to an operating division to carry out the policies formulated by Neumann, Marcuse, and Co. "The old foreign service people," H. Stuart Hughes recalled, "were very nervous. They saw their exclusive club being swamped by these characters, many of whom were foreign born, of improper social background, and suspected of leftist sympathies." Intellectual upbringing, as well as social differences, divided R & A from EUR. Both groups knew Europe very well, but their perspectives differed greatly. Those who had attended private schools in Switzerland had little in common with refugees from Hitler. Those who had spent four years in a Harvard undergraduate finishing school had a different outlook from Harvard history Ph.D.s trained by emigré social democrats. Hughes fell in between. "I was closer to the foreign service officers in social origins but different in intellectual origins. My grandfather had been secretary of state . . . very curious sandwich position between these people." Hughes described an incident that highlighted the disjuncture.

> One day I had a talk with the R & A branch chief for Western Europe who was, as chance would have it, the only Negro with any position of responsibility in the State Department. His name was Clinton Knox and he replaced Ralph Bunche as the State Department's Negro. Clinton, later ambassador to Africa, held a Harvard Ph.D. in history. He knew France and the Netherlands. At that point I knew only very few blacks. He was the third after John Hope Franklin and Ralph Bunche. We began to laugh and joke about these foreign service people. The fact that Clinton was black vanished. He and I were more similar because of our common background as Harvard Ph.D.s.[31]

If the Europeanists were stripped of the cable-drafting and monitoring process that generated the official picture of international events, their day was done. The OSS academics, they feared, would in a simple surgical move destroy the American diplomatic profession, and, Trotsky-like, turn the State Department into a left-wing propaganda organ. Roosevelt was dead, but his ghost was still haunting the diplomats. The nightmare, however, never became reality. The economy-minded members of the House Appropriations subcommittee, encouraged by foreign service officers who had built up ties with them over the years, refused the necessary funds to implement the reorganization. OSS Southeast Asian specialist Cora Dubois remembered the aftermath. "R & A was even lower than FE or Latin America in the eyes of the European offices. Their whole attitude was that the State Department *is* an intelligence office, a debating and reporting office. What are you people doing bothering us? We were beyond the pale, constantly rebuffed, with no access to anything. We were outcasts from the State Department establishment."[32]

The office geography, ever important, made this clear. The OSS academics, apart from all other considerations, were too far away to have much of an impact on daily business. "We were in an annex building in Foggy Bottom," Hughes relates. "The State Department was in the old State-War-Navy building. It was a ten-minute walk and you didn't undertake that lightly, particularly in the heat. We stayed where we had been under OSS. For all the organizational changes, the physical relations remained the same."[33] Acheson's new FE chief, John Carter Vincent, who was not hostile to his OSS FE counterparts, had the same feeling of futility.

> I never got to know most of them. They were always cooking up ideas. . . . It was almost an impossibility to bring them into the whole FE picture. So they were just busy analyzing and researching. . . . The day just wasn't long enough to figure out what kind of research you wanted.
>
> I never cleared cables with them. They were so to hell and gone anyway, you couldn't be clearing cables with them. . . . We seemed to have managed to get along without them before they came over there. They didn't get in the way, but I don't know what they contributed. Charlie Stelle, their chief, was certainly a smart boy.[34]

The academics ended up passing their time engaging in long philosophical discussions and waiting for offers from universities. Hughes describes the prevailing mood.

> I wasn't that busy. In a way it was the most leisurely time of my life. I occupied myself more than anything else the way I occupy myself as chairman of the history department, having staff meetings, answering the mail, writing memoranda. I spent a good deal of time editing and digesting reports from my division. I would edit one and then put on a shorter covering memorandum to try to make the points sharper. Though I don't

think they had any better fate than the longer ones. And then I had a certain amount of free time in which I would continue my own education. The pace was distinctly leisurely. Most of the time was spent in essentially bureaucratic activity. I would talk to the R & A Central European people more than anything else. And sometimes we'd be launched into half an hour or forty-five minutes of semiphilosophical discussion, the future of Germany, socialism, or the world, particularly with Neumann and Marcuse.

It was more like an academic bull session than policy talk. It might start with some statement by somebody like Franz Neumann, "Look what the idiots have done now . . ." but then we'd be off . . . the takeoff point for frustration. In such a frustrated situation the natural tendency is to go off into a slight abstraction. A lot of these people had a feeling that they were marking time waiting for a chance to get a suitable academic appointment. Why exert themselves that much?

There was a good deal of the atmosphere . . . one turned up at nine or shortly after nine in the morning and put in a facsimile of a working day. There was no point of going too fast. The work would be done conscientiously. The great energies and the best part of the mind was elsewhere. Actually the comparison that springs to mind is the group of specialist high-level prisoners in Solzhenitsyn's *The First Circle.* These are regular prisoners given specialized treatment kept in a kind of institute because of their talent. And they're given interesting assignments to which in general they devote their trained energies, but without knocking themselves out and with a sense that the timetable doesn't matter much, because they're all serving very long sentences.

In the novel occasionally the ministry gets awful angry because Stalin says "The new device has to be ready." That's part of the drama of the book. Occasionally we'd have a deadline. But the people I knew best, and I fell into the attitude myself, after a few months or the better part of a year thinking something could be done, simply felt that this was the particular sentence they were serving—not in any sense as prisoners deprived of their liberty though even so in a sense. It was hard for them to publish articles because they all had to be cleared by the State Department security system. There was a good deal of problem on this. They were cut off from the regular professional life of the universities . . . the feeling that here they had higher pay than at the universities. This was a period of inflation and low university salaries. Most of them were people who'd had trouble finding a job that was suitable for their talents. Most of them thought they would leave eventually and of the people I knew virtually all did, mostly to the academic life when a good opportunity presented itself.[35]

The failure of his reorganization angered Acheson. Noting the charge that he had wished "to shift control over the formulation of American foreign policy from the career Foreign Service officers," Acheson commented: "This was, indeed, where too many of them believed that it rested."[36] A key component in Acheson's failure was an alliance struck between Ray Murphy, ably supported by Henderson, and the communist-fearing members of the State Department subcommittee of the House Appropriations Committee.

Byrnes had appointed Donald Russell assistant secretary for administration primarily to protect his congressional flank. Russell's gumshoe was J. Anthony Panuch. As an aide to General Lucius Clay, Panuch had sifted the army service forces for communists. He met Byrnes when Clay became deputy director of the Office of War Mobilization and Reconversion (OWMR) under Byrnes in late 1944. When Byrnes became secretary of state, he asked Panuch to drag his FBI net through the foreign policy wartime agencies that the Bureau of the Budget had folded into State via the reorganization order Truman had signed. Russell, feeling the heat from conservative congressmen out to scuttle anything connected with the New Deal, worked through Panuch to encourage resignations or transfer undesirables to the UN.[37]

Ray Murphy, Dunn and Henderson's liaison with the FBI, directed the effort. FBI wiretaps were placed on the telephones of suspect officials. Economist Charles Kindleberger became aware of the practice when a conversation of his appeared in garbled and sinister form in a newspaper column. The nature of the newspaper account indicated that the conversation had been overheard by someone unfamiliar with the substance but looking for incriminating "leftist" plots.[38] The passport division, according to John Paton Davies, also had close ties to the FBI but was "not as sharp as Murphy who had tabs on the whole Comintern net in the United States."[39] Murphy was "a ferret," Dunn recalled. "He had the communist people all taped down."[40] In late October 1946, a *Time* reporter, Ray Brecht, interviewed Murphy.

> Murphy is the only State Department employee we ever saw who looks and acts like a cop, which could conceivably be a good thing. Murphy is grey and florid, lounges back in his chair, riffles [*sic*] through files, mostly newspaper clips, grins knowingly, smokes a lot of cigarettes, and talks in an intimate fashion not usually associated with the servants of DOS. . . . Murphy's cop-like advice . . . sounded as though it came from a character in Raymond Chandler. . . . [He made] the point several times that all this

is really J. Edgar Hoover's job—"and what do you get from him—nothing, huh?"[41]

In 1945 and 1946, Vincent remembered with distaste, "everybody was spying on everybody else." Henderson argued with Acheson for a security check on all American nationals going to the UN, but Acheson demurred. He considered the communist hunt in the department an underhanded EUR tactic to thwart his reorganization plans. In fact, to reduce the influence of what he felt was a morbid Catholic obsession with communism within the department, he took steps to reduce the number of Georgetown graduates accepted into the foreign service.[42] When Marshall succeeded Byrnes, the first thing Acheson did was to call in Fordham graduate Panuch and fire him.[43]

Part of the Budget Bureau plan to downgrade the career diplomats was a proposal to merge the career service with the departmental service. By eliminating the foreign service monopoly of the key cable-drafting positions, the foreign policy experts from OSS, OWI, and FEA, now merged into the department, could more easily rise into controlling positions. The political desks violently objected to this idea. It was a key point of conflict with McCormack—and Acheson. Ultimately the career officers won a complete victory, enshrined in the Foreign Service Act of 1946.[44] This detailed piece of legislation prepared jointly by foreign service officers and the House Foreign Affairs subcommittee strengthened the diplomats' monopoly rather than weakening it. The congressmen were eager to protect the career service from communist infiltration and supported the diplomats down the line. A detailed administrative history of this case notes: "Since [the subcommittee members] were concerned about charges of Communist infiltration in the departmental service of the Department of State, they were anxious to preserve a system for the Foreign Service that apparently had guarded successfully against such infiltration in that group."[45]

Russell, anxious not to create an open break between Byrnes and the career officers, instructed Panuch to back up the political desks and got Byrnes's approval of their draft. Russell's intimate ties with Byrnes left Acheson helpless to intervene. Appleby, aware that his good friend Acheson supported the Budget Bureau position, was reluctant to urge the undersecretary to defy the signed wish of his boss.

Thus, the Budget Bureau report on the State Department, apparent herald of a new régime at State, culminated in the Foreign Service Act of 1946—a strengthening of foreign service domination of the department. Acheson's reorganization designs in late 1945 fared no better than had Hopkins's and Roosevelt's a year earlier. Attacked from within by a capable undersecretary, inundated with grasping outsiders from the Roosevelt wartime apparatus, the diplomats drew in allies from Congress and the FBI to rout the invaders.

17 | BYRNES TURNS

DESPITE HIS EARLY responsiveness to EUR's picture of the Soviet leadership as uncivilized unmannered barbarians, Truman retained an open mind on the issue. He was as sensitive to domestic opinion as to bureaucratic opinion. In the summer and fall of 1945 the American public was far from ready for an anticommunist crusade.

Truman had liked Stalin's equable manner at Potsdam. "Stalin was a fine man who wanted to do the right thing," he told Henry Wallace. When they parted at Potsdam, Stalin said, in response to Truman's invitation to visit the United States, "I hope to, and, God willing, I shall." The problem, Truman thought, was that the people around Stalin lacked his broad view. When the Yalta agreement on the composition of the Polish government led to endless bickering, Stettinius and Eden blamed it on the Politburo. Stalin had desired a fair compromise, but when he got back to Moscow, the Politburo overruled him. "Stalin has a Politburo like the 80th Congress," Truman later said.

The "heavy" in the scenario was Molotov. When Molotov refused to come to the founding conference of the UN, an appeal to Stalin broke the ice. The Polish impasse was also resolved by direct negotiation between Stalin and Harry Hopkins. Reports that reached Truman in October and November 1945 that Stalin's health was deteriorating caused considerable alarm. If "Uncle Joe" died, the hardliners would probably replace him. Lord Inverchapel explained to Felix Frankfurter that Stalin had told him there were two factions in the Kremlin, the Easterners and the Westerners. Molotov led the Easterners, who had no faith in collaboration with the West; Stalin himself led the more moderate Westerners. The prospects for Soviet-American cooperation depended on Stalin's continued control of the Soviet government. Truman expressed his concern to Henry Wallace on October 15:

> The President, in speaking about Stalin, said he wasn't well at Potsdam, and he wasn't well now; and he was afraid that he was so tired he wanted to retire. He said this would be very unfortunate both for Russia and the United States, because then it would be a struggle for power between Molotov on the one hand and Zhukov on the other. He didn't like the prospect with either one of them. He returned to the fact that Stalin is an honest man who is easy to get along with—who arrives at sound decisions.

A week later, Truman met with Stettinius. Stalin, the president commented, was "a moderating influence in the present Russian government. . . . It would be a real catastrophe if Stalin should die at the present time." Prospects did not look good. On November 7, columnist Constantine Brown, a close friend of Admiral Leahy, relayed to him his evaluation of press dispatches from Moscow: "Stalin is on his way out of control of the government of Russia, either because of illness or by pressure from other aspirants for the place." On November 12, Caffery cabled from France a newspaper report that "Zhdanov has arrived in Moscow ready to take over direction of the Russian government in case Stalin's illness continues."

The blow fell just before Thanksgiving. J. Edgar Hoover informed Truman that Stalin had been toppled. Truman passed Hoover's analysis along to Byrnes.

> Stalin has probably been deposed as leader of Soviet Russia . . . removal of Earl Browder as head of U.S. Communist Party is part of a pattern of general turnover in the control of the Soviets in Russia. . . . Browder represented the Stalin group in the United States . . . his removal was interpreted in inner-Communist circles as being a clear indication that Stalin would shortly be deposed. Stalin's disappearance from the scene in the last few weeks . . . felt replaced by a new group . . . probably under Molotov domination.

Sitting in his office that November 24, Byrnes decided to make a last attempt at breaking the negotiating logjam he attributed to Molotov's stubborness. He cabled directly to Stalin proposing a conference of foreign ministers in Moscow to settle the problems among the allies. Such a conference would allow Byrnes to deal directly with Stalin, assuming Stalin were still in power. Perhaps Byrnes calculated that his initiative might strengthen Stalin's hand in the battle with his internal adversaries. He may have initiated the Moscow Conference to keep Stalin from being overthrown.[1]

Truman continued to retain a lively sympathy for Stalin's internal problems. After all, he, too, had to say things to appease his internal opposition. When Stalin gave an election speech in February 1946 calling for a renewed dedication to the triumph of communism, Justice William Douglas termed it "The Declaration of World War III." In a talk to the Women's Press Club a few days later, Truman commented that it was a political speech for home consumption. "Well, you know," he said, "we always have to demagogue a little, before elections."[2]

This tolerant outlook did not last long. In late February 1946 Kennan's famous long telegram arrived from Moscow and became the ideological basis for American policy toward Russia. Stalin or Molotov, Easterners or Westerners, Kennan cabled, the Soviet system was relentlessly expansionist, an animalistic force that would inexorably reach out to attain complete mastery of the shores of the Atlantic and the Pacific. In early March, Truman with complete foreknowledge of the text, sat on the platform in Fulton, Missouri while Churchill issued a plea for an Anglo-American military alliance aimed at Russia. Byrnes did not protest.

Truman and Byrnes now saw Russian foreign policy not in terms of a besieged Stalin who needed a conciliatory American gesture to discredit his hardline rivals, but as a remorselessly expanding machine independent of any personality. The reversal rested on the necessity for Byrnes to accommodate his own internal opposition. While trying to help out Stalin, he exposed himself to charges of "appeasement" from bureaucratic and political enemies who convinced Truman that Byrnes must be restrained. His enemies came home to haunt him.

In the White House, Admiral Leahy and speechwriter Samuel Rosenman teamed up to discredit Byrnes. Leahy, who originally applauded Byrnes's appointment, turned against him once he sought compromise with the Russians. Conservative to the roots, Leahy distrusted any political activity that appealed to the masses. The day after the Japanese surrender he noted in his diary: "To me the occasion seems appropriate for thoughtful appreciation of our good fortune in having gained the victory over fanatical enemies, but the proletariat considers noise appropriate and the greatest number of people in Democracies must have their way."[3] Leahy met regularly with Bullitt and representatives of the defunct Polish government-in-exile. He also offered the Europeanists a back-door entrance to the White House. Doc Matthews, head of EUR, had served under Bullitt in Paris and under Leahy in Vichy. When the Pentagon had stymied Kennan's efforts to negotiate an Azores treaty during World War II, Matthews had directed Kennan to Leahy who sent him to Hopkins and eventually Roosevelt.[4] The flow continued after Truman came in. Leahy's diary records visits by Messersmith, Berry, Harriman, and Carmel Offie, former secretary to Bullitt, to complain about Byrnes's handling of foreign policy.[5]

Military officers with complaints also visited Leahy. In addition, he funneled SWNCC reports and military intelligence on Soviet activities to the president. Admiral Sidney Souers and a staff of fifteen foreign service and military officers prepared a daily digest of international news for Truman, the only paper on the world situation that he read every day. Leahy and Souers were Truman's first two callers each morning, presenting the daily summary of Soviet aggressiveness. "Policy is based on facts," wrote the Alsops, reporting on Souers' group, "and the man who selects and prepares the facts for the highest authority cannot avoid making policy." The professional soldiers and diplomats had a direct pipeline to Truman's desk.[6]

Truman, who had found Leahy astride the Map Room cable traffic when he came into office, assumed that Leahy was a key adviser to Roosevelt on foreign policy. Although this was far from the truth, it inclined Truman to give the admiral's views great weight.[7] With Hopkins gone and the New Dealers dispersed, Leahy became the key White House voice on foreign policy. Speechwriter Sam Rosenman, although a New Dealer, had a personal hatred for Byrnes that made him a willing partner in any effort to discredit the secretary of state. Noted one *Time* report on the Roosevelt White House: "The Byrnes backers credit Judge Rosenman with a hand in cutting Jimmie out of the vice-presidential nomination—and Jimmie and Judge Rosenman never did get along too well."[8] Leahy and Rosenman collaborated on Truman's October 27 Navy Day speech which celebrated American military prowess and declared an unwillingness to compromise the standards of the Yalta Declaration on Liberated Europe.

When Byrnes returned from the Moscow Conference after Christmas with a compromise agreement on the composition of the Bulgarian and Rumanian governments, Leahy pointed out to Truman that Byrnes was violating the President's own policy as expressed in the Navy Day speech. "Mr. Byrnes has made concessions to expediency," Leahy wrote in his diary, "that are destructive of the President's announced intention to adhere strictly to policies that are righteous and in exact accord with his foreign policy announced in New York on Navy Day."[9] Leahy considered the communiqué issued at the conference "an appeasement document which gives to the Soviets everything they want and preserves to America nothing." Rosenman concurred. The communiqué "contains nothing of value to the United States," he told Leahy.[10] Soon after the turn of the year, informed columnists noted Byrnes's loss of favor with Truman. The president "is inclined to take Leahy's advice almost more than that of his Secretary," wrote Pearson. "Of all the men in President Truman's oddly assorted inner circle," reported Marquis Childs, "no one has more influence, and at the same time is less known to the public, than Admiral William D. Leahy."[11]

Dean Acheson had his own reasons for turning against Byrnes. After four years of frustration under Hull, he expected at last to have a chance to run things properly. He was irked by Byrnes's autocratic habits and felt that Byrnes's exclusion of Truman (and Acheson as well) from the foreign policy process was highly unconstitutional. He took it upon himself to "peach" to Truman when Byrnes was abroad.[12] As a result, the Soviet horror tales carried on the cable traffic from Eastern Europe poured into the White House day after day, giving the lie to Byrnes's hopes of reaching a compromise settlement. Leahy and Rosenman made sure they reached Truman's desk.

The Europeanists were pleased at Acheson's support. Their former nemesis had transformed himself into an ally. Henderson considered Acheson a naive New Dealer when he was first appointed, but soon changed his opinion. Although reluctant to hunt communists within the department, Acheson became a firm anticommunist overseas. Byrnes's bypassing of him made the undersecretary lend greater weight to the pleas for action that came across his desk from the geographic offices. Here was a hook to pull Byrnes back into the departmental cable process. At the same time that Acheson sought to modernize the department by diluting the Europeanists' monopoly, he came more and more to present their ideas to Truman as a way of countering Byrnes.

Probably of greater importance in hastening Acheson's transition to a cold warrior, though documentation is sketchy, was his growing awareness that nothing short of a Red scare could jolt Congress into voting a reconstruction loan to Britain and protecting the lifeline of the British Empire against Russian encroachment. Throughout the fall of 1945 and the winter of 1946, Clayton and Acheson, after an unsuccessful attempt to stretch out Lend-Lease shipments to Britain, campaigned in tandem to convince Congress of the necessity of voting a $3.75 billion loan. In return for the loan the United States would gain access to markets in the British Empire and British participation in a multilateral system of world trade. The autarky that contributed to World War II would be eliminated.

Clayton's vision of free-trade heaven and Acheson's desire to put Britain back on her feet ran into congressional indifference—and occasionally hostility. "There will always be a U.S.A.," read a manifesto issued by seventy-four Republican congressmen, "if we don't give it away." The unwillingness of the Senate leadership to comprehend the urgency of the situation exasperated Acheson. After one briefing he complained to Henry Wallace that he "never saw such stupendous ignorance in his life as that displayed by the senators." The loan passed in July 1946, but only after Acheson switched tactics and flooded the Congress with grisly stories about Soviet activities in Europe. One *Time* memo noted that Senator Owen Brewster "suspects that the rising anti-Russian note in official utterances may be part of a Machiavellian maneuver to help sell the British loan to Congress."

Churchill's Iron Curtain speech was part of the campaign. He had come to Washington primarily to lobby for the British loan. "Churchill's principal reason for coming to Washington," Keynes explained to Morgenthau, "was to try to bring pressure on his friend Baruch not to testify against the British loan." Davies noted how Churchill's speech altered the terms of debate. "It is no longer a question of maintaining the British economy; it has become a question of securing and aiding a partner in a military alliance to support Britain against Russia in Europe." John Carter Vincent speculated on how Churchill's talk influenced his friend Acheson. "I would think Churchill's Fulton, Missouri speech would have influenced Acheson. If Churchill saw the menace, Acheson could go further with such a policy . . . would have fortified any latent tendency in Acheson."[13]

The day after Churchill's speech Acheson gave a dinner reminiscent of Stimson's attempt to pacify the liberals at the time of the Darlan deal.

This time Acheson played the conservative. He invited Bohlen and the Australian minister, Richard Casey, to explain things to Wallace and columnist Walter Lippmann. "Mrs. Acheson spoke in lyrical terms," Wallace noted. "She has always admired Churchill and never more than yesterday." Wallace became aroused at the anti-Russian rhetoric. "Bohlen, Acheson, and Casey all think that the United States and England should run the risk of immediate war with Russia by taking a very hard-boiled stand and being willing to use force if Russia should go beyond a certain point."[14]

Anticommunist arguments were conclusive in switching many anti-British Irish-American congressmen to support of the loan. Congressman John McCormack voted for the loan to aid the Vatican's struggle against communism in Europe. The loan debate made it vividly clear to Clayton and Acheson that what they desired for economic reasons could only be approved on the basis of fighting communism. On this basis, Acheson came to see the Europeanists as valuable allies; Clayton deferred to the political desks. "Economics and politics can't be separated," one of Clayton's staff told a reporter in April 1946—and referred him to EE for any discussion of a loan to Russia.[15]

The soft spot in Frankfurter-Acheson liberalism—the mania for Britain—led them to abandon quickly the pro-Sovietism of the wartime period once the British Empire was threatened by Russia at the end of the war. Frankfurter and Acheson were antifascist in 1940 in part to save Britain; they became anticommunist in 1945 for the same reason. Having fought foreign service anticommunism during the war years as weakening the struggle against Hitler, they embraced it in 1946 to strengthen Britain economically and strategically. Pro-Soviet sentiment in the Frankfurter circle was derivative—based on solicitation for the Jews and the British. The Jews became indifferent to Russia at the end of the war; the British hostile.

Traces of the old Acheson still remained. In areas of the world that bored him—Latin America, the Far East—he could still be liberal. He backed John Carter Vincent's policy of detachment from the Chinese civil war and opposed the Pentagon desire to arm the Latin American republics. Count Sforza, an anti-Mussolini democrat of aristocratic lineage, had been a house guest of Acheson's parents during his days of exile. Acheson gave him the highest compliment. "It could be said of him, as it has been said of Balliol men, that he had a consciousness of effortless superiority." Sforza reported to Acheson on Peron's activities in Argentina, "taking over the universities, imprisoning the justices of the supreme court," as in Italy before Mussolini took over. Acheson argued to Byrnes that in the circumstances, the United States should not send military aid to Argentina. Supporting Peron, Acheson related to Frankfurter, "will appear to fall into the pattern of having us support reactionary regimes wherever the position arises—Darlan, the monarchy in Italy, King George in Greece, etc. etc." In areas marginal to Acheson's definition of civilization, he still retained vestigial New Deal reflexes.[16]

Byrnes's cavalier attitude, the steady flow of EUR memos through his office, the influence of his British friends, the frustrations of an isolationist-minded Congress, and Acheson's own assessment of world events all combined to turn him against Byrnes's policy of accommodation with Russia. *U.S. News and World Report* added one more cause. "In the postwar situation, Mr. Acheson, who is considered highly susceptible to liberal opinion, urged a liberal, friendly approach to Russia. As events developed, doubts grew, and perhaps he remembered his experience in the Treasury. At any rate, when policy toward Russia changed to one of firmness, Acheson swung with it."[17]

Acheson did not think much of Truman at first, but, unlike Byrnes, he disguised his disdain. An early experience of Truman's brisk agreeableness surprised him as it had Grew. "That man's got a lot more to him than you think," he told Vincent after an early meeting with the president. Nevertheless, Acheson retained a feeling of superiority to Truman, which he controlled in Truman's presence, but let out in private. "Truman is like a boy you tell not to stick peanuts up his nose," he told a friend. "The minute you turn around, there he is sticking peanuts up his nose." When one friend commented favorably on Truman's spontaneity, Acheson rejoined: "Do you see these gray hairs? That's Truman's spontaneity." Frankfurter considered Truman "second-rate." At the 1946 White House reception for the Supreme Court, Truman criticized a Walter Lippman column. Frankfurter superciliously noted in his diary:

> . . . the President indicated with a great deal of asperity how criticism gets under his skin. I am constantly impressed by the extent to which second-rate people around here are preoccupied with newspaper comments. The duty of a real statesman is to charge the atmosphere with his purposes and outlook. Columnists are important because mediocre and second-rate people treat them as important.[18]

Acheson, regardless of his private feelings, treated Truman with the respect his office deserved. Truman responded with trust and gratitude. This Brahmin aristocrat treated him with greater consideration than his unlettered senatorial colleague. A common feeling of irritation with Byrnes bound the two men close together. There is nothing like a common enemy to cement a friendship.[19]

Simultaneous with Leahy and Acheson's desertion, Senator Arthur Vandenberg's complaint that Byrnes was giving away atomic secrets to the Russians alerted Truman that Byrnes might be mishandling the Senate—the kind of foreign policy reality Truman understood. Harold Smith added to the indictment. Byrnes's administrative competence, he told Truman, "was actually nil according to estimates of people both in and out of the Department."[20] Smith was primed by Acheson's office, irate at his indifference to the undersecretary.

Truman, as president, could have it both ways—lay all the responsibility for foreign affairs on Byrnes's shoulders on the grounds of efficient administration and then, when Byrnes got into trouble, refuse to back him up and talk about being "bypassed." Truman found it easier to make Byrnes a scapegoat than to accept responsibility himself for what Byrnes did with a freely tendered grant of authority. Nonetheless, Byrnes's behavior was unwise. Truman out of obligation and respect for Byrnes—and his own newness—may have said too much to Byrnes and then resented being taken at his word. He leaned on Byrnes, but only at his peril did Byrnes interpret this as a license to ignore the president. Dukes should never forget that a king is still a king, no matter what he says, and is to be treated as such. "Byrnes ran out on me," Truman complained in later years. In this frame of mind, he easily fell in with the advice of those advisers, like Acheson and Leahy, who were justifiably tired of being bypassed themselves.

The list of Russian outrages Truman flung at Byrnes on his return from Moscow read like a yellow journalist's summary of the State Department cable traffic. "I do not think we should play compromise any longer," Truman concluded. "I'm tired of babying the Soviets." Thereafter, Byrnes's negotiating stance stiffened down the line. "Shortly after the Moscow conference," Henderson recalled, "Byrnes was a changed man. Ben Cohen's influence waned."[21]

Byrnes's about-face did not go unnoticed. The French, in particular, fearful that discord between American and Russia would destroy any hope of keeping Germany permanently disarmed, were dismayed at the new vigor. A "top French source"—either Foreign Minister Bidault or his deputy Couve de Murville—unburdened himself to a *Time* correspondent during the spring 1946 Council of Foreign Ministers' meeting. The conference was doomed from the outset, he said, because Byrnes, "primarily interested in . . . being intransigent enough to please American opinion," refused to make even minor concessions. Russian concessions were dismissed as unacceptable without the slightest attempt to probe for a solution. "In other words Byrnes was less concerned with narrowing the differences between the American and Russian viewpoints than he was with putting the onus for deadlock on the Russians." The French official was particularly struck by the contrast with Byrnes's stance at London the previous September. There, Byrnes had appeared as "a sincere American who was willing to make any reasonable sacrifice . . . in the interests of agreement." Six months later, he seemed "a foxy politician who arrived determined not to give away an inch on anything that mattered, but who, at the same time, was anxious that the world should get the impression he was a reasonable guy butting his head against a brick wall of Russian stubbornness."

If Byrnes's intransigence prevented a settlement between the victorious nations, the source concluded, "the impartial verdict of history on Byrnes . . . will be severe." Byrnes deserves a more charitable verdict. Squeezed by Truman, the Republicans, and the bureaucracy, he could only move in one direction and remain in office. His swing to a tougher negotiating stance completed the transition to a cold war mentality in the United States government.

With Acheson supporting EUR, Clayton neutralized, and Truman pressuring Byrnes, the only remaining cyst on the cable process was the UN office. The UN planners were hampered in creating a competing flow of cable traffic through the UN mission because the first meeting of the General Assembly did not occur until January 1946. Throughout 1945, they lacked a flow of daily actionable business to fill the minds and force the hands of their superiors. With the convening of the General Assembly, however, their opportunity to participate had arrived.

In the confrontation with the Soviet Union over Iran in the UN in early 1946, the UN surprisingly turned into a weapon in the anti-Soviet struggle.[22] Henderson led the campaign. In his eyes, the UN was a forum for publicizing the grievances of small nations under pressure from Russian imperialism, not an arena for the *in camera* reconciliation of Great Power differences. Henderson again did not shrink from open battle with the "leftists" in the UN office. He had constant disputes, in particular, with Harding Bancroft, later executive vice-president of the *New York Times.* Hiss and Cohen were against taking the issue of Soviet troops in Iran to the UN. In one staff conference on the subject, Henderson remembers Cohen arguing that "the age of small nations exercising total sovereignty had passed and that peace among the great powers was more important than a scrupulous regard for the rights of every small nation." NEA, by contrast, considered Iran the key to the entire Middle East. If it fell, Iraq and Turkey would go next. The desk officers cited a simple analogy:

> It is like one of those children's games of dominoes which in some old-fashioned families are called "domino snakes." You push the domino at one end of the snake. It knocks down the next domino; then the third domino goes, and so on until the last piece falls.[23]

In a series of cables in early March of 1946, Robert Rossow, the American vice-consul in Tabriz, portrayed Soviet troop movements in Iran as a full-scale combat deployment aimed at conquering Iran and then sweeping westward into Turkey and Iraq. Henderson's office prepared a blown-up map of Azerbaijan which indicated by arrows the direction of each thrust. Byrnes was galvanized into action by this apparent evidence of open aggression and fired off a note to Molotov demanding not merely an explanation but a decision as to Russian intentions. Simultaneously he prepared to place the Iranian case before the Security Council. State Department briefings and leaks of cables created the aura of a war scare and revived memories of Munich. *Newsweek* noted:

> Tension reminiscent of the early fall of 1938—the time of Munich and the series of crises that led to war—pervades the State Department. Officials with access to secret Soviet diplomatic reports are anxiously following Middle East troop movements on their maps. The situation looks no less serious to them than to headline readers.

For headline readers the situation looked serious indeed. The usually sedate *New York Times* carried an imposing eight-column headline: "Heavy Russian Columns Move West in Iran; Turkey or Iraq May Be Goal; U. S. Sends Note. . . ."[24]

The Iranian affair marked the final eclipse of the "nonprofessional" officials in the State Department. *U.S. News and World Report* revealed that Ben Cohen had definitely "lost out" as Byrnes's chief adviser on Russian policy. On the same day the department commended Vice-

Consul Rossow for his "energetic and thorough" reporting. Byrnes turned "more and more often" for advice, noted the *New York Times*, to "James C. Dunn, a specialist in general European diplomacy, and Charles E. Bohlen, an expert on Russia."[25]

The UN officials who had up until March presided over American mediation in the UN understandably felt uneasy at seeing the United States preparing a public confrontation with the Soviet Union and announcing it with a note sent directly to the Moscow embassy. They expressed their displeasure at the bypassing of the UN by arguing that the UN was the only valid forum for international protests. A unilateral note, they felt, should not have been sent to the Russians concerning a treaty to which the United States was not even a party. Finally, they deplored the publication of Russian troop moves as an ineffective action that could only increase tension.[26] Their suggestions were brushed aside. In the grip of a situation seemingly analagous to 1938, the phrase "upholding the UN" came to mean the sacrifice of Great Power unity to the protection of the sovereignty of small nations. The acceptance of the NEA interpretation of Russian troop movements entailed a revival of the vocabulary of "putsch," "appeasement," and "aggression." The successful dramatization of the "invasion" of Iran as a reenactment of the Sudetenland and a warning to avoid another "Munich" converted the ambiguity of Soviet foreign policy into a clear and simple picture that both the public and the top politicians could understand.

One official who joined the UN office in the spring of 1946 at the height of the Iranian crisis commented:

> It was an office of miscellaneous types of people, people who had come out of social work, university faculties, and public administration rather than out of the foreign service track. Ideologically you had more people there per cubic yard who were one-worlders than you had anywhere else in the government except perhaps in the research organizations.
>
> What I saw in that spring was the beginning of the erosion of that group and its transformation into a sort of straightline bureau. People like myself who joined the department because of our commitment to international cooperation rather than because we had been in the business of diplomacy were probably slower to accept the crumbling of the immediate postwar structure than those who had been predicting it. We represented a sort of hangover from the cooperative spirit of the war.[27]

The resignation of Alger Hiss as head of the UN office in late 1946 and his eventual replacement by Colonel Dean Rusk in early 1947 completed the transition. As the ideology of Great Power cooperation drained out of the UN office, its respectability increased in the eyes of the diplomats. The official quoted above comments:

> When Dean Rusk came in to take over, he asked for a security check on everyone in the bureau. For the next few years that office remained suspect as probably pretty soft towards the Russians, dreamy, nonprofessional. Then I would say it began to be reassimilated to the regular foreign service structure with the appointment of Jack Hickerson. [1949] He was in the tradition of the European bureau which had been the key to the foreign service through thick and through thin. His appointment clearly meant two things. First, it meant that the bureau would begin to be taken more seriously by the rest of the department. That was a definite plus in having an old-line foreign service officer take on the bureau. It meant, secondly, that his administration was not likely to fall back into some of the patterns of the Henry Wallace position of 1943 and 1944.[28]

The American ambassador in Tehran, Wallace Murray, pleaded with the Iranian foreign minister during March of 1946 to face the Russians with the vigor a "showdown" demanded. His cables to Washington revealed a fear that the foreign minister might be unduly inclined to negotiate with the Russians. Murray regularly lectured the foreign minister on the importance of being intransigent. When the Iranian minister attempted a more moderate course, the State Department persuaded the Iranian ambassador in Washington to disobey the prime minister and to leak news of the negotiations so as to embarrass the Russians and force a confrontation in the UN. American officials also actively discouraged UN Secretary General Trygve Lie's efforts to work out a quiet accommodation.[29]

Indeed, apparent Russian concessions in negotiations with Iran raised alarm in the State Department that the American case might appear overblown. An urgent cable was dispatched to Iran: "If no report of the status of the negotiations is made, the impression will be created that Soviet-Iranian negotiations are progressing smoothly and that the United States is pressing the case of Iran for its own purposes."[30] In fact, negotiations were progressing smoothly. The Iranian foreign minister Qavam was near to striking what was to him an acceptable bargain of an oil concession for troop withdrawal. Secretary of State Byrnes announced, however, that insistence on anything short of unconditional withdrawal would mean the death of the UN.

The final "lesson of Iran"—that toughness pays off—provided the general theme for postwar American foreign policy. Herbert Feis notes that the skirmish "left a lasting impression on Truman's disposition." He became convinced that the Soviet Union would "grab whatever it could" and would back down only if "firmly resisted."[31] Truman's attitude was widely shared.

The British view of these events was quite different. The British Foreign Office treated Iran as a traditional area of Anglo-Soviet rivalry and sought an agreement that would protect the oil interests of both powers. In contrast to the dramatic maps constructed in the State Department, British experts pointed out that the roads leading west, to Turkey and Iraq, were snowbound during March, and, strategically, led nowhere. They concluded that only the movement toward Tehran could hold any significance. In short, it was an extension of the war of nerves, not a military invasion and certainly not the prelude to a thrust into Turkey and Iraq.[32]

The *New York Times* correspondent supported the British analysis. After an overflight of northern Iran in mid-March, he verified the three-pronged thrust of Soviet troop movements but noted that each was directed toward the interior of the country, not toward Turkey or Iraq. He found, in general, neither large concentrations of troops nor evidence of great reinforcements. Shortly thereafter James Reston sharply criticized the State Department account of Soviet military activity in northern Iran. It was "hasty and ill-advised and gave the impression of imminent war that was not justified by the facts."[33]

By this point, however, the traumatic impression of the first explosive stories was impossible to erase. Nor was there any departmental desire to do so.

Acheson teamed up with Secretary of the Navy James Forrestal to bring George Kennan back from Moscow and establish him as the Department's leading expert on Soviet policy. The undersecretary also orchestrated the response of the permanent government to Soviet initiatives. When the Russians proposed a Soviet base along the Turkish Straits in mid-1946, Acheson seconded Henderson's desire for vigorous opposition. Henderson recalled: "Acheson had gotten all the important people together first, War, etc. before putting my idea before Truman." In a White House meeting with Truman and the military, Acheson portrayed the Soviet request as a desire to control Turkey and thence Greece, Iran, and the entire Middle East. Truman immediately concurred in a strong telegram. Turkish desk officer G. Lewis Jones was delighted at Acheson's agreement with NEA. After a year of timidity, the American government had at last caught up with his notion of Turkey as "the Beachhead of the Western World." Drafting the response to the Soviet note was easy. "It was simply a matter of taking out old, discarded memos and rewriting them."[34]

When Byrnes finally left in early 1947, Leahy and Acheson filled the gap until George Marshall took over. A conversation with Baruch confirmed Krock's impression that "with Byrnes out of the picture, Admiral Leahy's views had prevailed, that Byrnes and Leahy were very much apart in anti-Soviet procedure, though they agreed on the objective. . . ." When Henderson received the British notes announcing withdrawal from Greece and Turkey, he and Acheson immediately began to frame the issue for Truman. Unless the United States stepped in, Russia would take over the Middle East—at least. Acheson and Henderson limited consultation to EUR and NEA. They forbade discussions with Hiss and SPA as well as the economics offices until the response was drafted, foreclosing internal debate until they had put the face they preferred on the issue.[35]

Marshall was the only stumbling block. The new secretary's inclination was to view the issue in economic, not political, terms: the problem was not Soviet aggressiveness but Greek poverty. He wished to avoid a communist revolution in Greece, if possible, but was reluctant to launch a broadside at the Russians and risk embittering relations further. He was still hoping for some sort of wary accommodation. James Reston recorded in a private report:

> Marshall deplored the emotional anti-Russian attitude in the country and kept emphasizing the necessity to talk and write about Europe in terms of economics instead of ideologies. . . . He kept warning the reporters to try to understand their psychology, and he insisted that a way must be found to get more reparations for them without allowing them to control Germany.[36]

Marshall's unconvincing presentation of the need for aid to Greece and Turkey before a group of skeptical congressional leaders is usually explained as fumbling incompetence that, but for Acheson's masterful exegesis, might have doomed the aid program. But Marshall was far from inarticulate. His presentation was uninspiring because the face he put on the issue read "giveaway" to budget-conscious congressmen. When Acheson delivered a stunning portrayal of communism on the march, the legislators immediately sat up.

Marshall, accustomed to relying on staff work, soon became a spokesman for his subordinates. "General Marshall," observed Willard Thorp,

> was someone who insisted that all recommendations to him should be on one sheet of paper with an "approved" or "disapproved" typed down in the corner so he could initial it. . . . At the Council of Foreign Ministers, . . . he would never speak unless someone in the staff had jotted out the words that he should use and passed it up to him. It was very different from Mr. Byrnes. We all sat trembling for fear of what Mr. Byrnes would say. Mr. Marshall, we worried for fear he wouldn't say anything when there was an obvious requirement.[37]

Marshall did not disturb the Europeanists' domination of the department. If anything, his prestige reinforced it.

As Marshall's undersecretary, Dean Acheson became the strongest administrator the department had seen since Stimson—and in 1949 he took the secretary's chair himself. Having often opposed the Europeanists during the Roosevelt years and then collaborated with them to contain Russia, he knew whereof he spoke when he acknowledged their contribution to American diplomacy. "One fact," he wrote, "is clear to anyone with experience in government: the springs of policy bubble up; they do not trickle down."[38]

EPILOGUE

IN THE END, the diplomats outlived Roosevelt and outlasted the New Dealers. By 1945, when they finally had an opportunity to shape policy, their wait had been a long one. Grew and Phillips had joined the State Department in 1903 and 1904, a generation before the New Deal encamped in the capital. When the liberals folded up and left, they were still there. No longer a youth of twenty-four, Grew was now sixty-five. He retired when Acheson succeeded him as undersecretary. Phillips, two years older than Grew, had still looked like a smooth-skinned, glossy-haired prep school student when he greeted Litvinov in 1933. Phillips even then was fifty-five. When he finished his ambassadorship to Italy, he was sixty-two. As head of EUR briefly in 1945, he was a sprightly sixty-seven. Grew died in 1965, two days short of his eighty-fifth birthday; Phillips succumbed three years later, almost ninety. They had been friends for more than sixty years.

The younger generation that they reared proved equally as durable. Jimmy Dunn and Loy Henderson, born in the 1890s, saw their careers reach full flower in the late 1940s. Dunn became ambassador to Italy in 1946 at the age of fifty-six and held three more ambassadorships—France, Spain, and Brazil—before retiring at the statutory sixty-five in 1955. Henderson, after his NEA directorship, was ambassador to India and then Iran before serving as deputy undersecretary for administration during Eisenhower's second term.

The younger Russian experts—Kennan, Bohlen, Durbrow—all served as ambassadors in the 1950s. Kennan was Truman's last ambassador to Russia; Bohlen was Eisenhower's first. Durbrow was American ambassador to Vietnam from 1957 to 1961. John F. Kennedy was a teenager when Kennan and Bohlen were part of the first mission to Moscow in 1933. Thirty years later, they served as ambassadors under him—Bohlen in Paris and Kennan in Belgrade. Bohlen died on New Year's day in 1969. He had been a diplomat for thirty-nine years. Kennan and Durbrow—both over seventy—are still vigorous.

In October 1976, Secretary of State Henry Kissinger renamed the West Auditorium of the State Department the Dean Acheson Auditorium and lauded his predecessor as "the greatest Secretary of State in the twentieth century." The West Auditorium is too large for regular use. Most press conferences are held in the smaller International Conference Room. In the same ceremony Kissinger fittingly named this room, where the actual day-to-day briefing work is done, in honor of Loy Henderson, who was eighty-four at the time.

Hardiest of all is Jimmy Dunn. Now in his eighty-seventh year, he was interviewed at his flat in Rome. "I had ulcers continuously from 1932 until I retired in 1955," he recalled. "Today I could eat a tin can."

THE STATE DEPARTMENT
March 1933

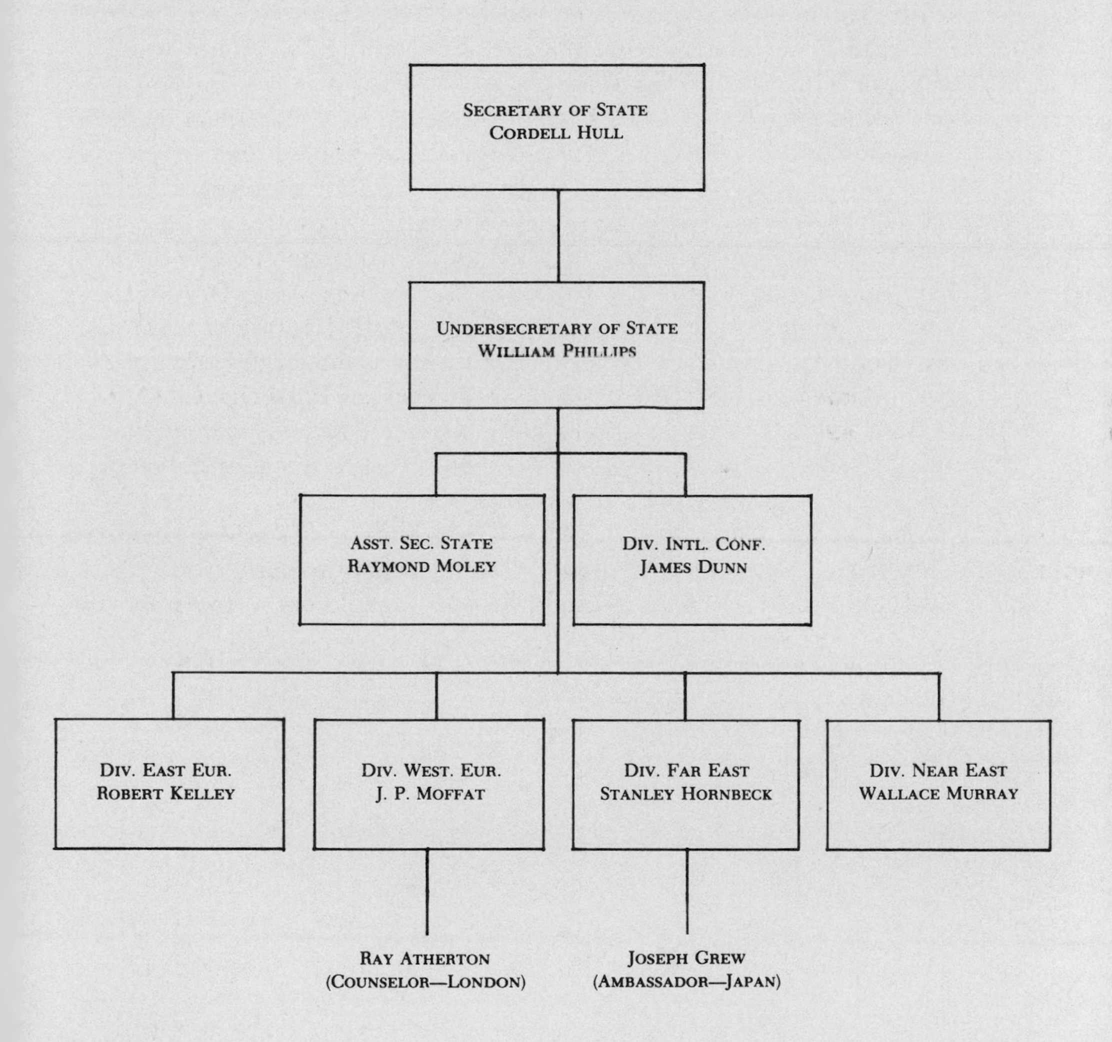

THE STATE DEPARTMENT
January 1939

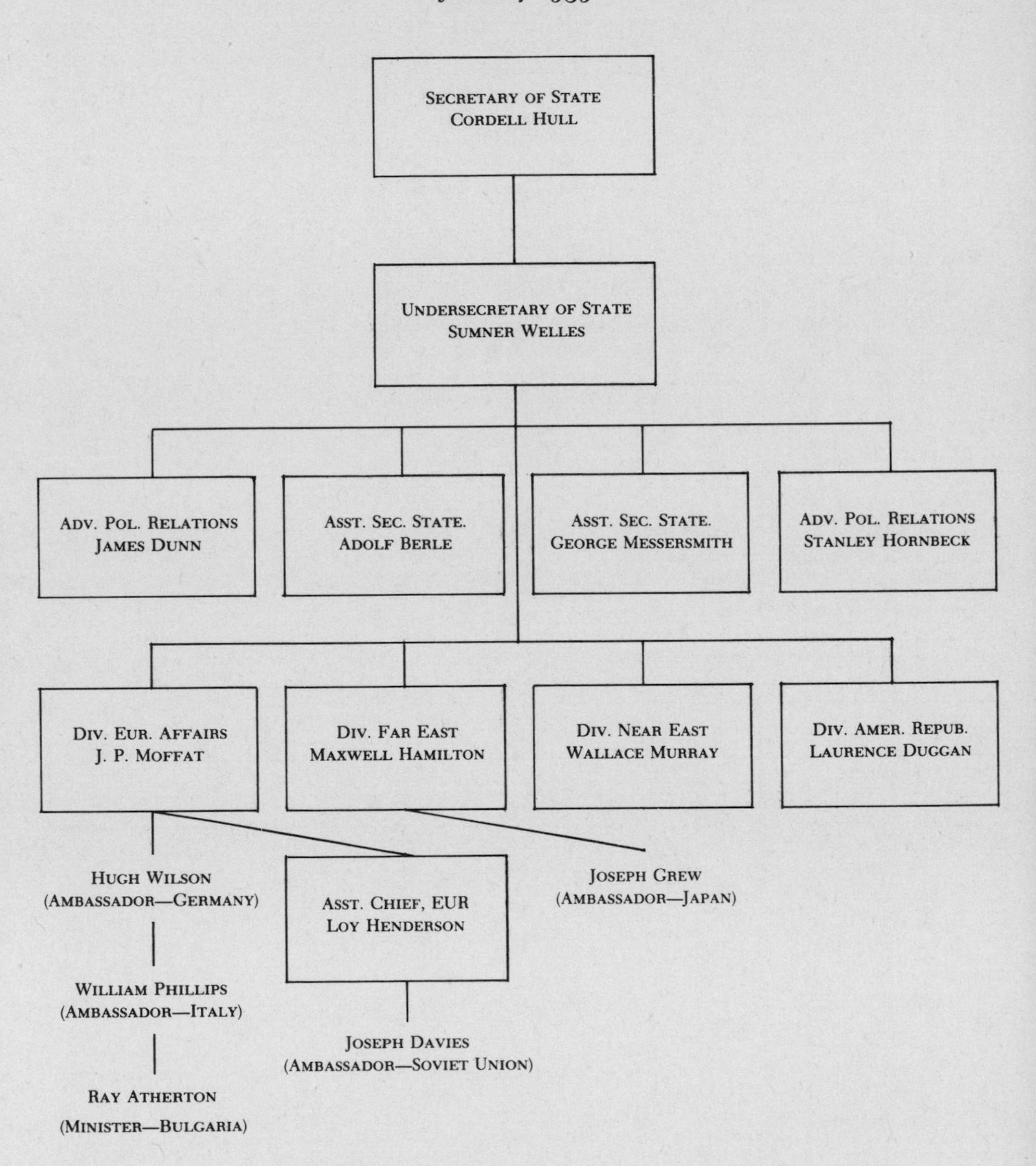

THE STATE DEPARTMENT
January 1942

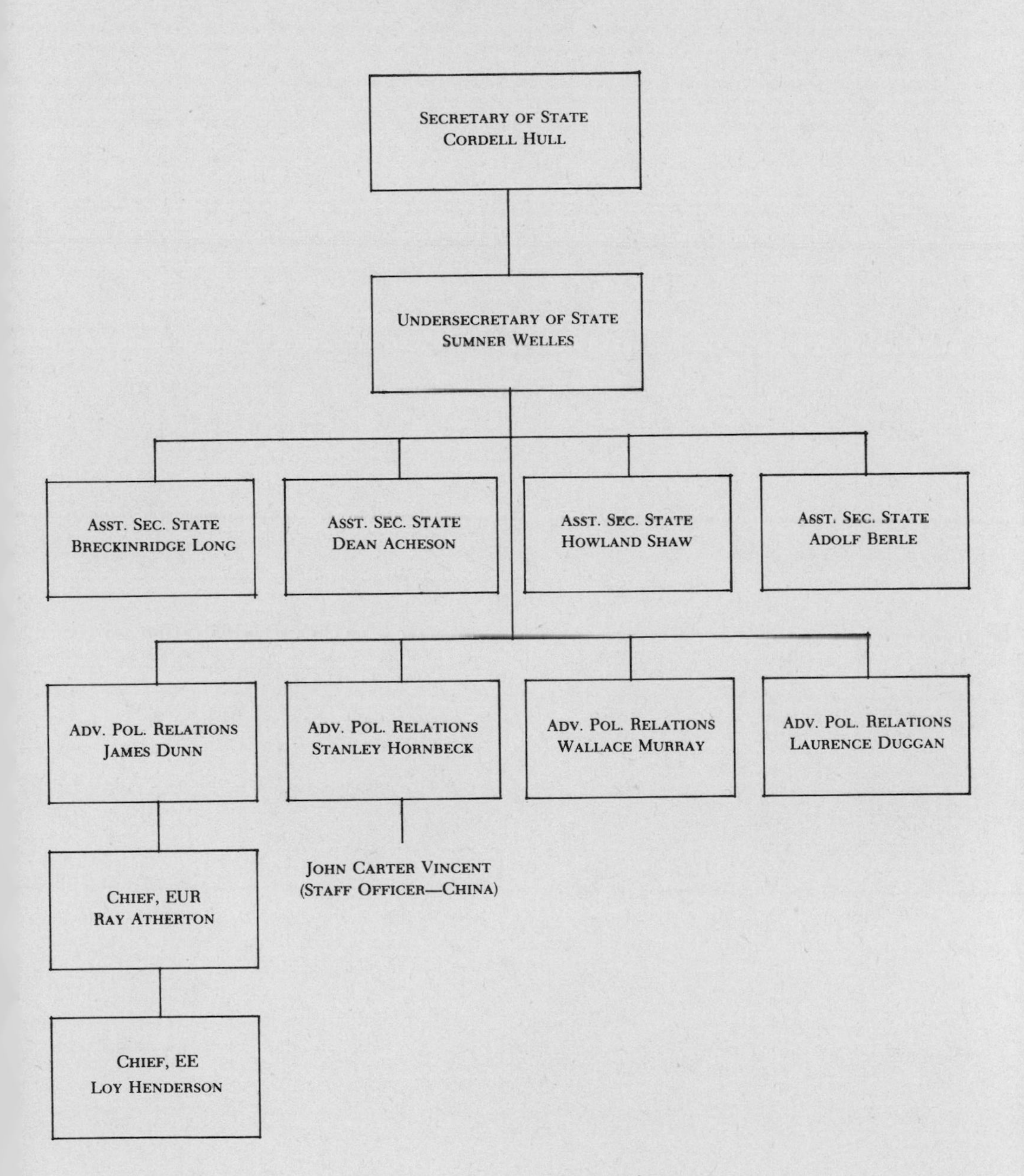

THE STATE DEPARTMENT
January 1945

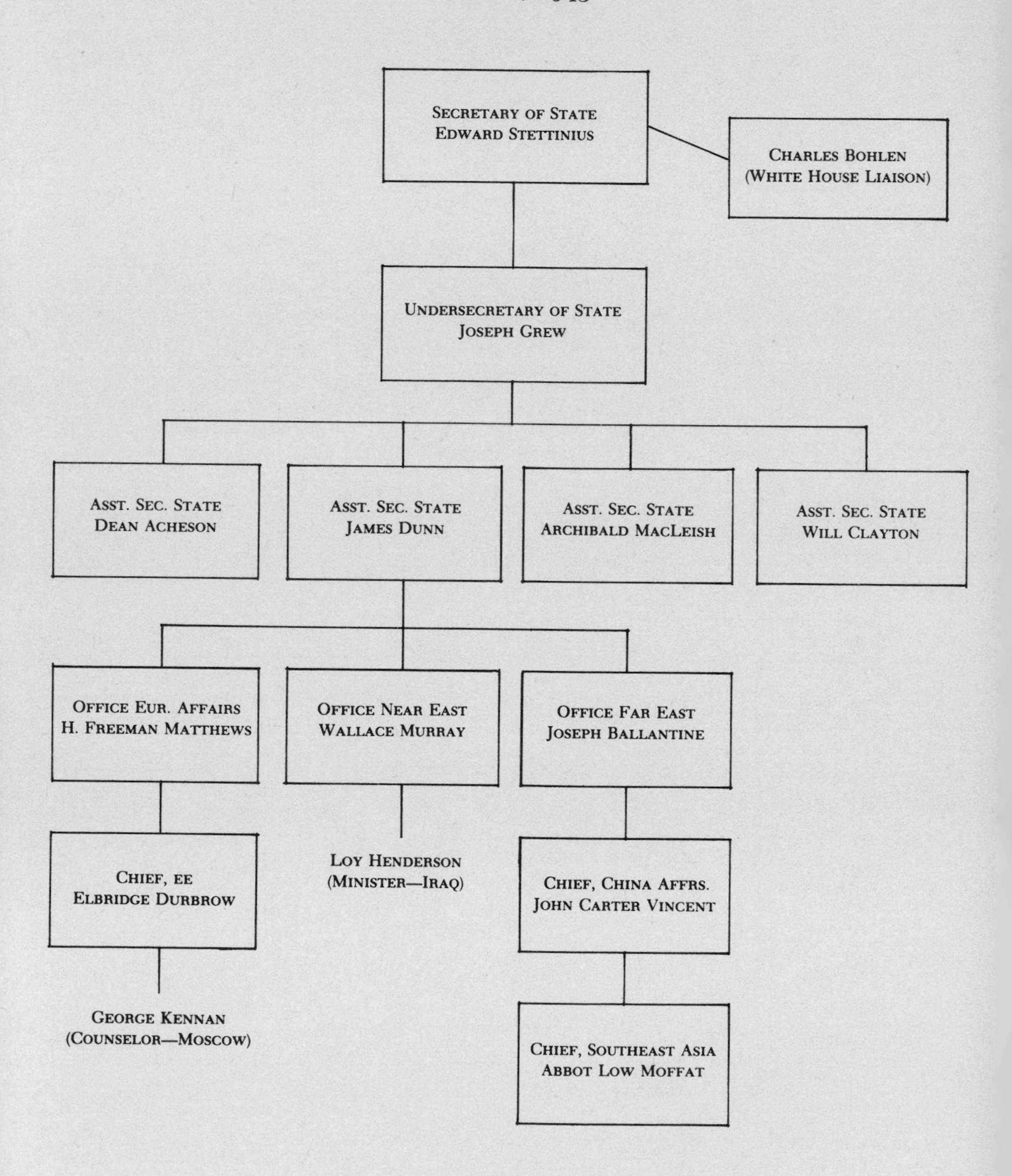

THE STATE DEPARTMENT
October 1945

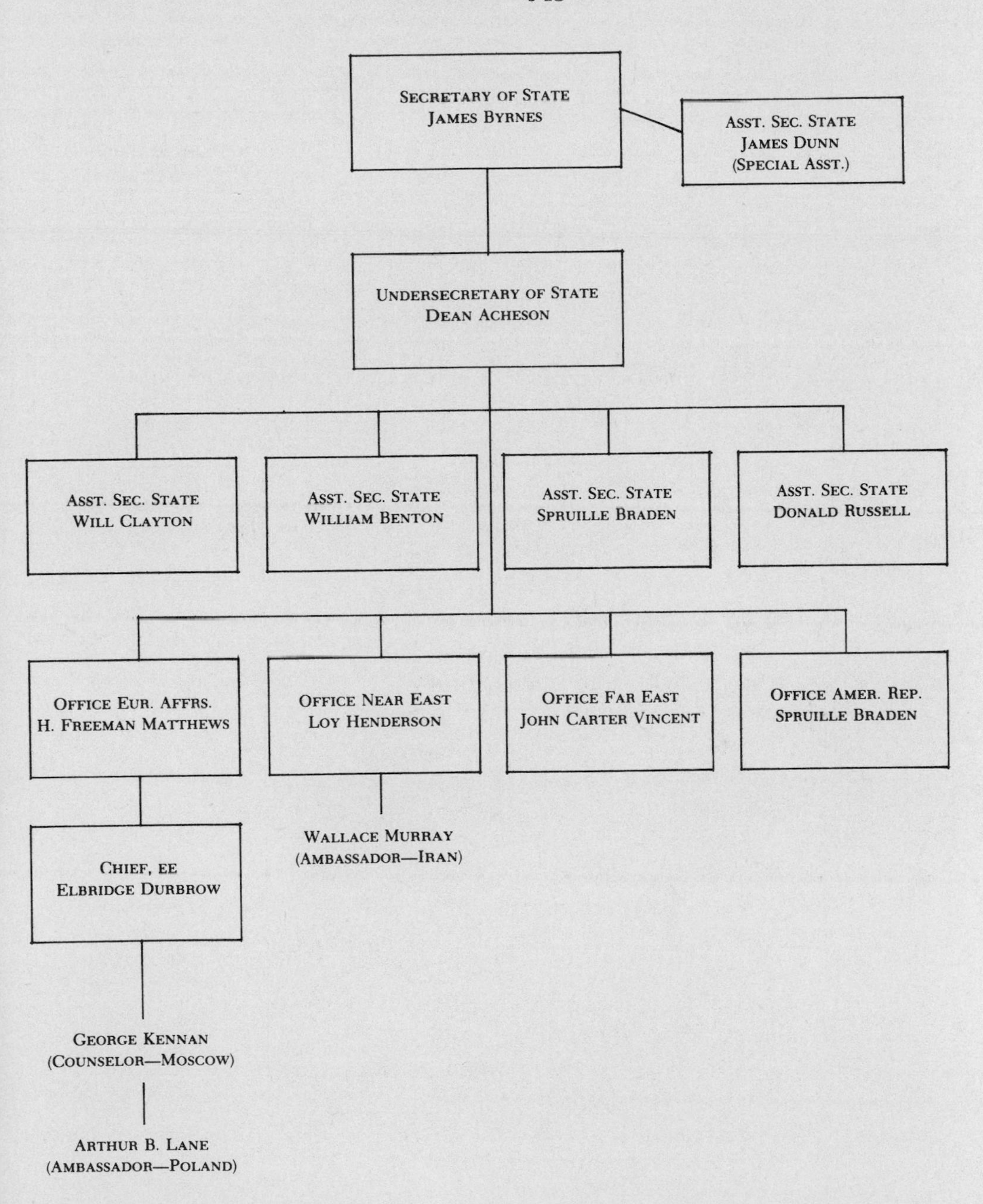

ABBREVIATIONS

ARA—Division of American Republics Affairs
EAC—European Advisory Commission
EE—Division of Eastern European Affairs
EUR—Division of European Affairs
FE—Division of Far Eastern Affairs
FEA—Foreign Economic Administration
FNB—Foreign Nationalities Branch of OSS
JCS—Joint Chiefs of Staff
NEA—Division of Near Eastern and African Affairs
OPA—Office of Price Administration
ORI—Office of Research and Intelligence
OSS—Office of Strategic Services
OWI—Office of War Information
OWM—Office of War Mobilization
OWMR—Office of War Mobilization and Reconversion
R & A—Research and Analysis Branch of OSS
SEA—Division of Southeast Asian Affairs
SPA—Office of Special Political Affairs
SWNCC—State-War-Navy Coordinating Committee
UDA—Union for Democratic Action
UNRRA—United Nations Relief and Rehabilitation Administration
WPA—Works Project Administration

NOTES

Chapter 1

1. James MacGregor Burns, *The Lion and the Fox* (New York, 1956), p. 14.
2. Alfred E. Stearns et al., *The Education of the Modern Boy* (Boston, 1928), pp. 110–111.
3. Ibid., pp. 8, 65, 112.
4. Theodore Roosevelt, *Realizable Ideals* (San Francisco, 1912), pp. 17–18, 37–40, 50.
5. Ibid., pp. 52–54.
6. Ibid., pp. 71, 75–77, 89–90.
7. Waldo Heinrichs, *American Ambassador* (Boston, 1966), p. 98.
8. Ibid., p. 9.
9. Ibid., pp. 10–15; Joseph Grew, *Turbulent Era* (New York, 1953), 1:21.
10. Heinrichs, *American Ambassador,* pp. 22–23.
11. William Phillips, *Ventures in Diplomacy* (Boston, 1952), pp. 1–2, 33–34.
12. Ibid., pp. 18–19.
13. Heinrichs, *American Ambassador,* pp. 48, 97–98.
14. Ibid., pp. 15, 96.
15. Ibid., pp. 46–47, 98; "Gibson Scans the Road to Disarmament," *New York Times Magazine,* June 21, 1931.
16. Stearns, *Education,* pp. 3–4, 36–37.
17. Heinrichs, *American Ambassador,* p. 49.
18. Ibid., p. 49.

19. Ibid., p. 19.
20. *Ibid.*, pp. 48, 401; Nancy Harvison Hooker, *The Moffat Papers* (Cambridge, Mass. 1956), p. 9.

CHAPTER 2

1. Hooker, *Moffat Papers,* p. 11.
2. Gibson to Lane, March 16, 1919, Lane Papers, box 1, Yale University Library.
3. Lane to Mr. and Mrs. James Lane, April 30, 1919, Lane Papers, box 56a.
4. Lane Diary, May 18, 1919, Lane Papers, box 56a.
5. Lane to Mr. and Mrs. James Lane, April 29, 1919, Lane Papers, box 56a.
6. Lane Diary, May 25, 1919.
7. Ibid., May 18, 1919.
8. Ibid., May 25, June 8, June 12, 1919.
9. Hooker, *Moffat Papers,* pp. 1, 2, 9.
10. Ibid., p. 43.
11. Hooker, *Moffat Papers,* p. 42.
12. Lane Diary, May 29, 1919.
13. *Moffat Papers,* p. 43.
14. Ibid., p. 37.
15. Lane Diary, May 29, 1919.
16. Hooker, *Moffat Papers,* pp. 43–44.
17. Ibid., p. 41. British Ambassador D'Abernon offered a novel suggestion for fostering national pride. "Poland," he wrote to the Foreign Office, "is an ideal country to fight in. I have not seen any European general, particularly any general of cavalry, whose mouth has not watered on surveying it. . . . It occurs to me, indeed, that if the League of Nations is not altogether successful on the original lines, it might by a slight alteration of its present constitution select Poland as an arena for a trial by arms between selected teams of potential litigants." (Ellis Dresel to Hugh Gibson, October 5, 1920, Hugh Gibson Papers, box 7A.)
18. These were Ellis Dresel, Hugh Wilson, Frederick Dolbeare, Allen Dulles, and Reggie Foster.
19. Louis Fischer, *The Soviets in World Affairs* (London, 1930), 1: 238–40; Piotr S. Wandycz, *Soviet-Polish Relations, 1917–1921* (Cambridge, Mass., 1969), pp. 128–34, 176.
20. Wandycz, *Soviet-Polish Relations,* p. 187.
21. Ibid., p. 160; Fischer, *Soviets,* 1:243.
22. U.S. Department of State, *Foreign Relations of the United States* (FRUS) 1920, 3: 375–76.
23. Gibson to Lane, January 19, 1920, Gibson Papers, box 8.
24. *FRUS,* 1920, 3: 377.

25. Moffat Diaries, January 2, 1920, Houghton Library, Harvard University.
26. *FRUS*, 1920, 3:378.
27. Moffat to Gibson, May 4, 1920, Moffat Diaries.
28. Moffat to Lane, May 19, 1920, Moffat Diaries.
29. Hooker, *Moffat Papers*, p. 41.
30. Moffat Diaries, January 7, 1920.
31. Heinrichs, *American Ambassador*, p. 67.
32. Hooker, *Moffat Papers*, p. 25.
33. Moffat to Gibson, July 31, 1920, Moffat Diaries.
34. Moffat to Gibson, July 6, 1920, Moffat Diaries.
35. Castle to Moffat, October 26, 1920, Moffat Diaries.
36. Moffat to Gibson, May 14, 1920, Moffat Diaries.
37. Gibson to Moffat, July 23, 1920, Moffat Diaries.
38. Gibson to Moffat, June 23, 1920, Moffat Diaries.
39. Gibson to Moffat, July 8, 1920, Moffat Diaries.
40. Gibson to Moffat, July 23, 1920, Moffat Diaries.
41. *FRUS*,1920, 3: 463–68.
42. Dulles to Gibson, October 14, 1920, Gibson Papers, box 7A.
43. Moffat to Gibson, August 8, 1920, Moffat Diaries.
44. Moffat to Gibson, April 19, 1920, Moffat Diaries.
45. Moffat to Gibson, May 4, 1920, Moffat Diaries.
46. Moffat to Gibson, June 2, 1920, Moffat Diaries.
47. Moffat Diaries, November 30, 1927.
48. Thaw to Gibson, April 11, 1921, Gibson Papers, box 7A.
49. See Gibson Papers, box 6, for clippings.
50. Grew to Gibson, November 2, 1921, Gibson Papers, box 7A.
51. Gibson to Lane, February 1, 1920, Gibson Papers, box 8.
52. Castle to Gibson, June 2, 1921; no date; September 22, 1921, Gibson Papers, box 7.
53. Moffat to Gibson, May 18, 1920, Moffat Diaries.
54. Aron Offen to American Ambassador—Warsaw, March 4, 1920, Gibson Papers, box 5; copy also in Moffat Diaries.
55. Moffat to Gibson, May 18, 1920, Moffat Diaries.

A hair-raising formulation of the Gibson-Moffat thesis is contained in the report of an American military observer in Poland, found in the Gibson Papers, box 6.

November 27,1920

To: Director of Military Intelligence, War Department

Subject: Jewish Migration to USA.

It is believed that this Jewish movement to America presents a serious menace to our civilization for the following reasons:

a/ The chief supporters of Bolshevism in Russia are the Jews and many of the Jews who go to the United States are agitators or Bolshevik agents.

b/ A large proportion of our radical agitators in the United States are Russian or Polish Jews and the entrance of this large number of Jews will only increase the number of radicals with whom we will have to contend.

c/ The Lithuanian and Polish Jews are filthy from a sanitary viewpoint. They have none of our ideas of sanitation and are carriers of typhus and other diseases. Their standard of living is very low.

d/ These Jews do not "melt" in the "melting pot" and will, later, form a troublesome racial minority.

e/ These Jews are international in their tendencies and do not strengthen, but rather weaken, our national spirit.

f/ These Jews will settle in cities and will not help cultivate the land, but will form filthy Jewish quarters in American cities.

In this connection, it is interesting to note that, while the desirable emigrants from the scandinavian countries, the British Isles and other parts of Northwestern Europe, members of the great Nordic race which founded and built up our civilization and who settle as small farmers and quickly become good, clean, conservative, hardworking American citizens, willing to fight and, if necessary, die for their adopted country, can get to the United States only with the greatest difficulty and many are refused permission, the way appears to be open for any Polish or Russian Jew who takes a notion to change his place of abode to America.

Viewed from this end, the matter appears to be one which might be investigated with interesting results, and one of great importance to all Americans who are interested in the preservation of the purity of our race and the suppression of any Bolshevistic movement in the United States.

T.W. Hollyday
Major, F.A.
Military Observer

56. *FRUS*, 1919, 2: 797.
57. Moffat to Gibson, May 18, 1920, Moffat Diaries.
58. Gibson to Mrs. Frank Gibson, June 1, 1919, Gibson Papers, family correspondence file.
59. See Gibson's reports in *FRUS*, 1919, 2: 65–69.

60. *FRUS,* 1919, 2: 756–58.
61. Lane Diary, June 1, 1919.
62. *FRUS,* 1919, 2: 749.
63. Lane to Mr. and Mrs. James Lane, June 1, 1919, Lane Papers, box 56a.
64. Lane Diary, June 8, 1919.
65. Dolbeare to Gibson, November 15, 1919; Gibson to Dolbeare, January 23, 1920, Gibson Papers, box 7; Grew to Gibson, October 29, 1919, Gibson Papers, box 7A.
66. Gibson to Mrs. Frank Gibson, May 30, 1919, Gibson Papers, family correspondence file; Gibson to Dolbeare, June 26, 1919, Gibson Papers, box 7; Gibson to Phillips, July 6, 1919, Gibson Papers, box 6.

Chapter 3

1. Heinrichs, *American Ambassador,* pp. 97–98, 106, 123.
2. I. F. Stone interview.
3. Alger Hiss interview.
4. I am indebted to Steven Shuker for these observations.
5. Henry Serrano Villard, *Affairs at State* (New York, 1965), p. 152.
6. Frankfurter Diary, February 25, 1943, Frankfurter Papers, box 2, Library of Congress.
7. This information is taken from Robert Murphy, *Diplomat among Warriors* (New York, 1964), ch. 1.
8. Ibid., p. 28.
9. Ibid., pp. 28, 30.
10. "Something New in Striped Pants," *Saturday Evening Post,* November 12, 1949.
11. William Phillips Diary, March 24, 1924, Houghton Library, Harvard University.
12. George F. Kennan, *Memoirs, 1925–1950* (Boston, 1967), p. 21.
13. Ibid., p. 28.
14. Ibid., pp. 29–30.
15. Ibid., p. 33.
16. Ibid., p. 49.
17. Ibid., p. 46.
18. Ibid., pp. 46–47.
19. Ibid., p. 57.
20. Ibid., p. 68.
21. Lane to Grew, June 26, 1925, Lane Papers.
22. Loy Henderson interview; Elbridge Durbrow interview; Graham H. Stuart, *The Department of State* (New York, 1949), p. 295.
23. Durbrow interview.

24. Charles Bohlen, *Witness to History* (New York, 1973), p. 11.
25. Ibid., p. 10.
26. Michael Forrestal to James Forrestal, April 19, May 22, 1947, Forrestal Papers, box 12, Princeton University.
27. Stone interview.
28. Samuel N. Harper, *The Russia I Believe In* (Chicago, 1945), p. 223.
29. Kennan, *Memoirs,* p. 82.
30. Michael Forrestal to James Forrestal, April 19, 1947, Forrestal Papers.
31. Bohlen, *Witness to History,* pp. 27–29, 85.
32. Don Cook, "Bohlen; Quintessential American Diplomat," *Los Angeles Times;* George Orwell, *The Road to Wigan Pier* (London, 1937).
33. Kennan, *Memoirs,* p. 67.
34. Bohlen adds a characteristic footnote. The purges were social darwinism in reverse, the survival of the stupidest. "Almost all the original Bolshevik leaders, such as Lenin and Trotsky, were men of considerable intellectual attainment. They were products of Western European civilization." Stalin, "purely a Russian-grown product . . . had little connection with the humane values of Western Christian civilization." The purges eliminated the last vestige of "Western-based intellect" in the Communist party. The result was a sharp drop in the IQ of the Soviet leadership. Georgi Malenkov, "a superior brain," was the only exception but "he, too, was basically a product of the West." His successors were right out of the Stone Age. "Khrushchev . . . could hardly be considered a cultivated or a civilized human being. Even less could be said for Leonid Brezhnev and Alexei Kosygin." Bohlen holds out a ray of hope that "in time the Russians can develop superb leaders" (*Witness to History,* p. 155).
35. Kennan, *Memoirs,* pp. 71–72.
36. Ibid., p. 72.
37. Gustav Hilger, *The Incompatible Allies* (New York, 1953), p. 142.
38. Carl E. Schorske, "Two German Ambassadors: Dirksen and Schulenburg," in *The Diplomats, 1919–1939,* ED. Gordon A. Craig and Felix Gilbert (Princeton, N.J., 1953), 2: ch. 15.
39. Kennan, *Memoirs,* pp. 119–23.
40. Moffat Diaries, April 3, 1934.
41. Moffat Diaries, January 1, 1934.
42. James B. Conant, *My Several Lives* (New York, 1970), pp. 140–45.
43. Hooker, *Moffat Papers,* pp. 153, 156.
44. Ibid., p. 183.
45. Ibid., pp. 240, 261.
46. Hugh Wilson, Jr., *A Career Diplomat* (New York, 1960), pp. 38–39, 44–45, 53, 65–66, 68, 80–81, 110–11.
47. See Villard, *Affairs at State,* for a characteristic statement.
48. Hugh Gibson, *The Road to Foreign Policy* (Garden City, N.Y., 1944), p. 10.

49. Ibid., pp. 32, 39, 63.
50. Kennan, *Memoirs,* p. 185.
51. Ibid., pp. 53–54.

Chapter 4

1. Caroline Phillips Journal, May 24, 1934.
2. William Phillips transcript, Columbia Oral History Collection (COHC), p. 104.
3. Caroline Phillips Journal, April 20, 1933.
4. Ibid., November 6, October 23, 1933.
5. Heinrichs, *American Ambassador,* p. 159.
6. Robert Bowers, "Hull, Russian Subversion in Cuba, and Recognition of the U.S.S.R.," *Journal of American History,* December 1966, p. 547.
7. Kennan, *Memoirs,* p. 57.
8. Moffat Diaries, April 12, 1934. See also April 21–22, 1934 for a restatement of the same point.
9. Hooker, *Moffat Papers,* pp. 93–94.
10. Caroline Phillips Journal, April 20, 1933.
11. Raymond Moley, *After Seven Years* (New York, 1939), p. 81.
12. Hooker, *Moffat Papers,* pp. 89–90; On Roosevelt's initial diplomatic appointments, see Frank Freidel, *Launching the New Deal* (Boston, 1973), pp. 355–68.
13. Caroline Phillips Journal, March 1, 1933.
14. Dulles to Gibson, April 20, 1933, Gibson Papers, box 22; Moffat to Gibson, April 30, 1933, Gibson Papers, box 26.
15. Raymond Moley, *The First New Deal* (New York, 1966), p. 455.
16. Moley, *After Seven Years,* p. 116.
17. Freidel, *Launching,* pp. 145–47.
18. Moley, *After Seven Years,* p. 131, 132.
19. Moley, *The First New Deal,* p. 395.
20. Norman Davis to Gibson, March 18, 1933, Gibson Papers, box 1.
21. Gibson to Wilson, April 14, 1933, Gibson Papers, box 30.
22. Gibson to Wilson, April 24, 1933, Gibson Papers, box 30.

Chapter 5

1. Hooker, *Moffat Papers,* p. 103.
2. Durbrow interview.
3. John Carter Vincent interview.
4. *Nation,* August 3, 1946.
5. Moley, *After Seven Years,* p. 116.
6. Herbert Feis, *1933: Characters in Crisis* (Boston, 1966), p. 80.
7. Ibid., pp. 98, 106.

8. Arthur Krock transcript, COHC, p. 39.
9. Feis, *1933*, p. 99.
10. Spruille Braden, *Diplomats and Demagogues* (New Rochelle, N.Y., 1971), p. 115; Freidel, *Launching*, pp. 491–940
11. Durbrow interview.
12. Heinrichs, *American Ambassador*, pp. 185–86; I am grateful to Steven Shuker for some of the ideas in this section.
13. Hull's memoirs are filled with frequent castigation of unnamed "leftists." Taxation for social welfare programs, administrative efforts to improve the lot of southern blacks, and the passage of labor legislation led to the formation of a conservative northern Republican-southern Democrat coalition in the late thirties aimed at stopping the New Deal. See James T. Patterson, *Congressional Conservatism and the New Deal* (Lexington, Mass., 1967).
14. Drew Pearson, "Washington Merry-Go-Round," *Washington Herald*, June 13, 1938.
15. Dunn to Gibson, January 22, 1928, Gibson Papers, box 22.
16. Pearson, "Washington Merry-Go-Round," *Washington Herald*, January 15, 1938.
17. Pearson, "Washington Merry-Go-Round," *Washington Herald*, June 13, 1938.
18. James Dunn interview.
19. Feis, *1933*, pp. 101–2.
20. Cordell Hull, *Memoirs* (New York, 1948), pp. 181–83.
21. Sterling was related to Curzon by marriage and his wife could not bear the thought of social life in Sofia. See Pearson, "Washington Merry-Go-Round," *Washington Herald*, January 4, 1938.
22. Moffat Diaries, February 5, 1934.
23. Edgar B. Nixon, ed., *Franklin D. Roosevelt and Foreign Affairs*, (Cambridge, Mass., 1969), 3: 234, 508–9.
24. Ibid., pp. 310, 314, 497–99.
25. Since Hickerson, unlike Dunn, did not have an independent income, his decision to become a permanent official may possibly have reflected the difficulties of managing an embassy on a Depression-reduced salary. (I am grateful to Ernest May for this suggestion.)

CHAPTER 6

1. Arthur Krock transcript, COHC, pp. 28–29.
2. Ibid., p. 28.
3. Ibid., p. 64.
4. See Krock, COHC, p. 30; Moley, *After Seven Years*, pp. 376–77.
5. Moley, *After Seven Years*, p. 114; Krock, COHC, p. 31.

6. Grace Tully, *F.D.R., My Boss* (New York, 1949), p. 174.
7. Harold Ickes, *The Secret Diary of Harold Ickes* (New York, 1954), 2:568.
8. Krock, COHC, p. 30.
9. Caroline Phillips Journal, October 27, 1933.
10. Braden, *Diplomats and Demagogues,* p. 115.
11. Nixon, ed., *Roosevelt and Foreign Affairs,* 3:442–43.
12. Sources for this sketch are: Edward L. and Frederick H. Schapsmeier, *Henry Wallace of Iowa, the Agrarian Years, 1910–1940* (Ames, Iowa, 1968); Frances Perkins, *The Roosevelt I Knew* (New York, 1946); Robert Sherwood, *Roosevelt and Hopkins* (New York, 1948), chs. 2, 3; Richard O'Connor, *The First Hurrah, a Biography of Alfred E. Smith* (New York, 1970); Matthew and Hannah Josephson, *Al Smith* (New York, 1969); John Morton Blum, *From the Morgenthau Diaries, Years of Crisis, 1928–1938* (Boston, 1959), chs. 4, 5; Harold Ickes, *Autobiography of a Curmudgeon* (New York, 1943); Joseph Lash, *Eleanor and Franklin* (New York, 1971), chs. 27–32.
13. Hubert Herring, "The Department of State," *Harper's,* February 1937.
14. Gibson to Lucy James, March 2, 1937, Gibson Papers, box 1.
15. Lucy James to Gibson, June 13, 1936, Gibson Papers, box 1.
16. Joseph P. Lash, *Eleanor and Franklin* (New York, 1972), p. 742.
17. Bohlen, *Witness,* p. 39.
18. Ibid., p. 44.
19. George Allen interview.
20. Henderson interview.
21. Henderson interview.
22. Bohlen rescued the library and found a home for it in the Library of Congress. Murphy managed to save a considerable portion of his files; they were later turned over to the CIA.
23. Ickes, *Secret Diary,* 2:93.
24. Ibid., pp. 321–22.
25. Ibid., p. 623.
26. Drew Pearson, *Washington Merry-Go Round* (New York, 1931), p. 144.
27. For evidence of Pearson's friendship with Ickes, see Ickes, *Secret Diary,* 2: 292, 640; 3:600.
28. "Washington Merry-Go-Round," *Washington Herald,* April 22, 1938.
29. Ibid., March 31, April 22, April 25, April 30, 1938, *Secret Diary,* 2: 377, 380.
30. Ickes, *Secret Diary,* 2:424.
31. Henry Morgenthau, "The Morgenthau Diaries," *Collier's Magazine,* October 11, 1947.
32. Ickes, *Secret Diary,* 2:676–77.
33. See Zara Steiner, *The Foreign Office and Foreign Policy, 1898–1914* (London, 1969), for a study of the population of Foreign Office professionals who originally introduced the anti-German orientation.

34. Moffat Diaries, July 14, 1941.
35. Ickes, *Secret Diary,* II: 670, 703–5.

CHAPTER 7

1. William Stevenson, *A Man Called Intrepid* (New York, 1976), pp. 315–16.
2. "Morgenthau Diaries," October 11, October 18, 1947.
3. Raymond H. Dawson, *The Decision, to Aid Russia* (Chapel Hill, N.C., 1959), pp. 62–63.
4. Kennan, *Memoirs,* pp. 133–34.
5. Quoted in John Gaddis, *The United States and the Origins of the Cold War* (New York, 1972), p. 5.
6. Paul Appleby transcript, COHC, p. 342.
7. Dawson, *Decision,* pp. 255–56.
8. Davies Diary, October 29, 1942, box 12, Library of Congress.
9. *New Republic,* January 12, 1942.
10. Braden, *Diplomats and Demagogues,* pp. 116–17.
11. Although Roosevelt had asked Hull to take Acheson into the department, the secretary readily assented. (Dean Acheson, *Present at the Creation* [New York, 1969], p. 3.)
12. Acheson, *Present,* p. 17.
13. Benjamin Stolberg, "Acheson of the State Department," *American Mercury,* May 1946.
14. Isaiah Berlin, "Felix Frankfurter at Oxford," in *Felix Frankfurter, A Tribute,* ed. Wallace Mendelson (New York, 1964), pp. 26, 30.
15. Liva Baker, *Felix Frankfurter* (New York, 1969), pp. 15, 36–37, 104.
16. Ibid., pp. 28, 83–84, 165, 169: Lash, *Eleanor and Franklin,1 pp. 731–32.*
17. *Harlan Phillips, Felix Frankfurter Reminisces* (New York, 1960), pp. 1276–77.
18. Baker, *Frankfurter,* pp. 169–73; Phillips, *Frankfurter Reminisces,* pp. 272, 277.
19. Berle Diary, October 10, 1941; Travis Jacobs and Beatrice Berle, eds., *Navigating the Rapids: The Diaries of Adolf Berle* (New York, 1973), p. 342.

    Frankfurter scuttled Fiorello LaGuardia's appointment as secretary of war in 1940. LaGuardia, as Berle's sponsor in New York City politics, automatically became Frankfurter's enemy. LaGuardia was for Berle what Thomas Dewey was for John Foster Dulles—a ticket to the top. Berle had backed LaGuardia for the 1940 Democratic presidential nomination. (Lash, *Eleanor and Franklin,* p. 826.)
20. Joseph P. Lash, *Eleanor Roosevelt: A Friend's Memoir* (New York, 1964), pp. 158–59.
21. State Department Economic Adviser Herbert Feis could have done the

job as well, but he was an old face who lacked the symbolic New Deal connections. His outlook was similar to Acheson's, but Hull needed fresh blood to invigorate the department's image. Feis kept his title but lost his job. He resigned in 1943, crushed between Acheson on one side and Henry Wallace's Board of Economic Warfare on the other. Stimson created a makework job for him to ease the pain.

22. Acheson, *Present,* pp. 3, 27, 47, 740.
23. Jacobs and Berle, eds., *Navigating the Rapids,* p. 358.
24. Appleby transcript, COHC, p. 318.
25. Ibid., p. 318.
26. Acheson, *Present,* p. 38.

Chapter 8

1. All of Appleby's recollections come from Appleby transcript, COHC, pp. 300–318.
2. Mayor Daley operated on the same principles as Hull—he helped those who showed respect. Issues came second. See Mike Royko, *Boss* (New York, 1971).
3. It is not surprising that Atherton and Acheson became close personal friends in the department. See Acheson, *Present,* pp. 115, 238.
4. Acheson, *Present,* p. 43.
5. Ibid.
6. Ibid., p. 36.
7. Murphy, *Diplomat,* p. 182; Sherwood, *Roosevelt and Hopkins,* pp. 676–77.
8. Harold MacMillan, *The Blast of War* (New York, 1967), p. 174.
9. Frankfurter Diary, February 25, 1942.
10. MacMillan, *Blast of War,* p. 201.
11. Murphy, *Diplomat,* pp. 173–75.
12. MacMillan, *Blast of War,* p. 160.
13. William D. Leahy, *I Was There* (New York, 1950), pp. 135, 137.
14. Ibid., p. 136.
15. Ibid., p. 146.
16. Donald Downes, *The Scarlet Thread* (London, 1953), p. 98.
17. Frankfurter Diary, February 25, 1942.
18. Leahy, *I Was There,* p. 100.
19. Frankfurter Diary, February 12, 1943.
20. John M. Blum, *From the Morgenthau Diaries: Years of War, 1941–1945* (Boston, 1967), pp. 148–50.
21. Murphy, *Diplomat,* pp. 171–72.
22. Leahy, *I Was There,* p. 140.
23. I. F. Stone, "Moral Issue for Mr. Hull," *Nation,* January 30, 1943. See also

"Trying to Justify Peyrouton," *New Republic,* February 8, 1943. For Murphy's version, see *Diplomat,* pp. 181–84.

24. *Nation,* April 10, 1943.
25. *Nation,* January 3, 1942.
26. *Nation,* January 30, April 10, 1943.
27. Stone interview.
28. As Murphy delicately expressed it, anti-Semitism in France was "aggravated by the fact that some prominent Communists were Jews, and that a Jewish premier, Leon Blum, was blamed by the French Armed Forces for their own military unpreparedness" (Murphy, *Diplomat,* p. 182).
29. Edgar Mowrer, "Our State Department and North Africa" (Union for Democratic Action pamphlet, 1943).
30. Freda Kirchwey, "The New Axis," *Nation,* March 6, 1943.
31. Blum, *Wallace Diaries,* pp. 151–52, 178.

CHAPTER 9

1. Moffat Diaries, August 24, 1937.
2. *New York Times,* August 22, 1937. Also, May 22, June 8, July 3, July 10, July 18, July 21, August 18, 1937.
3. Moffat Diaries, December 1–4, 1941.
4. See Henry L. Feingold, *The Politics of Rescue* (New Brunswick, N.J., 1970) and David Wyman, *Paper Walls* (Amherst, Mass., 1968).
5. Henderson interview.
6. *FRUS,* 1943, memo Atherton to Welles, June 15, 1943, SD 760C.61/2045.
7. Memo FDR to State Department, June 24, 1943; memo Atherton to Welles, June 24, 1943; memo Welles to Atherton, June 25, 1943, SD 860C.01/643.
8. Mem. con. Halifax-Welles, October 14, 1942; memo Welles to Atherton, October 14, 1942; memo Atherton to Welles (Bohlen draft), October 16, 1942; memo Welles to Atherton, October 17, 1942; memo Atherton to Welles (Bohlen draft), October 23, 1942, SD 861.404/485. Also *FRUS* (1942), 3: 470–71.
9. Letter Taylor to Welles, December 22, 1942; memo Bohlen to Atherton, December 24, 1942, SD 861.404/487.
10. Henderson interview.
11. Davies Diary, October 29, 30, 1942.
12. Henderson interview; Durbrow interview.
13. *FRUS* (1943), 3: 833; Henderson interview.
14. Henderson interview.
15. Ibid.

16. Davies Diary, March 12, 13, 1943; also Sherwood, *Roosevelt and Hopkins,* pp. 733–34.
17. Davies Diary, March 14, 1943, May 12, 1943. Davies found Dreyfus "an able man."
18. Sherwood, *Roosevelt and Hopkins,* p. 734.
19. City machine Democrats chuckled at Hopkins's idea of how to play politics—hand out a few patronage jobs and then expect automatic compliance with all White House requests. Hopkins's protegé Averell Harriman likened the Russian political system to that of a city boss backed up by the strong arm of the police. If Hopkins thought the same way, was the Henderson ouster a form of negative patronage for Boss Stalin—firing an enemy as opposed to hiring a friend? (Blum, *Wallace Diaries,* pp. 392–93.)
20. Henderson interview; Durbrow interview; Bohlen, *Witness,* pp. 124–25.
21. Memo Murphy to Henderson, June 29, 1942, SD 861.20211/175.
22. *New York Times,* June 25, 1943.
23. Memo K. Tolley to Capt. Smedberg, February 26, 1946, Forrestal Papers, box 24.
24. Lash, *Eleanor Roosevelt,* p. 86.
25. Acheson, *Present,* pp. 238–39.
26. Murphy, *Diplomat,* p. 48.
27. I. F. Stone, "The President and Sumner Welles," *Nation,* September 4, 1943.
28. Memo Stettinius to G. Howland Shaw, October 18, 1943; Stettinius Papers, box 215, University of Virginia Library.
29. Robert Lynch interview.
30. Appleby transcript, COHC, p. 303.
31. Archibald MacLeish interview.
32. Appleby transcript, COHC, p. 304.
33. Vincent interview.
34. Dunn interview.
35. Sherwood, *Roosevelt and Hopkins,* p. 757.
36. Durbrow interview.
37. I. F. Stone, "Stettinius and State," *Nation,* October 9, 1943.
38. Calendar Notes, Stettinius Papers, box 237.
39. Roosevelt to Hull, December 23, 1943; Roosevelt to Hull, December 4, 1943; Hull to Roosevelt, December 6, 1943, Hull Papers, box 53, Library of Congress; Winant to Hull, December 15, 1943, FRUS (1943), I: 809; Calendar Notes, January 31, February 1, 1944, Stettinius Papers, box 239; Henderson interview.
40. Calendar Notes, October 6, November 27, 1943, Stettinius Papers.
41. Stettinius to Roosevelt, February 21, 1944, Stettinius Papers.

42. Ray Brecht Report, November 29, 1944; John Metcalfe Report, November 29, 1944, *Time* Reports, Houghten Library, Harvard University.
43. Memo Stettinius, Dunn, Shaw, Hachworth to Hull, "Proposed Organization Plan of the Department," December 8, 1943, Stettinius Papers, box 394; "Notes on First Meeting of Reorganization Plan," November 29, 1943, Stettinius Papers, box 394; Memo Stettinius to FDR (not sent), February 22, 1944, Stettinius Papers, box 238; *New York Times,* January 16, February 10, 1944; W. C. Laves and Francis Wilcox, "The Reorganization of the Department of State," *American Political Science Review,* April 1944.
44. Joseph Ballantine transcript, COHC, pp. 50, 53.
45. Vincent interview; *Biographic Register of the Department of State,* October 1, 1945; Hornbeck Autobiography, pp. 346–48, Hornbeck Papers, box 497, Hoover Institute, Stanford; "Notes on Fourth Meeting on Reorganization Plan," December 2, 1943, Stettinius Papers, box 394.

CHAPTER 10

1. Memo Byrnes to Roosevelt, September 3, 1943, President's Secretary File, Franklin D. Roosevelt Library (FDRL).
2. Vincent interview.
3. Mem. con. Louis Fischer-Hull, January 19, 1944, Fischer Papers, FDRL.
4. Henderson interview.
5. Mem. con. Fischer-Hull.
6. Metcalfe Report, December 31, 1943, *Time* Reports.
7. Mem. con. Fischer-Hull.
8. Durbrow interview.
9. Sherwood, *Roosevelt and Hopkins,* p. 757.
10. Durbrow interview.
11. Kennan, *Memoirs,* p. 130.
12. Bohlen, *Witness,* p. 8.
13. Ibid., pp. 12, 40, 57–58, 125.
14. Durbrow interview; Henderson interview; Ben Cohen interview.
15. Bohlen, *Witness,* pp. 125–26, 160, 164, 176, 177.
16. Ibid., pp. 121, 135.
17. Durbrow interview.
18. Durbrow interview; *FRUS* (1943), 3: 722–23.
19. Memo Dubrow to Jones, Matthews, Atherton, Dunn, November 9, 1943, SD 865.00B/50.
20. *FRUS* (1944), 4: 813–19. Similarly, *FRUS* (1943), 3: 372–73, 459–60, 584.

Chapter 11

1. See George Kennan, *The Decision to Intervene* (Princeton, N.J., 1958), for a description of Poole's activities in the American consulate in Russia during the chaotic months after the October revolution.
2. Memo Cecil W. Barnes to Poole, February 9, 1943, FNB Correspondence, 1941–45, OSS Records, National Archives; DeWitt C. Poole, "The Study of Foreign Political Developments in the United States" (Poole Report), December 31, 1944, SD 711.00/2–545.
3. Poole Report, pp. 11–12.
4. Poole Report, pp. 14–15; Professor Robert Reynolds, "European Minorities as American Majorities," March 1, 1943, FNB Correspondence, 1941–45, OSS Records.
5. "The USSR and Foreign Nationality Groups in the United States," February 27, 1943, FNB Correspondence, box 1, OSS Records.
6. Poole Report, p. 23; memo Poole to Davies.
7. "The Reverend Stanislaus Orlemanski," FN Number 13–166, March 10, 1944, Jonathan Daniels Papers, box 31, folder 459, University of North Carolina, Chapel Hill.
8. Roosevelt press conference, May 9, 1944, pp. 12–13.
9. Mem. con. Orlemanski-Poole, May 17, 1944, Daniels Papers, box 31, folder 467.
10. Memo Berle to Shaw, Dunn, Bohlen, May 20, 1944, SD 760C.61/2331.
11. Durbrow interview.
12. Roosevelt to Hull, May 31, 1944; Hull to Roosevelt, June 2, 1944, SD 760C.61/2334.
13. Stettinius to Matthews, June 14, 1944, Stettinius Papers, box 216; Jan Ciechanowski, *Defeat in Victory,* (Garden City, N.Y., 1947), pp. 308–9.
14. Mem. con. Poole and Durbrow, August 24, 1943, SD 860C.00/924 1/2.
15. "Poland and the USSR," January 20, 1944, SD 760C.61/2235. Memo A. H. Kulikowski to Alan Cranston, "Polish Problem," January 25, 1944, *Amerasia Papers,* p. 341.
16. Daniels Diary, May 13, October 25, 1942, Daniels Papers, box 29.
17. Josephus Daniels to Jonathan Daniels, May 28, 1943, Daniels Papers, box 29.
18. These included Isador Lubin (White House staff), Oscar Chapman (Interior), Aubrey Williams (Wallace aide), Abe Fortas (Interior), Mordecai Ezekiel, Paul Porter (DNC), Ed Pritchard (OWMR), Harry White (Treasury). Also Lauchlin Currie (White House staff), Wayne Coy (Lend-Lease), Dave Niles (White House staff), Paul Appleby (Agriculture), Ben Cohen (OWMR), Bob Nathan, Michael Strauss, Randolph Paul.

19. Daniels Diary, November 25, 1942, June 28, 1944, Daniels Papers, box 29, 33 (folder 489).
20. Daniels to McIntyre, May 8, 1943, Daniels Papers, box 29; "Polish Politics in the U.S.," December 5, 1942, OSS (FN) #25320, December 21, 1942, OSS (FN) #25787.
21. Davies Diary, April 28, May 26, 1943, Davies Papers, box 13.
22. Davies Diary, April 30, 1943, Davies Papers, box 13, 14.
23. Roosevelt to State Department, June 24, 1943; Atherton to Welles, June 24, 1943; Welles to Atherton, June 25, 1943; Welles to Roosevelt, June 29, 1943, SD 860C.01/643.
24. Harry Hopkins, like his boss, was not averse to deflecting criticism from the White House to the State Department. When the Polish foreign minister asked for an unequivocal statement of opposition to Soviet territorial demands, Hopkins demurred. He couldn't "interfere" in such matters. "I never encroach upon matters within the competence of the Department of State," he said—and then broke out laughing. One can imagine that Hopkins and FDR shared many a late-night joke at the department's expense. All unpopular actions were laid at Hull's door.
25. Stettinius Calendar Notes, February 11, February 18, 1944, Stettinius Papers, box 239; Stettinius to Dunn, February 19, 1944, Stettinius Papers, box 216; Matthews to Stettinius, February 15, 1944, SD 860C.00/2–1544; Bohlen to Stettinius, February 17, 1944, SD 760C.61/2232; Stettinius to Roosevelt, February 18, 1944, ibid.; Ciechanowski, *Defeat in Victory*, p. 274.
26. F. C. Gowen to Fullerton, April 12, 1944, SD 760C.61/2287; Daniels Diary, May 16, 1944, Daniels Papers, box 33, folder 489; Richard Neustadt interview.
27. Daniels to Roosevelt, June 2, 1944, Daniels Papers, box 32, folder 469; Lubin to Roosevelt, "Polish Propaganda in the U.S.," June 5, 1944, PSF: Poland, January-June, 1944, FDRL; Niles to Tully, June 6, 1944, ibid.
28. Ciechanowski, *Defeat in Victory*, pp. 293–94.
29. *FRUS* (1944), 3: 1307, 1432; SD 760C.61/8–1444.
30. *FRUS* (1944), 3: 1328–30; memo Stettinius to Roosevelt, October 28, 1944, SD 760C.61/10–2844; Calendar Notes, October 30, 1944, Stettinius Papers, box 242.
31. Davies Diary, November 20, 1944, Davies Papers, box 15.

CHAPTER 12

1. Davies Diary, September 25, October 2, October 6, 1943, Davies Papers, box 14; memo Davies to Roosevelt, May 17, 1944, ibid.
2. Wallace Diary, May 9, October 6, 1944; Davies Diary, June 10, 1944.
3. Davies Diary, November 26, October 13, 1944, January 22, 1945.

4. Vincent interview. The Grew appointment, despite Vincent's explanation, remains a mystery. Did Roosevelt or Hopkins consider him a paper tiger by this stage? (He was sixty-four.) Was it just a slip-up? The appointment of Charles Bohlen as White House liaison officer is similarly ambiguous. According to Bohlen's account, Hopkins wanted State Department "expertise" to contribute to the consideration of postwar problems. Bohlen may have appeared in Hopkins's mind as a simpler device than Sumner Welles for Roosevelt to get what he wanted out of the State Department machine. Stettinius, a tame rabbit, could sit there and look pretty. Hopkins would use Bohlen to monitor and prod the machine as necessary. Just what Roosevelt and Hopkins had in mind is unclear. In the end, especially after Roosevelt's death and Hopkins's departure, Bohlen became an FSO emissary to the White House. See Bohlen, *Witness,* pp. 165–66; Neustadt interview.
5. *Washington Post,* December 20, 1944; "Toward Imperialism," *Nation,* December 30, 1944.
6. Acheson, *Present,* p. 89; Calendar Notes, November 29, 1944, Stettinius Papers, box 242; memo John Ross to Robert Lynch, December 19, 1944, Stettinius Papers, box 394.
7. Adolf Berle interview; Blum, *Wallace Diaries,* p. 173; MacLeish interview; Frankfurter Diary, January 24, 1943, Frankfurter Papers, box 2.
8. Berle interview; Willard Thorpe interview; MacLeish interview; Wallace Diary, January 12, 1945.
9. *New York Times,* December 6, 1944; I. F. Stone, "New Front, Old Firm," *Nation,* December 16, 1944.
10. *Nation,* December 16, 1944; Stone, "Only the Fig Leaf," *Nation,* December 23, 1944.
11. Eleanor to Franklin, December 4, 1944, in Lash, *Eleanor and Franklin,* p. 918.
12. Stone, "Millionaires' Club," *Nation,* December 9, 1944.
13. Blum, *Morgenthau Diaries, 1941–1945,* p. 353; *Washington Post,* December 29, 1944.
14. Henry Morgenthau, "Presidential Diary," FDRL. An abbreviated account is in Blum, *Morgenthau Diaries, 1941–1945,* pp. 417–18.
15. Lash, *Eleanor and Franklin,* p. 920; *Washington Post,* December 21, 1944.
16. Hiss interview; Dunn interview.

Chapter 13

1. Dunn interview; MacLeish to Daniels, September 15, 1948, Daniels Papers, box 42; Tyler Abell, ed., *Drew Pearson Diaries, 1949–1959* (New York, 1974), p. 341; Wallace Diaries, January 21, 1945.

2. Policy Committee Document A-B/1, "Principal Problems in Europe," by Adolf Berle, September 26, 1944; SD lot 60D224, box 6; "Berle at Reading," April 10, 1943, *Time* Reports.
3. *FRUS*, 1944, 4: 1025–26.
4. Letter Leland Morris to Wallace Murray, December 30, 1944, SD 711.-61/12–3–44.
5. Letter Murray to Morris, February 9, 1945, SD 711.61/12–30–44.
6. London Cable 2659, February 3, 1945, Stoyan Pribichevich to David Hulburd, *Time* Reports; Staff Committee Minutes, July 5, 1945, SD lot 122, box 58.
7. John Scott Cable 11, January 24, 1946, *Time* Reports.
8. "The U.S. Foreign Service," *Fortune*, July 1946.
9. Bill Lawrence, *Six Presidents, Too Many Wars* (New York, 1972), pp. 144–47.
10. PC #55, June 8, 1944, SD lot 60D224, box 6.
11. *FRUS*, 1944, 3: 499.
12. *FRUS*, 1945, 4: 191.
13. *FRUS*, 1945, 4: 155–56; I have profited from a seminar paper written for Ernest May by Wayne R. Strasbaugh, "The Origins of the Cold War: Bulgaria, a Case Study."
14. *FRUS*, 4: 1944; *FRUS*, 5: 1945; See Ernest May, *"Lessons" of the Past* (New York, 1973), ch. 2, for an excellent survey of American diplomatic reporting in early 1945.
15. James F. Byrnes, *Speaking Frankly* (London, 1947), p. 331; Herbert Feis, *Churchill, Roosevelt, and Stalin* (Princeton, N.J., 1957), p. 549; Diane Clemens, *Yalta* (New York, 1970), pp. 262–64.
16. Lord Gladwyn, *The Memoirs of Lord Gladwyn* (London, 1973), pp. 129, 155–56.
17. DS 740.0011 EW/2–2045.
18. SD 740.0011 EW/2–2045, Barnes to Secretary of State, February 20, 1945.
19. *FRUS*, 1945, 4: 168; Staff Committee Minutes, February 22, 1945, State Department Records, lot 122, box 58; *FRUS*, 1945, 4: 171.

CHAPTER 14

1. Pasvolsky, wrote a *Time* reporter, "is one of the most unusual looking men in Washington. He looks like an ostrich egg with a billiard ball on top of it. His pate is likewise billiard ball. His face is moon-round and his myopic eyes look on the world through thick lenses encircled by thick black horn rims" ("Leo Pasvolsky Quits," March 16, 1946, *Time* Reports).
2. Letter to author, August 13, 1969.
3. Memo Pasvolsky to Byrnes, October 23, 1945, SD 711.00/10–2745.
4. Letter to author, August 13, 1969.

5. All of Vernon's comments in this section are from an interview on September 30, 1969.
6. On Clayton, see Frederick J. Dobney, ed., *Selected Papers of Will Clayton* (Baltimore, 1971).
7. "Roosevelt's Harem," January 4, 1945, *Time* Reports.
8. Thorp's comments are from an interview at his Amherst home on September 25, 1969.
9. Ballantine transcript, COHC, pp. 59,221.
10. "U.S. Foreign Service," *Fortune,* p. 202.
11. William Phillips transcript, COHC; Staff Committee (SC) Minutes, April 16, 1945, SD lot 122, box 58.
12. John Jay Iselin, "The Truman Doctrine," Ph.D. dissertation, Harvard University, 1965, p. 180.
13. Henderson interview.
14. SC Minutes, March 23, 1945, SD lot 122, box 58.
15. Raymond Thurston interview.
16. Henderson interview.
17. SC Minutes, May 1, April 4, May 19, 1945, SD lot 122, box 58.
18. SC Minutes, May 21, 1945; Mem. cn. Raymond Swing-Bohlen-MacLeish, May 22, 1945, SD 711.61/5–2245; mem. cn. MacLeish-Lippmann, May 23, 1945, memo MacLeish to Grew, May 26, 1945, SD 711.61/5–2345; memo MacLeish to Grew, May 26, 1945, SD 711.61/5–2645; letter MacLeish to Wilfred Lumen, May 31, 1945, SD 711.61/5–2945.
19. Vincent interview; Acheson, *Present,* pp. 112–13.
20. All of Vincent's comments from Vincent interview.
21. Walter Millis, ed., *Forrestal Diaries* (New York, 1951), pp. 90–91.
22. Ballantine transcript, COHC, p. 219.
23. Ibid., pp. 50–51.
24. Ibid., p. 30.
25. Ibid., p. 218.
26. Vincent interview.
27. SC Minutes, April 22, 1945, SD lot 122, box 58; Summaries of SC meetings, April 24, 1945, SD lot 60D 224, box 6.
28. This episode is described in a letter from Moffat to Vincent, November 5, 1971.

Chapter 15

1. Gaddis, *Origins of the Cold War,* p. 199.
2. Allen interview.
3. *Wallace Diaries,* p. 451; Gaddis, *Origins of the Cold War,* p. 230.
4. Charles S. Maier, "Revisionism and the Interpretation of Cold War Origins," *Perspectives in American History* (1970).

5. Davies Diary, April 30, 1945.
6. Vincent interview.
7. Dunn interview.
8. Davies Diary, July 21, 1945.
9. Abell, ed., *Pearson Diaries,* p. 26.
10. Blum, *Wallace Diaries,* p. 437.
11. Harold Smith Diary, April 26, 1945, Harry S. Truman Library (HSTL).
12. Appleby transcript, COHC, p. 353.
13. Morgenthau Presidential Diary, April 27, 1945.
14. Smith Diary, April 26, 1945; *Detroit Free Press,* December 28, 1945.
15. Daniels interview with Truman, Daniels Papers; Morgenthau Presidential Diary, June 6, 1945; *Pearson Diaries,* pp. 201, 234; Neustadt interview.
16. Blum, *Wallace Diaries,* p. 465.
17. Abell, ed., *Pearson Diaries,* pp. 11, 49.
18. Stone interview.
19. I. F. Stone, *In a Time of Torment* (New York, 1968), p. 437.
20. Joseph Baldwin transcript, COHC, p. 44.

CHAPTER 16

1. Lynch interview.
2. Stettinius interview, October 10, 1948, Stettinius Papers, box 876.
3. Allen interview; Neustadt interview.
4. Lynch interview; mem. con. Hull-Stettinius, June 6, 1945, Stettinius Papers, box 238.
5. Appleby transcript, COHC, p. 234.
6. Blum, *Morgenthau Diaries, 1941–1945,* p. 70.
7. Appleby transcript, COHC, pp. 234, 240.
8. Blum, *Morgenthau Diaries, 1941–1945,* p. 424.
9. Ibid., pp. 46–71.
10. Davies Diary, September 6, 1946, Davies Papers, box 24; Stanley Surrey interview.
11. Alsop interview; Smith Diary, July 6, September 18, 1945; Vincent interview.
12. *Washington Post,* December 31, 1945.
13. Gaddis, *Origins of the Cold War,* p. 285; Cohen interview.
14. Cohen interview; Blum, *Wallace Diaries,* p. 475.
15. Stone interview.
16. Cohen interview.
17. Durbrow interview.
18. Cohen interview.
19. Dunn interview. Byrnes developed considerable affection for Dunn.

After the peace treaties were in hand, he took pleasure in appointing Dunn as ambassador to Italy.

20. Cohen interview; Acheson, *Present,* pp. 114–21.
21. Acheson to Frankfurter, August 20, 1945, Frankfurter Papers, box 19.
22. I. F. Stone, "Shake-up in the State Department," *Nation,* August 25, 1945. Also, "The State Department Reorganization," *Nation,* September 15, 1945.
23. *New Republic,* August 27, 1945; Benjamin Stolberg, "Acheson of the State Department," *American Mercury,* May 1946.
24. Acheson, *Present,* pp. 47, 120; Vincent interview.
25. Vincent interview.
26. Smith Diary, September 13, 1945.
27. H. Stuart Hughes, "The Second Year of the Cold War," *Commentary,* August 1969, p. 30. Hughes argued in a memo written in 1947 that the destruction of Ferme Nagy's Smallholders' party in Hungary was a "routine and anticipated move on the part of the USSR to plug an obvious gap in its security system." And he added "The enunciation of the Truman Doctrine accelerated the process," as did "The removal of the Communist ministers from the governments of France and Italy. . . ."
28. "The Capabilities and Intentions of the Soviet Union as Affected by American Policy," paper by Geroid T. Robinson for Charles E. Bohlen, December 10, 1945, SD 711.61/12–1045.
29. For accounts of participants, see Acheson, *Present,* pp. 167–73; Braden, *Diplomats and Demagogues,* pp. 346–50; Winthrop McCormack, "The State Department Loses the Lead in National Intelligence, 1945–46," Honors thesis, Harvard University, 1967.

    In a letter to Byrnes, Acheson described McCormack's responsibilities in this way:

> The Special Assistant and his organization would be responsible for the collection, evaluation and dissemination of all information regarding foreign nations. These functions are now spread throughout the Department. To unite them in one organization, which would become the Department's encyclopedia, would free the operating offices of the intelligence function and thus relieve them of a very considerable burden. Intelligence would furnish the data upon which the operating offices would determine our policy and our actions. (McCormack, "State Department," p. 50)

30. Henderson interview.
31. H. Stuart Hughes interview.
32. Cora Dubois interview.

33. Hughes interview.
34. Vincent interview.
35. Hughes interview.
36. Acheson, *Present,* p. 162.
37. Vincent interview.
38. Vincent interview; Charles Kindleberger interview.
39. John Paton Davies interview.
40. Dunn interview.
41. "Communist Fronts," October 25, 1946, *Time* Reports.
42. Abell, ed., *Pearson Diaries,* p. 314.
43. Braden, *Diplomats and Demagogues,* p. 351.
44. See Harold Stein, "The Foreign Service Act of 1946," in Harold Stein, ed., *Public Administration and Policy Development* (New York, 1952).
45. Ibid., p. 710.

CHAPTER 17

1. Gaddis, *Origins of the Cold War,* pp. 275–76; Arthur Krock interview with Truman, April 7, 1948, Krock Papers, Princeton University; Blum, *Wallace Diaries,* p. 490; William D. Leahy Diary, November 7, 1945 Library of Congress; Caffrey to Secretary of State, November 12, 1945, SD 861.00/11–1245; Truman to Byrnes, November 24, 1945, SD 861.00/11–2445.
2. Davies Diary, February 9, 1946, Davies Papers, box 23.
3. Leahy Diary, August 14, 1945.
4. Kennan, *Memoirs,* pp. 156–62.
5. Leahy Diary, September 25, December 27, 1945; February 13, February 21, 1946; Alsop column, *New York Herald Tribune,* March 1, 1946.
6. Truman, *Memoirs* (New York, 1958), 2: 58; *Washington Post,* March 1, 1946.
7. Neustadt interview.
8. "Roosevelt's Harem," January 4, 1945, *Time* Reports.
9. Leahy Diary, December 26, 1945.
10. Ibid., December 28, 1945.
11. *Washington Post,* February 12, March 9, 1946.
12. Joseph Alsop interview. Acheson circumspectly wrote in his memoirs about Byrnes's successor: "General Marshall was meticulous that when the door to his aircraft closed, the command passed. . . . Mr. Byrnes was inclined occasionally . . . to give us instructions while he was away from Washington. . . . The Marshall procedure seemed better to me." Anxious to take command of the department in Byrnes's absence, Acheson bridled when Byrnes left him in a vacuum, unwilling to delegate authority to run the department in his absence. The OSS humiliation was one

result. After four years of frustration under Hull, Acheson's enthusiasm at finally occupying a position of line authority dissipated in frustration. Although in most circumstances, the undersecretary automatically deals with the president in the secretary's absence, Byrnes did not wish this. Acheson stretched this formal prerogative because of the way Byrnes treated him. See Acheson, *Present*, p. 138.

13. "Summary of Staff Committee Meeting, May 9, 1945, SD lot 60D224, box 6; "Washington Memo," March 6, 1946, "British Loan," July 5, 1946, *Time* Reports; Morgenthau Presidential Diary, March 2, 1946; Davies Journal, March 15, 1946; Vincent interview; Blum, *Wallace Diaries*, pp. 526–27.
14. Blum, *Wallace Diaries*, pp. 556–57.
15. "Russian Loan Talks," April 26, 1946, "British Loan," July 5, 1946, *Time* Reports.
16. Frankfurter Diary, October 21, 1946; Acheson, *Present*, pp. 187–90, 328; Braden, *Diplomats and Demagogues*, pp. 356–70.
17. *U.S. News and World Report*, February 7, 1947.
18. Frankfurter Diary, October 15, 1946. Acheson and Frankfurter delighted in finding people second-rate. The impulse came straight from Holmes, who had commented on FDR, "A second-class intellect—but a firstclass temperament."
19. See Frankfurter Diary, October 15, 1946, for one instance of commiseration.
20. Smith Diary, December 5, 1945.
21. Truman, *Memoirs*, 1: 551–52; Henderson interview.
22. See Thomas Platt, "The Iranian Crisis and the Origins of the Cold War," Honors thesis, Harvard University, 1970, for a detailed study of the Iranian crisis.
23. Henderson interview; Alsop column, February 17, 1946, *Washington Post.*
24. FRUS, 1946, 7: 340–48; *Newsweek*, March 25, 1946; *New York Times*, March 13, 1946.
25. *New York Times*, March 9, 1946.
26. FRUS, 1946, 7: 306–9, 359; *U.S. News and World Report*, March 15, 1946; Arthur Krock columns, *New York Times*, March 18, 21, 1946.
27. Lincoln Bloomfield interview.
28. Ibid.
29. Platt, "Iranian Crisis," pp. 129–32; Trygve Lie, *In the Cause of Peace* (New York, 1954), pp. 75–76, 80, 85–86.
30. FRUS, 1946, 7: 390.
31. Herbert Feis, *From Trust to Terror*, (New York, 1970), p. 186.
32. *New York Times*, March 14, 1946.
33. *New York Times*, March 15, 20, 1946.
34. Henderson interview; Iselin, "The Truman Doctrine," pp. 158–62, 180–81.

35. Mem. con. Krock-Baruch, March 25, 1947, Krock Papers; Iselin, "Truman Doctrine," p. 195; Henderson interview.
36. Reston memo, undated; Krock Papers.
37. Thorp interview.
38. Dean Acheson, "Thoughts about Thought in High Places," *New York Times Magazine,* October 11, 1959.

BIBLIOGRAPHY

Archives and Manuscript Collections

Alsop, Joseph, and Stewart Alsop. Library of Congress. Washington, D.C.
Appleby, Paul. Columbia Oral History Collection. New York, N.Y.
Baldwin, Joseph. Columbia Oral History Collection. New York, N.Y.
Ballantine, Joseph. Columbia Oral History Collection. New York, N.Y.
Daniels, Jonathan. University of North Carolina Library. Chapel Hill, N.C.
Davies, Joseph. Library of Congress. Washington, D.C.
Fischer, Louis. Franklin D. Roosevelt Library. Hyde Park, N.Y.
Forrestal, James. Princeton University Library. Princeton, N.J.
Frankfurter, Felix. Library of Congress. Washington, D.C.
Gibson, Hugh. Hoover Institute, Stanford University. Palo Alto, Ca.
Grew, Joseph. Houghton Library, Harvard University. Cambridge, Mass.
Hornbeck, Stanley. Hoover Institute, Stanford University. Palo Alto, Ca.
Hull, Cordell. Library of Congress. Washington, D.C.
Krock, Arthur. Columbia Oral History Collection. New York, N.Y.
——. Princeton University Library. Princeton, N.J.
Lane, Arthur Bliss. Yale University Library. New Haven, Conn.
Leahy, William D. Library of Congress. Washington, D.C.
Messersmith, George. University of Delaware Library. Wilmington, Del.
Moffat, Jay Pierrepont. Houghton Library, Harvard University. Cambridge, Mass.

Morgenthau, Henry. Franklin D. Roosevelt Library. Hyde Park, N.Y.
Niles, David. Brandeis University Library. Waltham, Mass.
Office of Strategic Services (OSS). National Archives. Washington, D.C.
Phillips, Caroline. In possession of family.
Phillips, William. Columbia Oral History Collection. New York, N.Y.
——. Houghton Library, Harvard University. Cambridge, Mass.
Roosevelt, Franklin D. Franklin D. Roosevelt Library. Hyde Park, N.Y.
Smith, Harold. Harry S. Truman Library. Independence, Mo.
Stettinius, Edward. University of Virginia Library. Charlottesville, Va.
Time Reports. Houghton Library, Harvard University. Cambridge, Mass.
U.S. Department of State Archives, 1941–45. National Archives. Washington, D.C.

INTERVIEWS (1969–70)

George Allen
Joseph Alsop
Adolf Berle
Lincoln Bloomfield
Benjamin V. Cohen
John Paton Davies
Cora Dubois
James Clement Dunn
Elbridge Durbrow
James Farley
Loy Henderson
Alger Hiss
H. Stuart Hughes
Charles Kindleberger
William L. Langer
Robert Lynch
Archibald MacLeish
Richard E. Neustadt
Samuel Rosenman
Arthur Schlesinger, Jr
Raymond Sontag
I. F. Stone
Stanley Surrey
Willard Throp
Raymond Thurston
Raymond Vernon
John Carter Vincent
Benjamin Welles

UNPUBLISHED MATERIAL

Iselin, John Jay. "The Truman Doctrine." Ph.D. dissertation, Harvard University, 1965.
Mayes, Edythe Beam, ed.. "Room 474: Posthumous Memoirs of Leroy H. Mayes." In private possession.
McCormack, Winthrop. "The State Department Loses the Lead in National Intelligence, 1945–1946." Honors thesis, Harvard University, 1967.
Strasbaugh, Wayne R. "The Origins of the Cold War: Bulgaria, a Case Study." Harvard Seminar Paper, 1971.

Published Material

Abell, Tyler, ed. *Drew Pearson Diaries, 1949–1959.* New York, 1974.

Acheson, Dean. *Present at the Creation.* New York, 1969.

Baker, Liva. *Felix Frankfurter.* New York, 1969.

Bendiner, Robert. *The Riddle of the State Department.* New York, 1942.

Berlin, Isaiah. "Felix Frankfurter at Oxford." In *Felix Frankfurter, a Tribute,* edited by Wallace Mendelson. New York, 1964.

Biographic Register of the Department of State. October 1, 1945.

Blum, John Morton. *From the Morgenthau Diaries: Years of Crisis, 1928–1938.* Boston, 1959.

———. *From the Morgenthau Diaries: Years of War, 1941–1945.* Boston, 1967.

———. *The Price of Vision: The Diaries of Henry Wallace, 1942–1946.* New York, 1973.

Bohlen, Charles. *Witness to History.* New York, 1973.

Bowers, Robert. "Hull, Russian Subversion in Cuba, and Recognition of the U.S.S.R." *Journal of American History,* December 1966.

Braden, Spruille. *Diplomats and Demagogues.* New Rochelle, N.Y., 1971.

Byrnes, James F. *Speaking Frankly.* London, 1947.

Ciechanowski, Jan. *Defeat in Victory.* Garden City, N.Y., 1947.

Clemens, Diane. *Yalta.* New York, 1970.

Conant, James B. *My Several Lives.* New York, 1970.

Craig, Gordon A., and Felix Gilbert, eds. *The Diplomats, 1919–1939.* Princeton, N.J., 1953.

Crawford, Kenneth. *Report on North Africa.* New York, 1943.

Dawson, Raymond H. *The Decision to Aid Russia, 1941.* Chapel Hill, N.C., 1959.

Dobney, Frederick J., ed. *Selected Papers of Will Clayton.* Baltimore, 1971.

Downes, Donald. *The Scarlet Thread.* London, 1953.

Feiling, Keith. *Life of Neville Chamberlain.* London, 1947.

Feingold, Henry L. *The Politics of Rescue.* New Brunswick, N.J., 1970.

Feis, Herbert. *Churchill, Roosevelt, and Stalin.* Princeton, N.J., 1957.

———. *1933: Characters in Crisis.* Boston, 1966.

———. *The Birth of Israel.* New York, 1969.

———. *From Trust to Terror: The Onset of the Cold War, 1945–50.* New York, 1970.

Fischer, Louis. *The Soviets in World Affairs,* vol. 1. London, 1930.

Freidel, Frank. *Launching the New Deal.* Boston, 1973.

Gaddis, John. *The United States and the Origins of the Cold War.* New York, 1972.

Gibson, Hugh. *The Road to Foreign Policy.* Garden City, N.Y., 1944.

"Gibson Scans the Road to Disarmament." *New York Times Magazine,* June 21, 1931.

Gladwyn, Lord. *The Memoirs of Lord Gladwyn.* London, 1973.

Gosset, Renée. *Conspiracy in Algiers.* New York, 1945.
Grafton, Samuel. *An American Diary.* New York, 1943.
Grew, Joseph. *Turbulent Era.* New York, 1952.
Harper, Samuel N. *The Russia I Believe In.* Chicago, 1945.
Heinrichs, Waldo. *American Ambassador.* Boston, 1966.
Herring, Hubert. "The Department of State." *Harper's,* February 1937.
Hilger, Gustav. *The Incompatible Allies.* New York, 1953.
Hooker, Nancy Harvison. *The Moffat Papers.* Cambridge, Mass., 1956.
Hughes, H. Stuart. "The Second Year of the Cold War." *Commentary,* August 1969.
Hull, Cordell. *Memoirs.* New York, 1948.
Ickes, Harold. *The Secret Diary of Harold Ickes.* New York, 1954.
Israel, Fred L., ed. *The War Diary of Breckinridge Long.* Lincoln, Nebraska, 1966.
Jacobs, Travis, and Beatrice Berle, eds. *Navigating the Rapids: The Diaries of Adolf Berle.* New York, 1973.
Kennan, George F. *The Decision to Intervene.* Princeton, N.J., 1958.
——. *Memoirs, 1925–1950.* Boston, 1967.
Kirchwey, Freda. "The New Axis." *Nation,* March 6, 1943.
Lash, Joseph P. *Eleanor Roosevelt, A Friend's Memoir.* New York, 1964.
——. *Eleanor and Franklin.* New York, 1971.
Laves, W. C., and Francis Wilcox. "The Reorganization of the Department of State." *American Political Science Review,* April 1944.
Lawrence, Bill. *Six Presidents, Too Many Wars.* New York, 1972.
Leahy, William D. *I Was There.* New York, 1950.
MacMillan, Harold. *The Blast of War.* New York, 1967.
May, Ernest R. "An American Tradition in Foreign Affairs." In *The Historian and the Diplomat,* edited by Francis Loewenheim, New York, 1967.
——. *"Lessons" of the Past.* New York, 1973.
Millis, Walter, ed. *Forrestal Diaries.* New York, 1951.
Moley, Raymond. *After Seven Years.* New York, 1939.
——. *The First New Deal.* New York, 1966.
Morgenthau, Henry. "The Morgenthau Diaries." *Collier's Magazine,* October 11, 1947.
Mowrer, Edgar. "Our State Department and North Africa." Union for Democratic Action pamphlet, 1943.
Murphy, Robert. *Diplomat among Warriors.* New York, 1964.
Nixon, Edgar B., ed. *Franklin D. Roosevelt and Foreign Affairs.* Cambridge, Mass., 1969.
Offner, Arnold. *American Appeasement.* Cambridge, Mass., 1969.
Orwell, George. *The Road to Wigan Pier.* London, 1937.
Patterson, James T. *Congressional Conservatism and the New Deal.* Lexington, Mass., 1967.

Pearson, Drew. *Washington Merry-Go-Round.* New York, 1931.
Phillips, Harlan. *Felix Frankfurter Reminisces.* New York, 1960.
Phillips, William. *Ventures in Diplomacy.* Boston, 1952.
Roosevelt, Eleanor. *This I Remember.* New York, 1949.
Rowse, A. L. *Appeasement.* New York, 1961.
Royko, Mike. *Boss.* New York, 1971.
Schmidt, Hans. *The United States Occupation of Haiti, 1915–1934.* New Brunswick, N.J., 1971.
Sherwood, Robert E. *Roosevelt and Hopkins.* New York, 1950.
Smith, R. Harris. *OSS.* Los Angeles, 1972.
"Something New in Striped Pants." *Saturday Evening Post,* November 12, 1949.
Stein, Harold. "The Foreign Service Act of 1946." In *Public Administration and Policy Development,* edited by Harold Stein, New York, 1952.
Steiner, Zara. *The Foreign Office and Foreign Policy, 1898–1914.* London, 1969.
Stolberg, Benjamin. "Acheson of the State Department." *American Mercury,* May 1946.
Stone, I. F. "Aid and Comfort to the Enemy." *Nation,* January 3, 1942.
____. "Moral Issue for Mr. Hull." *Nation,* January 30, 1943.
____. "The President and Sumner Welles." *Nation,* September 4, 1943.
____. "V for Vituperation." *Nation,* September 11, 1943.
____. "Stettinius and State." *Nation,* October 9, 1943.
____. "Millionaries' Club." *Nation,* December 9, 1944.
____. "New Front, Old Firm." *Nation,* December 16, 1944.
____. "Only the Fig Leaf." *Nation,* December 23, 1944.
____. *In a Time of Torment.* New York, 1968.
Stuart, Graham H. *The Department of State.* New York, 1949.
Taylor, F. J. *The United States and the Spanish Civil War.* New York, 1956.
"Toward Imperialism." *Nation,* December 30, 1944.
Traina, Richard P. *American Diplomacy and the Spanish Civil War.* Bloomington, Ind., 1968.
Truman, Harry S. *Memoirs.* 2 vols. New York, 1958.
"Trying to Justify Peyrouton." *New Republic,* February 8, 1943.
Tully, Grace. *F.D.R., My Boss.* New York, 1949.
U.S. Department of State. *Foreign Relations of the United States* (FRUS). Annual volumes, 1919–21, 1941–46. Washington, D.C., 1930–70.
"The U.S. Foreign Service." *Fortune,* July 1946.
Villard, Henry Serrano. *Affairs at State.* New York, 1965.
Wandycz, Piotr S. *Soviet-Polish Relations, 1917–1921.* Cambridge, Mass., 1969.
Wilson, Hugh, Jr. *A Career Diplomat.* New York, 1960.
Wyman, David. *Paper Walls.* Amherst, Mass., 1968.

INDEX